The Origins

of

American

Capitalism

The Origins

of

AMERICAN
CAPITALISM

Collected Essays

JAMES A. HENRETTA

NORTHEASTERN UNIVERSITY PRESS

BOSTON

Northeastern University Press

Library of Congress Cataloging-in-Publication Data
Henretta, James A.
The origins of American capitalism : collected essays / James
Henretta.
p. cm.
Includes bibliographical references and index.
ISBN 1-55553-109-1
1. United States—Economic conditions—To 1865. 2. United
States—
Social conditions—To 1865. 3. United States—Industries—
History.
4. Capitalism—United States—History. I. Title.
HC104.H46 1991
330.973—dc20   91-16315
CIP

Designed by Daniel Earl Thaxton

This book was composed in Janson by Coghill Composition
Company, Richmond, Virginia. It was printed and bound by
The Maple Press in York, Pennsylvania. The paper is Sebago
Antique, an acid-free sheet.

Manufactured in the United States of America
96 95 94 93 92 91   5 4 3 2 1

For Patricia Wilson
who learned some of this history from me,
taught me some of it—
and much more besides.

Contents

List of Tables   ix

Preface   xi

Introduction   xv

Part I   Society and Economy
in Colonial America, 1600–1775   3

1   The Morphology of New England Society
in the Colonial Period   7

2   The Weber Thesis Revisited: The Protestant
Ethic and the Reality of Capitalism
in Early America   35

3   Families and Farms: *Mentalité* in
Preindustrial America   71

4   Economic Development and Social Structure
in Colonial Boston   121

5   Wealth and Social Structure   148

Contents

Part II   Toward a New Order, 1775–1800   199

6   The War for Independence
and American Economic Development   203

7   The Transition to Capitalism in America   256

Suggested Reading   295

Index   297

Tables

Table 4.1   Real Estate Ownership in Boston
            in 1687 and 1771
            128–29

Table 4.2   Distribution of Assessed Taxable Wealth
            in Boston in 1687
            130–31

Table 4.3   Distribution of Assessed Taxable Wealth
            in Boston in 1771
            138–39

Table 5.1   The Growth of Wealth: Selected
            Statistics
            168

Table 5.2   Regional Wealth Composition, 1774
            174

Table 6.1   Percentage of Maryland and Virginia
            Estates with Yarn- or Cloth-Making Tools
            224

Table 6.2   Production in Newtown and Woodbury,
            Connecticut, 1770–1824
            251

Preface

I wrote the oldest essay in this volume as a graduate seminar paper for Bernard Bailyn, and one of the most recent for a *festschrift* honoring his distinguished career as a teacher and scholar. His scholarship has shaped my own in myriad ways and I welcome the opportunity to acknowledge my many debts to him—intellectual, professional, and personal. Over the years, I have drawn inspiration from my personal contact with four other master historians: the late Marcus Cunliffe, Lawrence Stone, Carl Schorske, and Eugen Weber. Their engagement with the life of the mind has enriched and expanded my intellectual and personal horizons, and I record my thanks to them as well.

This book owes a great deal to Deborah Kops of Northeastern University Press. She planted the seed of this project a number of years ago, helped to define its character, and, most important of all, pushed it forward to completion. Mrs. Catherine Donohue, my secretary at the University of Maryland, not only typed the manuscript with unfailing patience and care, but also saved me from a number of errors. The History Department of the University of Maryland,

College Park, has provided many benefits—intellectual, financial, collegial—during my tenure as Priscilla Alden Burke Professor of American History, for which I am deeply appreciative. I wish to acknowledge The German Historical Institute of Washington, D.C. for providing me with the opportunity to prepare the essay on "The Weber Thesis Revisited." Finally, I want to thank the following institutions, publishers, and journals for assigning me the copyright or granting permission to reprint the essays that originally appeared under their auspices:

The MIT Press, Cambridge, Massachusetts, and the editors of *The Journal of Interdisciplinary History* for:
"The Morphology of New England Society in the Colonial Period," vol. 2 (1971): 379–98. © 1971 by The Massachusetts Institute of Technology and the editors of *The Journal of Interdisciplinary History*.

William and Mary Quarterly for:
"Families and Farms: *Mentalité* in Preindustrial America," 3d ser., 35 (1978): 3–32, and "Economic Development and Social Structure in Colonial Boston," 3d ser., 22 (1965): 75–92.

The Johns Hopkins University Press for:
"Wealth and Social Structure," in *Colonial British America: Essays in the New History of the Early Modern Era*, ed. Jack P. Greene and J. R. Pole (1984), 262–89.

The University Press of Virginia for:
"The War for Independence and American Economic Development," in *The Economy of Early America: The Revolutionary Period, 1763–1790*, ed. Ronald Hoffman, John J. McCusker, Russell R. Menard, and Peter J. Albert (1988), 45–87.

Alfred A. Knopf, Inc., for:

"The Transition to Capitalism in America," in *The Transformation of Early American History: Society, Authority and Ideology*, ed. James A. Henretta, Michael Kammen, and Stanley N. Katz (1991), 222–43.

The essays appear here essentially as originally published; however, I have made a few editorial changes and put all of the footnotes into a common form.

Introduction

Recent scholarship has transformed our understanding of early American history. It has done so in part by vastly increasing our knowledge of the colonial period. Hundreds—even thousands—of books and articles have revealed that era in all its complexity, probing the lives and experiences of the poor and oppressed as well as the rich and the powerful.

Knowledge is not understanding. The small mountain of newly discovered facts about early America might well have buried us under a heap of antiquarian information. Certainly the politics-focused scholarship of the "old" history nearly suffocated the nimble mind of Woodrow Wilson. As a graduate student at Johns Hopkins University a century ago, Wilson approached his examination in colonial history "crammed with one or two hundred dates and one or two thousand minute particulars about the quarrels of nobody knows who with an obscure Governor, for nobody knows what." "Just think of all that energy wasted," the future president of Princeton and the United States lamented, "The only comfort is that this mass of information won't burden me. I shall forget it with ease."[1]

This fate will probably not befall the "new" social history of early America—of which the seven essays in this volume form a small part. For the accumulation of facts is not the prime contribution of this history, although it has produced a mind-numbing amount of data. We now have scores of minibiographies of ordinary Americans—red, black, and white—and hundreds of statistical tables describing the behavior of tens of thousands of people. And yet much of this material can be comprehended relatively easily, for the scholarship of the past generation has given us new tools of understanding by elucidating the structure and logic inherent in what Wilson called the "minute particulars" of history. In many important respects, the analysis of pattern, configuration, and direction has replaced the study of discrete acts, facts, and events as the major concern of historical scholarship.[2]

Or so it has been for a generation. Historians know—or should know—that their work is the product of a specific intellectual period. Like other forms of cultural expression, historical scholarship reflects, and helps to shape, the outlook of the time. As intellectual concerns and cultural circumstances change, so also does the saliency of certain issues and perspectives. The "understanding" of the American past conveyed by the new social history will itself be super-

---

1. Woodrow Wilson to J. H. Kennard, Jr., 18 November 1884, quoted in Bernard Bailyn, *The Origins of American Politics* (New York, 1967), vii–viii.
2. As I suggested in James A. Henretta, *The Evolution of American Society, 1700–1815: An Interdisciplinary Analysis* (Lexington, Mass., 1973), iii.

seded by new modes of comprehension. This scholarship will then be seen, not as a mass of information to be forgotten, but as an important intellectual phase in the ongoing dialogue between historians and the past.

Moreover, the controversies generated by this scholarship will remain important. It should be remembered that Frederick Jackson Turner's seminal essay, "The Significance of the Frontier in American History," was the product of an intense debate over the origins of American social institutions. Did they represent the flowering of a Teutonic "seed," a primordial cultural germ that was first transplanted from Germanic Europe to England and then carried to the English settlements in North America? The influential German-trained historian Herbert Baxter Adams thought so. Or did Turner, educated in Wisconsin, in a far corner of the European intellectual world, have it right? Were the institutions and characteristics of white Americans more the product of material forces, and especially the settlers' confrontation with the geographic environments of the American continent?

That debate hinged not only on issues of fact but, to an even greater extent, on those of perspective and philosophy. Turner's more modern materialist conception of historical change quickly triumphed over Adams's idealist notions of institutional "germs" and nineteenth-century conceptions of the genetic transmission of cultural traits.[3] More importantly, Turner's thesis shaped scholarly debate on a wide variety of

---

3. Not until the recent publication of David Hackett Fischer's *Albion's Seed: Four British Cultures in North America* (New York, 1990) has a major American historian embraced the major tenets of Adams's world view.

issues for the next two generations. Not until the 1950s did Turner's analytical categories lose their intellectual cogency.[4]

II

It is impossible to predict the life span of the historiographic issues raised by the new social history. But one of them, the emphasis on the "pastness" of the past, has already profoundly altered our understanding of early America.

Regardless of their intellectual outlook, most historians writing before 1960 had emphasized the continuities between colonial America and the postrevolutionary United States. Adams's germs, Turner's frontier, Charles Beard's class-conscious social analysis: these interpretations assumed a similarity of historical experience across the generations. And so of course did those of the so-called "consensus" historians of the 1950s. "Where did the liberal heritage of the Americans come from in the first place?" Louis Hartz asked rhetorically in *The Liberal Tradition in America*. His answer was twofold. First, he argued that it was transplanted by "the men of the seventeenth century who fled to America from Europe," leaving behind forever "its basic feudal oppressions." Second, he suggested that these liberal notions (seeds?) came to fruition because of the frontier, the "abundance of land" that pushed forward "the distinctive element in

---

4. In this regard, see my review of Merle Curti et al.'s Turnerian study of Trempealeau County, "*The Making of An American Community*: A Thirty-Year Retrospective," *Reviews in American History* 16 (1988): 506–12.

American civilization: its social freedom, its social equality."[5] With this formulation, Hartz had not only effected a synthesis between the substantive views of Adams and Turner but also postulated an essential continuity between the distant past and the present. From John Locke to John D. Rockefeller to Herbert Hoover, America was a society of liberal individualists.

Recent historians of colonial America, regardless of their interpretative differences, have challenged—even repudiated—that belief in the essential continuity of American history. The world of the Puritan settlers, Kenneth Lockridge declared in *A New England Town: The First Hundred Years* (1970), "is in many respects irretrievable. It was too long ago, too different, its beliefs are too strange to be reconstructed with accuracy." With society, so also with politics: "The story of politics in the colonial period is not that of a distinct evolution toward the modern world," Bernard Bailyn argued in 1965; it "has no climax in the state and national party politics of later periods of American history." This historical experience was, as Peter Laslett cogently put it in a parallel study of early modern England, "the world we have lost."[6]

Other scholars have deepened our understanding

---

5. Louis Hartz, *The Liberal Tradition in America: An Interpretation of American Political Thought since the Revolution* (New York, 1955), 35, 64–66, 14, 60, 5, 46n. For a critique of Hartz, see my "The Slow Triumph of Liberal Individualism: Law and Politics in New York, 1780–1860," in *American Chameleon: Individualism in United States History*, ed. Richard O. Curry and Eugene Goodheart (Kent, Ohio, 1991).

6. Kenneth Lockridge, *A New England Town, The First Hundred Years: Dedham, Massachusetts, 1636–1736* (New York, 1970), xii; Bailyn, *Origins*, ix; Peter Laslett, *The World We Have Lost* (London, 1965).

of the "pastness" of early American history. John Murrin and Rowland Berthoff called attention to a "feudal revival" of landholding titles in mid-eighteenth-century colonies, while a host of historians have demonstrated the importance of "classical republican" thought to Americans of this era. Indeed, this "republican synthesis" of the Revolutionary era has become a new orthodoxy, confounding the liberal continuities postulated by Hartz and his scholarly successors.[7]

The essays in this book seek to confound an uncritical "liberal" interpretation of American history. They do so in two ways. First, they contest the assumption of many scholars working in the liberal or consensus tradition that there were few social divisions or conflicts in early America. For example, my analyses of Boston in chapter 4 and of rural society in chapter 5 demonstrate significant inequalities in the

---

7. John Murrin and Rowland Berthoff, "Feudalism, Communalism, and the Yeoman Freeholder: The American Revolution Considered as a Social Accident," in *Essays on the American Revolution*, ed. Stephen G. Kurtz and James H. Hutson (Chapel Hill, N.C., 1973), 256–88. On republicanism, see J. G. A. Pocock, "Machiavelli, Harrington, and English Political Ideologies in the Eighteenth Century," *William and Mary Quarterly*, 3d ser., 22 (1965), 549–83; Gordon S. Wood, *The Creation of the American Republic, 1776–1789* (Chapel Hill, 1969); Robert E. Shalhope, "Toward a Republican Synthesis: The Emergence of an Understanding of Republicanism in American Historiography," *William and Mary Quarterly*, 3d ser., 29 (1972): 49–80; and Lance Banning, "Jeffersonian Ideology Revisited: Liberal and Classical Ideas in the New American Republic," ibid., 43 (1986): 3–19. Scholars who have revived parts of Hartz's argument include John P. Diggins, *The Lost Soul of American Politics: Virtue, Self-Interest, and the Foundations of Liberalism* (New York, 1984), and Joyce Appleby, *Capitalism and a New Social Order: The Republican Vision of the 1790s* (New York, 1984). See also Appleby's reply to Banning, "Republicanism in Old and New Contexts," *William and Mary Quarterly*, 3d ser., 43 (1986): 20–34, and the impressive synthesis by Isaac Kramnick, "The 'Great National Discussion': The Discourse of Politics in 1787," ibid., 45 (1988): 3–32.

distribution of wealth, while my study of rival systems of political economy at the end of chapter 7 shows how these economic divisions affected governmental policies. Second, these essays affirm the distinctive character of the colonial period. In particular, they argue that capitalist practices and values were not central to the lives of most of the inhabitants of British North America before 1750. Rather, there was a transition to capitalism during the generation following the American Revolution. By 1800 enterprising European merchants and entrepreneurs had been active in North America for nearly two centuries, but only then did they operate within a system—economic, political, and cultural—that was genuinely conducive to capitalist enterprise. In its economic system, as in society and politics, an older American world had given way to a new reality.

III

Debate is the heart of the scholarly enterprise. Reviews and commentaries reveal errors or omissions in published work while suggesting how new data, insights, and interpretations can be used to construct a more complex and accurate picture of historical reality. Some historians have accepted my interpretation of the economy and society of the northern colonies. Other scholars have revised my argument or restricted its applicability to New England.[8] In either case, it

---

8. Scholars who have largely accepted my interpretation include Richard Bushman, "Family Security in the Transition from Farm to City, 1750–1850," *Journal of Family History* 6 (1981): 238–56; Steven Hahn, *The Roots of Southern Populism: Yeoman Farmers and the*

has become part of a broader and more refined interpretation of early American history.

Still other historians have not been persuaded by
my depiction of the *mentalité* of farm families. Some
of them seem not to have realized that my argument
grants the presence of a market economy in which
most farmers participated to a limited extent, and that
I have acknowledged the existence of capitalist values
and activities among a *portion* of the rural population
even as I have argued for the dominance of a rather
different worldview among the *majority* of farm families.[9] Given this confusion, it seems appropriate to use
the present occasion to clarify my interpretation and,
in the process, to provide an intellectual and historiographic context for the essays that follow.

In chapter 3, "Families and Farms," I conclude
that the majority of northern farmers were not agrarian entrepreneurs and that their prime goal was not a
simple maximization of profits. As I state it there:
"Economic gain was important to these men and
women, yet it was not their dominant value. It was
subordinate to (or encompassed by) two other goals:
the yearly subsistence and long-term financial security

Transformation of the Georgia Upcountry, 1850–1890 (New York,
1983); Christopher Clark, *The Roots of Rural Capitalism: Western
Massachusetts, 1780–1860* (Ithaca, N.Y., 1990); and Daniel Vickers,
"Competency and Competition: Economic Culture in Early
America," *William and Mary Quarterly*, 3d ser., 47 (1990): 3–29.
See also the fine interpretative synthesis by Allan Kulikoff, "The
Transition to Capitalism in Early America," ibid., 46 (1989): 120–
44. Gary Nash accepts the validity of my argument, but only for
New England. See his "Social Development," in *Colonial British
America: Essays in the New History of the Early Modern Era*, ed. Jack
P. Greene and J. R. Pole (Baltimore, Md., 1984), 233–61.

9. Timothy Breen, "An Empire of Goods: The Anglicization of
Colonial America, 1690–1776," *Journal of British Studies* 25 (1986):
467–99.

of the family unit." This interpretation does not assume that individual farmers were "self-sufficient," although it suggests that many communities did form largely self-contained economic units. Nor do I embrace the notion that ordinary farm families followed a "precapitalist" way of life. Their economic and social lives were too complex to be subsumed into such a one-dimensional historical category.

Rather, my essay suggests that most farm families operated in a three-tiered economic world. Their first concern was subsistence. Consequently, most families raised a diversified mix of crops to feed themselves and their livestock. They did not engage in specialized production with market sale in mind, nor, in point of fact, did they dispose of most of their produce or labor in the market. Families made these decisions both for reasons of safety and because opportunities for specialized market sales were limited, especially before 1750.

Second, northern farm families exchanged (and did not *sell*) labor, foodstuffs, and handmade goods with neighboring farmers and artisans. That system of exchange enhanced the cohesiveness of hundreds of local communities and, through the exchange of labor and capital goods among family units, expanded their productivity. Third and finally, farmers sold the surplus that remained after subsistence and exchange in the market economy, receiving cash or store credit in return. Many farmers referred to those sales as consisting of their "surplus," explicitly affirming that participation in the market was not their prime goal.

My interpretation is consistent with the evidence in farm account books and similar documents. Indeed, it is even supported by the ledgers of merchants, storekeepers, and traders who did business with farm families. When William Moore, a "petty chapman," arrived in the isolated village of Berwick, Maine, in

1721, residents eagerly inspected his stock of imported goods, but they bought only a few items and (as a student of this episode reports) "none of the purchases amounted to more than a few pennies."[10]

In sum, my position is that most northern families were "subsistence plus" farmers (to use the apt phrase of Toby Ditz)[11] who disposed of a small percentage of their total production in the market economy. Their society was neither "self-sufficient" nor deeply enmeshed in the capitalist world economy. It had some precapitalist features and some characteristics of a market system; considered abstractly, "on the family level there was freehold property ownership, a household mode of production, limited economic possibilities and aspirations, and a safety-first subsistence agriculture within a commercial capitalist market structure" (chapter 3).

This complicated (and contradictory) set of circumstances meant that there was no necessary dichotomy between family values and market production. Indeed, most colonial Americans had to participate in the market in order to provide for the short-term subsistence and the long-term landed security of their families. For example, there is a story in "Families and Farms" of a self-styled "honest farmer" in Pennsylvania who bought land for his many children by "accu-

---

10. Ibid., 467, 468. Bruce H. Mann, *Neighbors and Strangers: Law and Community in Early Connecticut* (Chapel Hill, N.C., 1987), notes that promissory notes and other legal instruments replace account books as evidence in court cases between debtors and creditors after 1720. That change probably indicates the spread of a rural capitalism, as Mann argues; however, these books continued to serve as the main accounting device in the local exchange system for the subsequent half century or more.

11. Toby Ditz, *Property and Kinship: Inheritance in Early Connecticut, 1750–1820* (Princeton, N.J., 1986), chapter 1.

mulat[ing] capital through the regular sale of his surplus production on the market" (chapter 3). Here "rational" marketplace behavior and family welfare went hand in hand.

In other cases, family values prompted decisions that were not economically rational. For example, some parents divided their small farms among all male and female heirs rather than passing a viable estate to one of their children.[12] With this behavior in mind, I argue that those families "were enmeshed also in a web of social relationships and cultural expectations that inhibited the free play of market forces" (chapter 3). Indeed, decisions that lacked economic rationality were inevitable in a society in which the basic economic institution, the family, was also the prime emotional and cultural unit.

Thus the market was not sovereign in the rural society of preindustrial America. Rather, it was only one of several "institutions" that affected the economic decisions made by small-scale producers. The actions of those men and women were determined as well by concerns for their family, their status in the community, and the traditional (often anticapitalist) moral norms of their religious congregations.

IV

Nonetheless, those families operated in an increasingly dynamic economic system. Because the world of

---

12. Christopher M. Jedrey, *The World of John Cleaveland: Family and Community in Eighteenth-Century New England* (New York, 1979). See also Christine Leigh Heyrman, *Commerce and Culture: The Maritime Communities of Colonial Massachusetts, 1690–1750* (New York, 1984), for a discussion of "a-rational" economic behavior among merchants.

1800 was different from that of 1700, a convincing analysis of American society must present a coherent analysis of change. How and why did the economy develop? What were the causal forces in the origins of American capitalism? These questions, which arise naturally from my interpretation of the *mentalité* of the farm population during the colonial period, are addressed at some length in the two concluding essays in this volume.

It is necessary here only to place those questions in a historiographic context. In recent years, various scholars have propounded the thesis of a "consumer revolution" during the eighteenth century, a thirst for consumption goods that was "the driving engine of economic change" in Great Britain and its North American colonies.[13] In my view, there are two flaws in that thesis. First, the advocates of a consumer revolution assume that a demand for goods is the crucial causal factor. In fact, it is much more likely that an increased supply of manufactures was the key ingredient. That surplus of goods was the product of the English industrial revolution, which increased output through technology and the more rigorous organization of labor. Over the decades the continuing revolution in production resulted in *falling* prices for manufactured goods, particularly in relation to the cost of farm crops, a clear sign that supply was increasing faster than demand.[14]

---

13. Breen, "Empire of Goods," 481; Neil McKendrick, John Brewer, and J. H. Plumb, *The Commercialization of Eighteenth-Century England* (Bloomington, Ind., 1982); Ronald Hoffman and Cary Carson, eds., *Of Consuming Interest: The Style of Life in the Eighteenth Century* (Charlottesville, Va., 1992).

14. Sidney Pollard, *Peaceful Conquest: The Industrialization of Europe, 1760–1970* (Oxford, 1981).

Thus the expansion of manufacturing, not the growth of consumer demand, was the principal economic "revolution" of the eighteenth century. The primacy of production informs the treatment of economic change in part II of this volume. As I argue there, the transformation of the American economy after 1775 stemmed from two developments: first, the integration of domestic manufacturing—the traditional handmade production of goods such as cloth and cheese—into the market economy and, second, the expansion of artisan output through the merchant-run putting-out system.

The timing of this transition to a capitalist rural economy reveals the second flaw in the "consumer revolution" thesis. It fails to provide a convincing explanation of the economic values and behavior of the white residents of British North America during the colonial period. Before the American Revolution, the settlers were not avid consumers; their purchases of imported goods increased at a snail's pace during the first three-quarters of the eighteenth century. On a per capita basis, the annual imports from England (and Scotland) rose modestly from roughly £1 sterling in 1700 to £1.2 in 1770, and most of this increase occurred after 1750.[15]

What were the economic goals of Americans during this "preconsumer" era, which comprised most of the colonial period? Advocates of the "consumer revolution" believe that most farmers always wanted to produce for the market and to buy manufactured goods. In their view, there was no "preconsumer" era, but only a period in which consumer wants could not

---

15. Breen, "Empire of Goods," 479, 485, 486.

be satisfied. Conversely, my position is that a market mentality and consumer values were not dominant among most northern farm families before 1750 and achieved a prominent position only after 1800. In my view, most Americans were ambivalent toward new (and externally generated) credit and market opportunities.

These contrasting interpretations lead to distinct views of the preindependence crisis. Advocates of the "consumer revolution" suggest that the transatlantic debts resulting from increased imports of British manufactures threatened many Americans with "the loss of their own independence." Eventually, it prompted them to redefine "the symbolic meaning of imported goods" by engaging "in a series of increasingly successful boycotts against British manufactures."[16] On this reading of the evidence, Americans become nonimporters because they could not control the market economy that they had eagerly embraced. Conversely, my view (presented in chapter 6, "The War for Independence and Economic Development") is that northern farm families joined the boycott movement because many of them already wore homespun clothes; many others feared a full commitment to market forces and values. Nonimportation thus flowed naturally from many aspects of their present existence.

How can scholars decide between our interpretations? This question raises two points of disagreement—one methodological, one epistemological—between my view and that of scholars who stress the importance of foreign trade, either in the form of staple crop exports or imported consumer goods. In

---

16. Ibid., 498, 499.

methodological terms, we look at American economic life from different perspectives. Those who emphasize foreign trade view the world primarily from the floor of merchants' warehouses and through their letters and account books. Their interpretations reflect what they find in those documents—bulging inventories of imported manufactures or large shipments of rice, tobacco, and wheat to overseas markets.[17] Conversely, my essays depict the world primarily from the floor of farmers' barns and through the ledgers of local artisans. These inventories and entries suggest the relative unimportance of imported consumer items. Or do they? Here is a key question to be placed on the research agenda. A related issue is the proportion of the farmers' total production that was sold in the market economy.[18]

These matters remain in dispute. Some historians echo my argument that the market had a limited effect in the towns of rural New England throughout the colonial period. As Gary Nash has stated, "New En-

---

17. For a sophisticated statement of the staple thesis (which argues that the export of the staple crops of tobacco, rice, and eventually wheat was the driving force in the colonial economy), see John J. McCusker and Russell R. Menard, *The Economy of British America, 1607–1789* (Chapel Hill, N.C., 1985).

18. Thus Carole Shammas's conclusion that "nearly a quarter of all expenditures" of Massachusetts families went for imported goods is not based on evidence found in financial ledgers of individual households. Rather, it is the product of a macrostatistical analysis that contains debatable assumptions. More important, her category of "expenditures" does not include the value of housing or of family-produced goods used for subsistence; hence, purchases of imported goods probably account for a very small proportion of the total value of the resources used by those families in a given year. See Carole Shammas, "Consumer Behavior in Colonial America," *Social Science History* 6 (1982): 81, 67–86; idem, "How Self-Sufficient Was Early America?" *Journal of Interdisciplinary History* 13 (1982): 247–72.

gland's communities [were] unusually stable and relatively static in comparison with communities in other parts of colonial America. . . . [It remained] a hierarchically structured society of lineal families on small community-oriented farms."[19] At the same time, they argue that farmers in other regions were heavily involved in the export of staple crops or in the consumer revolution, what one historian has called the "empire of goods."

Even here this issue is not settled. Consider the situation of the yeoman and tenant farm families in the export-oriented Chesapeake region. The careful research of Lorena Walsh has demonstrated that by the 1750s the probate inventories of middling and poorer Chesapeake families contained a growing variety of material items, some of them imported. However, the value of these items in relation to decedents' total wealth was still relatively small. Moreover, Walsh's scholarship (and that of Lois Green Carr) has also showed that, with each passing decade, the inventories of more and more of these families contained cloth-making items, such as spinning wheels and looms.[20] Their data therefore offer support both for advocates of a transatlantic "empire of goods" and for

---

19. Nash, "Social Development," 236.
20. Lorena Walsh, "Urban Amenities and Rural Sufficiency: Living Standards and Consumer Behavior in the Colonial Chesapeake, 1643–1777," *Journal of Economic History* 43 (1983): 109–17; Lois Green Carr and Lorena Walsh, "Inventories and the Analysis of Wealth and Consumption Patterns in St. Mary's County, Maryland, 1658–1777," *Historical Methods* 13 (1980): 81–104; Carr, "Diversification in the Colonial Chesapeake: Somerset County, Maryland, in Comparative Perspective," in *Colonial Chesapeake Society*, ed. Lois Green Carr, Philip D. Morgan, and Jean B. Russo (Chapel Hill, N.C., 1989), 342–88.

my emphasis on increasing American household production.

Contemporary observers likewise remarked on the limited participation of many southern farmers in the broader market economy. Charles Varley was a farmer born in Yorkshire who lived in Ireland and Wales as well. Varley traveled to America in 1784 and stayed about a year, residing mostly in the northern states. But he took a trip to Washington's Mount Vernon, stopping at Baltimore, Annapolis, and various Maryland towns near the Chesapeake Bay. "The country farmers" in Maryland, Varley reported, "seem to have the least desire to lay up treasure of any people I ever met with, for if they can raise as much of everything this year as will serve to bring in the next year's crop it is all they aim at. One thing indeed may discourage them," he continued by way of explanation, "which is, markets are thin and at a great distance, and there are scarce any fairs in America." More enterprising farmers obviously sought out markets, for Varley also noted that "there are many waggons that go from twenty to sixty miles to the market of Philadelphia, New York, and Baltimore."[21] Yet this anecdotal evidence, in conjunction with the statistical calculations of Walsh and Carr, suggests the complexity of the Chesapeake economy and the limited access of many farmers to foreign goods or markets.

Still, the discovery of "mere" factual evidence will probably not resolve the argument, given the existence of different epistemological assumptions

---

21. Charles Varley (or Varlo), *The Unfortunate Husbandman: An Account of the Life and Travels of a Real Farmer in Ireland, Scotland, England, and America* (London, 1964), 115–16. My thanks to Barbara Sarudy for bringing Varley's comments to my attention.

about how it should be interpreted. For example, how can scholars establish the life goals and day-to-day motivation of ordinary farm families who left few written records? My assumption in chapter 3, "Families and Farms," is that "the behavior of the farm population constitutes a crucial (although not a foolproof) indicator of its values and aspirations." Beyond that, my argument calls attention to how the "structural possibilities and limitations of the society" affected the behavior of its inhabitants and even their "cultural propensities or economic aspirations." In my view, the relative absence of a market and of imported goods before 1750 (or even 1775) shaped the values and goals of individual farmers. In this regard, I adopt the "environmentalist" perspective of Percy Bidwell, an important early twentieth-century historian of agriculture. Why should the farmer without access to a market "exert himself to produce a surplus," Bidwell asked, when "the only return he could expect would be a sort of psychological income?"[22]

Advocates of the consumer revolution ascribe greater importance to this psychological income, reflecting their "culturalist" perspective on human motivation. They maintain that increases in consumption occurred not only because of changes in the "environment," such as the diffusion of elite tastes, the greater availability of British goods and credit, and the entrepreneurial activities of American and Scottish merchants and traders, but also because farm families had long been psychologically eager for it. Evidence that would prove (or disprove) their argument is hard to

22. Percy W. Bidwell, "Rural Economy in New England at the Beginning of the Nineteenth Century," *Transactions of the Connecticut Academy of Arts and Sciences* 20 (1916): 330.

come by; for the time being at least, the epistemological controversy must remain unresolved.

In any event, it is clear that the material well-being and the financial goals of many American farmers rose over the course of the eighteenth century. But it remains my view that this change occurred primarily because of the growing maturity of the domestic economy. Here I will only mention the point (explicated in chapter 6) that the proportion of the mainland settlements' "gross national product" stemming from foreign trade decreased steadily from 1700 to 1790.

Moreover, I continue to maintain that the consciousness of the farm population in a given chronological period cannot be divorced from its actual condition. For if an acquisitive or capitalist mentality is compatible with all historical circumstances and forms of behavior, then what is its causal or explanatory significance? We need a conceptual framework that acknowledges the importance of *changes* in economic values as well as in the structures of economic life.

Perhaps there are grounds for optimism. Winifred Rothenberg has long argued that a market economy was important in Massachusetts from the time of its earliest settlement.[23] Recently, Rothenberg has introduced a chronological dimension into her interpretation and no longer equates mere market exchange with a capitalist way of life. Instead, she calls attention to the sudden appearance of substantial holdings of liquid capital—bonds, mortgages, promissory notes—

---

23. See Winifred Rothenberg, "A Price Index for Rural Massachusetts, 1750–1855," *Journal of Economic History* 39 (1979): 975–1001; idem, "The Market and Massachusetts Farmers, 1750–1855," ibid., 41 (1981): 283–314; idem, "Markets, Values, and Capitalism: A Discourse on Method," ibid., 44 (1984): 174–78.

and a highly developed credit economy in the 1780s. As Rothenberg has explained,

> The enhanced liquidity of rural portfolios *is* the transformation of the rural economy. This phenomenon, it seems to me, must henceforth loom large in whatever is meant by the coming of capitalism to the New England village economy. Capitalism is necessarily, even if not sufficiently, the creature of a developed credit market. And that market, in eastern Massachusetts, can be dated to the early years of national independence.[24]

This hypothesis suggests that market relations in the colonial economy were different in quantity and quality from those of the postrevolutionary period, a point I heartily endorse. And it lends support to my thesis in chapter 7, "The Transition to Capitalism," that the emergence of a new system of economic behavior, values, and institutions occurred at the beginning of the nineteenth century.

V

These essays were written over a period of twenty-five years, yet they have considerable unity in both approach and argument. How is that coherence to be explained?

Most academic historians, like most novelists, treat a limited number of significant ideas or issues in their creative work. In some cases that restrictive focus

---

24. Winifred Rothenberg, "The Emergence of a Capital Market in Rural Massachusetts, 1730–1838," *Journal of Economic History* 45 (1985): 806.

is conscious, the result of the historian's deliberate decision to explore a massive set of documents in its entirety or to develop a unique methodological perspective. Thus Charles McLean Andrews wrote a great institutional history of the first British empire, a project that rested on years of labor in the Colonial Office archives and yielded a distinct "imperial" view of early American history. More recently, J. G. A. Pocock has offered a "republican" reading of the intellectual history of the early modern Anglo-American world, a vision that challenges both traditional interpretations of this period and existing conceptions of the historical process.[25]

The essays gathered in this volume are much more modest contributions to historical knowledge than those of Andrews and Pocock, and they were not the product of a conscious strategy. And yet they also cohere around a distinct set of historical and philosophical issues. To my mind, two concerns inform this body of work. First, these essays address the distribution of social and economic power and do so in a critical fashion. My analysis is empirical and historical, seeking to specify the ownership of wealth in precise quantitative terms; it is also moral, raising issues of social power and economic justice. This two-

---

25. Charles McLean Andrews, *The Colonial Period of American History*, 4 vols. (New Haven, Conn., 1934–38); idem, *The Colonial Background of the American Revolution* (New York, 1924); Lawrence Henry Gipson, "The Imperial Approach to Early American History," in *The Reinterpretation of Early American History*, ed. Ray Allen Billington (San Marino, Calif., 1966), 185–200; J. G. A. Pocock, *The Machiavellian Moment: Florentine Political Thought and the Atlantic Republican Tradition* (Princeton, N.J., 1975); idem, *Virtue, Commerce, and History: Essays on Political Thought and History, Chiefly in the Eighteenth Century* (New York, 1985); idem, ed., *Three British Revolutions: 1641, 1688, 1776* (Princeton, N.J., 1980).

fold concern, with the past and the present, *is* part of a conscious strategy. My goal is to compose a work of scholarship that simultaneously respects the integrity of the past and comments critically on the values and behavior of historical actors and institutions. As Paul Hernadi has argued, the contemporary historian should not pretend "to *mirror* what really happened" but should freely admit that he or she "mediates." The responsibility of the scholar is, in fact, "to make us see the past from within and from without at the same time—as evolving drama and as the fixed target of distanced retrospection."[26] Throughout these essays, the continuing object of this complex process of scrutiny is "social power."

The second *problematique* begins from a philosophical concern with the nature of human action. In my historical treatment of this issue, I focus on the "constraints" placed on individuals by the institutional structures and social customs of their society. Thus my work pays particular attention to *patterns* of existence, such as the "social morphology" of New England communities; to economic *structures*, ranging from the unequal distribution of wealth to proto-industrial systems of production; and to *frameworks* of cultural values. In my view, historical actors must fashion their individual identities and lives from within the range of options afforded by those institutions and customs.

This emphasis on social constraints rubs against

---

26. Paul Hernadi, "Re-Presenting the Past: A Note on Narrative Historiography and Historical Drama," *History and Theory* 15 (1976), 45, 47, and my commentary on these and other issues in James A. Henretta, "Social History as Lived and Written," *American Historical Review* 84 (1979): 1321, 1293–1333.

the grain of modern American culture which, in both its liberal and conservative forms, emphasizes the moral primacy of the unfettered individual. It also accounts for my intellectual doubts about the descriptive accuracy of the ideology of individualism and my unwillingness to write history according to its precepts, whether moral or methodological.[27] Even as my more recent essays focus on individual men and women, recounting their life stories and depicting the world from their perspective, they continue to call attention to the institutions and conditions that constrict people's lives and limit their choices. The challenge seems ever more complex and difficult—of writing the paradoxical story of individuals acting and yet acted upon by the structures of their own existence.

---

27. See my comments in Henretta, "Slow Triumph."

The Origins

of

American

Capitalism

I

Society and Economy
in
Colonial America,
1600–1775

To write history is to compose stories about the past, and therein lies a problem. Many scholars coming of age in the 1960s wanted to write a new history, an account of ordinary people and of their society. But how could such a story be composed? Who would be the leading characters? How would it be organized? What themes or issues would give shape and meaning to the infinity of social facts and individual lives?

Traditional political approaches and frameworks seemed of little use. The history of politics consisted of stories about kings and presidents, judges and legislators. These individuals pursued power or exercised authority within institutions that persisted across the generations. Such frameworks—the life accomplishments of individual political actors or the evolution of an institution—gave coherence and direction to the accounts written by political historians. To compose a complex and convincing narrative remained a difficult task, as Louis Mink has demonstrated,[1] but the scope and analytic categories of the enterprise were well defined.

To tell their story, "new social historians" had to invent a new form of discourse. The first problem was to define a central "character," someone or something to carry the narrative line. The solution came in a variety of forms. Some authors told the story of a "community." They began with a geographically defined communal entity and then told its story. Other authors focused on the "family," using this basic social institution to give form to the experiences of the individuals who composed it. A second problem involved chronology. Political narratives were usually restricted in time, perhaps to a year of crisis, or a decade of change, at most to a generation of development. By contrast, societal change came slowly and imperceptibly; the inner dynamic of the story often appeared only over the course of a century. Social historians had therefore to establish an extended chronology, to plot change over three or four generations or to posit the *longue durée* of social institutions.

The five essays in part 1 illustrate the discourse of the new social history. The concept of "social morphology" has provided a way of analyzing the evolution of New England communities over the entire colonial period. Similarly, the notion of "economic development" suggests a pattern of change that re-

---

1. See in particular Louis Mink's "History and Fiction as Modes of Comprehension," *New Literary History* 1 (1970): 541–58; reprinted in idem, *Historical Understanding* (Ithaca, N.Y., 1987), chapter 2.

sulted, over time, in the creation of a new "social structure." Finally, the idea of a mental world unique to the yeoman farm families of preindustrial America has provided yet another means of giving shape and significance to the lives and activities of hundreds of thousands of ordinary women and men.

These essays also comment critically upon this new mode of historical discourse. The discussion of Max Weber's pathbreaking essay on the Protestant ethic points up dangers of "reification" in historical analysis—of depicting motive forces apart from the lives of individuals and the actual society in which they lived. Likewise, the analysis of the *mentalité* of farm families exposes the philosophical and methodological weaknesses of those historical works that posit "liberal individualist" cultural norms in early America. Finally, the essay "Wealth and Social Structure" provides a systematic and extended examination of historians' treatment of these topics—and the general problem of social change—over the past three decades.

I

The Morphology
of New England Society
in the Colonial Period

For nearly three-quarters of a century the colonial history
of New England has been organized around a single
dominant theme: the erosion of traditional English institutions, customs, and ideas by the corrosive force of the
American wilderness. For the intellectual as much as for
the social historian, for Perry Miller no less than for
Frederick Jackson Turner, the theme of disintegration, of
declension, provided a generalization that was at once
elemental in its force, striking in its simplicity, and
nationalistic in its impact. The story was simply told:
Medieval Englishmen of peasant stock and deep religious
beliefs came to the New World intent upon transplanting
a traditional communal society to new soil; instead, they
were transformed by the American environment. A new
type of society was created as the culture of the past was
rendered irrelevant by the primitive logic of necessity,
and as the constricting social and psychological bonds of

the premodern world were dissolved by the corrosive forces of nature. This long, silent revolution took an explicitly political form in the War for Independence, itself the logical culmination of a century and a half of social change.

Interpretations of this process might differ, but the thrust was the same. The society that appeared in the northern states in the aftermath of revolution was not a positive creation, the end product of the organic growth of a coherent social system. It was the individualistic residue, an atomistic congeries of "new men," that remained in the aftermath of the decay and dissolution of the traditional social fabric of European civilization.

The present essay constitutes an extended critique of this "negative" approach to the American past. It builds on the work of four young historians who have brought the assumptions and techniques of modern social science to bear upon the history of the colonial period.[1] Ultimately, it attempts to make more explicit certain aspects of their findings and to place their results within a common framework. This takes the form of a more positive vision of historical change, a morphology of societal evolution that, like its biological counterpart, seeks an organic explanation for the changing form and structure of colonial society.[2]

---

1. John Demos, *A Little Commonwealth: Family Life in Plymouth Colony* (New York, 1970); Philip J. Greven, Jr., *Four Generations: Population, Land, and Family in Colonial Andover, Massachusetts* (Ithaca, N.Y., 1970); Kenneth A. Lockridge, *A New England Town: The First Hundred Years: Dedham, Massachusetts, 1636–1736* (New York, 1970); and Michael Zuckerman, *Peaceable Kingdoms: New England Towns in the Eighteenth Century* (New York, 1970).

2. Bernard Bailyn suggested the concept of a "social morphology" but should not be held responsible for the way this theme is developed here. For Emile Durkheim, "social morphology" consisted of the study of the environmental basis of social organization

Of the four books under consideration, Kenneth Lockridge's history of Dedham, Massachusetts, conforms most closely to the traditional accounts. If this is not obvious at first sight, it is because Lockridge has translated the old arguments, with their overtones of Darwinian environmentalism, into the language of the modern anthropologist. For fifty years after its foundation in 1636, the author tells us, Dedham was essentially a "closed corporate peasant community," very similar to those that have formed the substructure of agricultural societies in all parts of the world in many ages. As such, this tightly knit community of Puritan saints carefully restricted its membership, maintained close control over the distribution and alienation of land, and enforced common standards of behavior:

> The tendency of medieval peasants to look on the villages of an imaginary golden past as their model for the future regeneration of society was repeated in the Puritan idealization of the communes of the primitive Christian church and in the use of these communes as a model for some features of Dedham's organization. . . . Whatever the exact nature of the mixture, Dedham was at once a Puritan and a peasant utopia.

This argument is dramatic, but distorted. In this instance, as in others, Lockridge consciously sacrifices historical detail and complexity in his search for the striking generalization and the simplifying concept. In

---

and the investigation of population, especially its size, density, and spatial distribution. It is in these senses that the term is used here. The best introduction to the concept of social morphology is Leo F. Schnore, "Social Morphology and Human Ecology," *American Journal of Sociology* 58 (1958): 620–35.

precisely what sense were the first Massachusetts towns "peasant" communities when, as Lockridge himself tells us, they were settled by families drawn "from the broad ranks of the English middle classes"; when the initial inhabitants were complete strangers to one another; and when nearly one-third of the original settlers of Dedham eventually lived in at least three different New England towns? To fashion an *enduring* peasant society from the heterogeneous members of a geographically mobile middle class would have been an accomplishment. In point of fact, the intense religious ideology that prompted the migration from England was simply not strong enough to recreate the type of community that could be held together only by unconscious assumptions and traditional practices. Within the lifetime of the first generation the open-field system had vanished, the nuclear pattern of settlement had been challenged, the control of the original proprietors seriously shaken, and membership in the church reduced to a minority of the inhabitants. From the beginnings of settlement there was an inherent dynamism in these New England communities that made them fundamentally different from their medieval counterparts.

For all its superficial brilliance, Lockridge's interpretation is so schematized, so highly conceptualized, and so removed from the reality it purports to explain, that at times it seems more like arbitrary invention than serious history. Those who came to America were peasants neither in condition nor in consciousness. They were the products of a country already in the process of dramatic social and demographic change. As the work of E. A. Wrigley, Peter Laslett, Lawrence Stone, and others has demonstrated, the years between 1500 and 1620 were marked by a doubling of the population of England and Wales, extensive enclosures and a remarkably active land market, considerable geographical mobility, and the disruption of traditional economic alignments and social patterns by a sustained rise in prices.[3] In short, the England from which the settlers of Dedham came was at the end of a century-long process of transition that had largely destroyed the earlier peasant society. By 1641, as E. E. Rich has pointed out, "only 16% of our agricultural population had a hundred years in the same village behind them."[4]

Lockridge's analysis of Dedham is nearly as questionable as his description of its antecedents. Take the matter of chronology. The first half of the book, "A Utopian Commune," carries the story to 1686. Upon inspection, however, it becomes clear that this choice of a date is the result of the author's desire to discuss the history of the town in two periods of equal length; nothing happened in 1686 to cause or even to symbolize the end of the utopian experiment.

The result has been to distort the real character of those years. On Lockridge's own evidence there were two periods of major change during the first half century of settlement. The first came in the 1670s with the death of the original minister and of several influential selectmen, the outbreak of religious controversy, the failure to enforce the laws restricting the

---

3. See, for example, Peter Laslett, *The World We Have Lost* (New York, 1965); Peter Laslett and John Harrison, "Clayworth and Cogenhoe," in *Historical Essays, 1600–1750, Presented to David Ogg*, ed. H. E. Bell and R. L. Ollard (London, 1963), 157–84; and Lawrence Stone, "Social Mobility in England, 1500–1700," *Past and Present* 33 (1966): 16–55.

4. E. E. Rich, "The Population of Elizabethan England," *Economic History Review* 2 (1950): 247–65, as quoted in Greven, *Four Generations*, 265. See also Jack M. Potter, May N. Diaz, and George M. Foster, *Peasant Society: A Reader* (Boston, 1967), esp. 2–14, 35–41, 230–45, 300–323.

entrance of strangers into the town, and the most severe demographic crisis in Dedham's history.[5] The second cluster of important events came in 1691 and 1692 with the acceptance of the Halfway Covenant, after a resistance of thirty years, and the dismissal of all of the selectmen, apparently because of their acquiescence in the regime of Sir Edmund Andros, the deposed governor of the abortive Dominion of New England. These "natural" turning points are neglected in the pursuit of symmetry and simplicity. As a result, the author's organization of the town's history bears little relation to the actual life experiences of its members. There are brilliant passages and convincing interpretations in every chapter of the book, especially in those sections based on earlier journal articles, but the total effect is disappointing. The actual Dedham experience is obscured by Lockridge's continual quest for a wider synthesis, and the history of one town is too meager a scaffolding to support a comprehensive interpretation of early American history.

John Demos's study of the pattern of social existence in Plymouth colony, between its settlement in 1620 and its incorporation into the province of Massachusetts Bay in 1691, is much better in depicting the concrete reality of the early settlements. Eschewing chronological analysis, Demos offers a careful topical investigation of the character of family life and of the nature and functioning of the household unit. Within these rather narrow limits he is remarkably successful. In consecutive chapters on the housing, furnishings,

---

5. There were twenty-five recorded deaths in the year 1675–76, many caused directly or indirectly by an Indian war. See Kenneth A. Lockridge, "The Population of Dedham, Massachusetts, 1636–1736," *Economic History Review*, 2d ser., 19 (1966): 318–44.

and clothing of the colonists, Demos evokes the physical setting of these relatively primitive village communities with considerable skill and understanding. He does not resort to dramatic coloration or curious anecdote to bring these historical materials to life. Instead, he captures the attention of the general reader by explicitly casting the historian in the role of a detective attempting to extract the essence of the past from the barren artifacts it has bequeathed to posterity.

Demos's excursion into the mundane description of housing arrangements in Plymouth serves a larger interpretive purpose. It is his contention that the crowded confines of the rough houses of the seventeenth century exacerbated the normal frustrations and problems inherent in family life, and at the same time made it imperative that they be controlled. The aggressive behavior that was suppressed within the household, Demos suggests, was then "displaced" upon other members of the community. As corroborating evidence, Demos points to the relatively large number of interfamily disputes that found their way into the courts, especially when compared to the relative harmony within the nuclear family unit.

Like so much else in *A Little Commonwealth*, this suggestion is frankly presented as a hypothesis without proof in the hope that it will stimulate further research and thought. That is fair enough, but it is important at the outset to establish the a priori character of this type of argument and to insist upon the formulation of testable propositions. For Michael Zuckerman uses Puritan literary evidence that calls for the suppression of antisocial impulses to arrive at another conclusion. Employing different psychological assumptions, Zuckerman argues that New England towns were "peaceable kingdoms," because the socialization of children and the political institutions of the society were functionally designed to make them so. In his view, familial aggression was not displaced upon others; it was either sublimated or directed into more socially acceptable channels.

Demos and Zuckerman are in greater agreement with regard to the significance of the clothing worn by children during the colonial period. Building on the foundations laid by Philippe Ariès in his *Centuries of Childhood*,[6] both authors argue persuasively that the identity of dress among children and adults implies a view of human development in which the young are conceived of as adults in miniature. Starting from this aesthetic observation, Demos then proceeds to adduce considerable evidence from other sources in support of his proposition. In the final and most original section of his book, "Themes of Individual Development," Demos maintains that significant biological changes occur in all children at precisely that age at which the young in Plymouth colony began to be dressed as adults. Further, he contends, it was exactly at this point as well that considerable numbers of children (perhaps one-third) were sent to serve as apprentices or servants in the homes of others. In this instance, at least, there would seem to be a clear fit between traditional types of historical evidence and the eight-stage model of human development proposed by Erik Erikson and used by Demos as a guide to the life cycle of the inhabitants of Plymouth colony during the first two generations of settlement.

In other cases the relationship between fact and theory is not conclusively demonstrated. The paucity

---

6. Philippe Ariès, *Centuries of Childhood: A Social History of Family Life*, trans. Robert Baldick (New York, 1962).

of written evidence prevents the author from proving that the Puritans systematically repressed their children's "natural" impulse for autonomy during the early years of life. More disturbing is Demos's failure to indicate the effect of such child training on the development of the adult personality, or to consider at length the personality structure of the mature members of the Puritan community. Did the authoritarian nature of family life produce, as Richard Bushman has suggested, "steady and resolute personalities sure of the world in which they lived"?[7] Demos skirts this question at several points in the text and always refuses to confront it directly.

The limited range of many of the statements in *A Little Commonwealth* and their hypothetical nature are not as serious as the author's unwillingness to exploit the full potential of the Eriksonian model. For Erikson, human development is the result of a continuing interplay among individual propensities, cultural traditions, and environmental forces. A change in any one of those variables inevitably affects the others; this alteration, and the chain of events it sets in motion, also reveals the precise influence of a given factor in the behavior of the human organism. It is therefore crucial for the historian to apply this model over time in order to indicate the ways in which small changes in the wider social environment effect subtle mutations in the cultural pattern and in the life experiences of a particular generation. Both because of his methodological commitment to the approach of a developmental psychologist and because of his choice of a

---

7. Richard Bushman, *From Puritan to Yankee: Character and the Social Order in Connecticut, 1690–1765* (Cambridge, Mass., 1967), 20.

narrow chronological period, Demos is not sufficiently appreciative of changes on a larger scale—the alterations in the historical context that made family life very different for successive generations, even as it left largely undisturbed the basic structure of the household unit.

For a detailed analysis of historical change, we must turn to the work of Philip J. Greven, Jr. Greven's investigation of the relationship between land, population, and family in colonial Andover is presented with a wealth of data, including twenty-nine tables and five graphs covering a multitude of demographic and social phenomena. It provides a most complete and suggestive analysis of the ecological basis of early American society.

From an isolated settlement of twenty families in 1646, Andover grew rapidly to a town of 600 inhabitants by 1685. That number more than doubled during the next forty years, as the population climbed to 1,305 in 1725; by 1764 there were 2,356 people within the once-ample boundaries of the town. A major factor in this impressive rate of population growth was a low death rate. Plague and famine, the twin scourges of Europe until the mid-eighteenth century, were largely absent from the New England colonies. In the case of famine, this was especially true once the initial settlements had exploited the fruitfulness of the land, and because of the closeness of most towns and villages to navigable water. Except in the port cities along the Atlantic coast, there were relatively few epidemics during the first century of settlement.

The result was little less than spectacular. At the age of twenty the average colonist in America could expect to live well past his or her sixtieth birthday. This was true not only in Andover but in Dedham and Plymouth as well; and that long expectancy of life at maturity continued in New England until the end of the colonial period. The situation was rather different in Europe. It was only the generation of children born to British *ducal* families between 1730 and 1779 whose life expectancy at age twenty equaled that of the early settlers of Massachusetts Bay; and only in the first decades of the nineteenth century did the general population of Norway achieve the same expectation of life at maturity.[8]

The data on child mortality are even more striking and, indeed, hold perhaps the main key to the rapid expansion of American population. Both in Andover and in Plymouth, nearly nine of every ten infants born during the first years of settlement survived to age twenty, although this percentage decreased considerably during succeeding generations. Of those born in Andover between 1670 and 1690, only about 80 percent lived to maturity; this proportion then dropped to 66 percent of those born during the first three decades of the eighteenth century, and to 50 percent of those born between 1730 and 1759. At midcentury the rate of childhood mortality in Andover had regressed to the European standard.[9]

Behind this continuous decline was the increased incidence of scarlet fever, dysentery, and diphtheria, epidemic diseases that struck particularly hard at the ranks of the young but that left relatively unscathed

---

8. T. H. Hollingsworth, "A Demographic Study of British Ducal Families," in *Population in History: Essays in Historical Demography*, ed. D. V. Glass and D. E. C. Eversley (Chicago, 1965), 361 (table 9); Michael Drake, *Population and Society in Norway, 1735–1865* (Cambridge, 1969), 45–49, table 3.5.

9. See, for example, the mortality data in Louis Henry, "The Population of France in the Eighteenth Century," in Glass and Eversley, *Population*, 445–48; Thomas McKeow and R. G. Brown, "Medical Evidence Related to English Population Changes in the Eighteenth Century," in ibid., 298–99.

the mature portion of the population. In time this increase in child mortality affected the rate of population growth as a smaller percentage of the young survived to bear offspring themselves. The first generation of settlers in Andover produced an average of 8.3 children per completed marriage (where both partners survive until the woman reaches the end of her childbearing years). Of these, 7.2 survived to maturity. Those totals fell to 8.1 and 6.6 respectively by the time the second generation began to have children in the years between 1670 and 1690. The offspring of the third generation, born mostly between 1705 and 1735, were still fewer in number. Only 7.2 children were born on an average per completed marriage, and of these only 5.1 survived to adulthood.

As these figures indicate, it was not only the increase in childhood mortality that was responsible for the steady decline in the rate of population growth. Those who did survive to adulthood were having fewer children as well. The number of births per marriage in Andover declined continually during the eighteenth century. From an average of 7.6 in 1700, the number dropped to 4.2 by the 1770s. Two specific factors accounted for this decline: an increase in the length of the interval between births and a rise in the marriage age of women. Because of the severely imbalanced sex ratio during the first generation in Andover and in Plymouth, the average age at marriage for women was exceedingly low: at Plymouth 20 years, in Andover a mere 19 years. In Andover this average rose to 22.3 for the next generation, 24.5 for the third, and then dropped slightly to 23.2 for the fourth generation. The increase of four or five years was particularly dramatic, for it meant that those women who married in the eighteenth century would have at least one and probably two fewer live births during their fertile years than those who had begun to raise a family in the preceding century.[10]

The studies of Greven and Demos suggest, therefore, that the high rate of population growth in colonial New England was the result both of low childhood mortality in isolated frontier settlements—a condition duplicated in certain parts of Scandinavia—and a sharp decrease in the age of marriage for women during the first fifty years of a new community. Because the area of settlement was continually expanding during the eighteenth century, it seems likely that these prime demographic conditions were repeated again and again. This assumption would account for the fact that in 1800, when the first national figures are available, the crude birthrate of the white population of the United States was in the range of 40 to 50 per 1,000, or an average of five or six births per marriage.[11]

---

10. At Crulai, France, in the period from 1674 to 1742, "the mean number of children per completed family is approximately 8, 6, and 4, for women who marry at 20, 25, and 30 respectively." (Henry, "Population of France," 450). It is also likely, as Robert Wells has pointed out to me, that the continual decline in births per marriage was caused in part by the migration of couples married in Andover who departed before the end of the woman's childbearing period. That the number of births per completed marriage falls much less slowly than does the number of births for all marriages suggests as much (see Greven, *Four Generations*, tables 6, 15, 21).

11. J. Potter, "The Growth of Population in America, 1700–1860," in Glass and Eversley, *Population*, 672; Ansley J. Coale and Melvin Zelnik, *New Estimates of Fertility and Population in the United States: A Study of Annual White Births from 1855 to 1960 and of Completeness of Enumeration in the Censuses from 1880 to 1960* (Princeton, N.J., 1963), chapter 4; Gustaf Utterström, "Two Essays on Population in Eighteenth-Century Scandinavia," in Glass and Eversley, *Population*, 528, 530. The lower fertility of women in long-settled areas (more unmarried women and later age at marriage because of disproportionate male immigration to the frontier)

By that date the number of births per marriage in Andover had fallen to three. Given the high incidence of death in childhood, it was doubtful if the members of the town were even reproducing themselves. Indeed, the total population of the town actually declined between 1776 and 1800. The cause of this depopulation—the conjunction of a high age at marriage for women, high infant and child mortality, and declining marital fertility (as measured by an increase in the average interval between births)—appeared also in Colyton, Devon, during a period of disease and economic decline.[12] The simultaneous appearance of three demographic characteristics of a stationary or declining population was not accidental and points directly to the central ecological question: the intricate interaction between land, population, technology, and culture.

To state the problem is easier than to resolve it, but the valuable investigations of Greven and Lockridge permit us to begin.[13] Three distinct phases, corresponding roughly to the passage of generations, appear to characterize the social life of the towns of colonial New England. The first, which Greven has referred to as a reversion to a "traditional" patriarchal

---

would be more than offset by the increased birthrates in the new areas, and especially by the much lower rates of child mortality there.

12. E. A. Wrigley, "Family Limitation in Pre-Industrial England," *Economic History Review*, 2d ser., 19 (1966): 101–5. As Wrigley is at pains to point out, this rather strange mixture of demographic characteristics can be explained only by reference to a wider ecological crisis.

13. Two fine articles by Lockridge are "Land, Population, and the Evolution of New England Society, 1630–1790," *Past and Present* 39 (1968): 62–80, and (with Alan Krieder) "The Evolution of Massachusetts Town Government, 1640 to 1740," *William and Mary Quarterly*, 3d ser., 25 (1968): 549–74.

society, was inaugurated by the first settlers and persisted, to some extent, during the lifetimes of their sons and daughters. Its distinctive features were an elitist political system in which effective authority resided in the hands of long-serving selectmen; patriarchal control over the disposition of family lands, a practice that kept the age of marriage for men at a European level; and low rates of geographic mobility. In Dedham, for example, less than 1 percent of the adult males of the town would emigrate in a given year. The inhabitants of these first communities were content to farm their ample lands and to take directions from their ministers and leaders; their sons likewise acquiesced in the hierarchical pattern of authority because of limited economic opportunities elsewhere and their expectation of a considerable landed inheritance.

There was a dynamic element to these settlements as well, and this "expansive" feature soon became the predominant one. For sixteen years following the initial settlement at Plymouth in 1620, Governor William Bradford led a successful effort to prevent the dispersion of population. Then, in a massive surge caused both by internal discontent and external immigration, seven new towns were founded between 1636 and 1641. The chronology was much the same within the geographically more extensive towns of Massachusetts Bay. During the first twenty years of settlement the proprietors of Dedham distributed only 3,000 acres of the two hundred square miles bestowed upon them by the General Court; the next twelve years, however, witnessed the allocation of an additional 15,000 acres. In Andover, three divisions of land between 1646 and 1658 resulted in the allotment of only 2,700 acres; but in the fourth division of 1662 the settlers divided up more than 5,000 acres. The immediate effect of this expansion was a breakup of the nucleated open-field pattern and an increase in the significance of the individual family, now settled on lands of its own at an appreciable distance from the center of the community.

A second dynamic factor was the growth in the size of the family. The birthrate reached 50 per 1,000 in Dedham during the first decade of settlement, a level that was never subsequently surpassed. In Andover and Plymouth the process was slower. The number of births per marriage rose from the first generation to the second, just at the time that the town was beginning to make a liberal dispensation of its landed wealth. Significantly, this increase in marital fertility occurred at the same time as an increase in the average age of women at marriage. This rise in age was more than offset, however, by a decrease in the average interval between births from twenty-eight to twenty-four months. This development, in turn, would seem to have been the result of the perception of favorable economic conditions and of the great demand for labor.

If the connection between agricultural abundance and marital fertility is conjectural, the relationship between inheritance patterns and geographical mobility in this first phase of town history is clear. Greven finds that in Andover, partible inheritance was endorsed in practice as well as in theory. Over 96 percent of the sons of the first generation of settlers eventually received land from their fathers. As a result, 78 percent of the men of the second generation remained in the town for their entire lives. And why not? With large tracts of land still untouched by a plow, there was no incentive to move on in search of a landed estate.

That abundance had decreased significantly by the time the third generation came to maturity during the first decades of the eighteenth century, and this change marked the end of the "expansive" stage in the social morphology of the New England town. Only about 66 percent of the male members of the third generation received land from their fathers, and only 60 percent of those who survived to the age of twenty-one in Andover remained in the town all their lives. Many of those men purchased their inheritance from their fathers; other sons were given gifts of money in lieu of a section of land. Finally, a large proportion (20–25 percent) of the male members of this generation took up a trade, an index not only of growing occupational specialization within the community but also of the need for an alternative means of support. The diminishing agricultural resources of the family had been accompanied by a decrease in the extent of patriarchal authority within the household. Unable to provide for his offspring, the father could not hope to control them.

It was at this point in the history of the community that the average number of births per marriage began to decline. Those married between 1700 and 1710 averaged 7.5 births per completed family. The rate dropped sharply to 5.7 for those beginning married life in the succeeding ten years, and to 4.8, 4.1, and 4.0 in the three decades between 1720 and 1750.

By the time the fourth generation came to maturity between 1730 and 1769, Andover had become overcrowded. The density of the population reached forty-one per square mile in 1764, and fifty per square mile in 1776, relatively high figures given the relatively primitive agrarian technology of the period. There was a consequent decrease in the number of estates that were divided among all sons as Andover moved into the third, or "static," phase of its colonial history. Whereas 95 percent of the estates of the first generation had been divided among all of the male heirs, only 75 percent were so distributed by the next generation. The proportion declined even further, to 58 percent, when the third generation came to divide its property in the second half of the eighteenth century. The result was that only 43 percent of the males of the fourth generation who survived to maturity remained in Andover for the rest of their lives. The majority of men moved off into other localities, often with the assistance of their families, and settled in no fewer than fifty-two different New England communities. The dynamic of natural population increase, present since the early years of the town, had finally outrun the capacity of the land to sustain it, given the essential continuity of economic production, agrarian technology, and social organization.

Andover was not the only town to experience the oppressive effects of the pressure of population upon resources. Charles Grant's study of Kent, Connecticut, delineates the same configuration. Settled in 1738 by forty families, many of which were composed of fourth-generation descendants of the first English settlers, Kent supported an adult male population of 321 forty years later. But 500 adult males had lived in the town between 1774 and 1777; over fifty men were moving out of the community each year in search of new land. That process continued until 1796, when a census of the town indicated that 209 adult males were settled on 103 separate homesteads; the subdivided farms of Kent would support only a single heir. New England society had to expand geographically or it would die.[14]

By the end of the American Revolution, Kent,

---

14. Charles Grant, *Democracy in the Connecticut Frontier Town of Kent* (1961; reprint, New York, 1972), 99–103.

like Andover, had reached the third, or "static," phase of its social development. There was an inner dynamic to this process. Once unleashed by the favorable ecological conditions of the New World, the deep-rooted biological force of sustained population growth had come to constitute an independent variable in the historical process, shaping and molding cultural patterns. The "traditional" community of the first generations, with its emphasis on patriarchy, hierarchy, and stability, had been inexorably superseded by an "expansive" society with very different social characteristics. And this, in turn, gave way to the "static" town of the late eighteenth century. Epidemics, technological advances, religious conflicts, increased trade—all of these could (and sometimes did) impinge upon or distort the basic morphology of the life cycle of the town. But in much of New England during the colonial period, these exogenous variables were so weak in their substance and so scattered in their incidence that they can best be considered as deviations from the norm, as "accidents" within a larger framework of organic historical development.

Before making one very important qualification to this social morphology of the New England town, it is necessary to establish the connection between demographic change and political development. As Lockridge brilliantly demonstrates in the case of Dedham, there was a direct causal link between the growth of population and certain types of political change. The doubling of the town's size within a period of forty years produced a surplus of potential political leaders. Because of the increased competition for the same number of offices, the average length of service for a selectman of the town dropped from 7.6 years to 4.8 years. Nor was this all. The number and length of town meetings increased during the second stage of Dedham's social development. There were more issues to discuss and more voices to be heard. New institutional procedures were adopted as ad hoc committees were named to deal with specific problems.

In the end these various developments converged to transform the basic political character of the town. A small group of respected and experienced selectmen, well advanced in age, no longer decided the affairs of the town in informal meetings; the pressure of population had created new leaders and a more open, more responsive, and more democratic town meeting. Like many other aspects of town life, "middle-class democracy" was the manifestation of a discrete and transient stage of political development. In time it would give way to the "organized social system" that Henry Adams discerned in his compelling portrait of New England in 1800 as "the cordial union between the clergy, the magistracy, the bench and the bar," which dominated the life of the community.[15]

This evolution was related to significant changes in the social structure. From 1740 until 1777 the permanent "proletariat" in Kent, Connecticut, had never numbered more than 4 percent of the adult male population; by 1796 the proportion had risen to 11 percent. In Dedham the share of the town's wealth owned by the poorest 20 percent of the taxpayers fell from 10 percent in 1690 to half that ratio in 1730. During the same period, the landless element in the population increased from 5 to 10 percent of the adult males. As geographical mobility was hampered by the custom of partible inheritance, the members of this

---

15. Henry Adams, *The United States in 1800* (Ithaca, N.Y., 1955), 54.

new subgroup of landless workers would eventually facilitate the establishment of small industrial enterprises in New England at the beginning of the nineteenth century. Here, then, was the important legacy of the third phase of town development: a surplus population that could be employed in a subsequent process of technological and industrial advance.[16]

The interrelationship between demographic change and the political and social life cycle of a town could be traced in greater detail,[17] but the argument is clear enough. It remains only to place this social morphology within a larger chronological context. The members of the fourth Andover generation who left the town of their birth to settle in fifty-two different New England communities did not have the same religious fervor, social attitudes, and political outlook as did the original settlers of the town. The history of the settlements they would help to create, therefore, would not be completely congruent with that of An-

---

16. A number of English historians have demonstrated the link between partible inheritance and the rise of important centers of domestic industry. See Joan Thirsk, "Industries in the Countryside," in *Essays in the Economic and Social History of Tudor and Stuart England*, ed. F. J. Fisher (London, 1961), and H. J. Habakkuk, "Family Structure and Economic Change in Nineteenth Century Europe," *Journal of Economic History* 15 (1955): 1–12.

17. For example, it was not completely fortuitous that epidemic diseases appeared during the "expansive" phase of the history of Andover. "Given a constant birth rate," Ernest Caulfield has noted, "a steady growth in population density obviously produced a more and more rapid renewal of concentrated groups of nonimmune children, a fact which explains the orderly increase in frequency of epidemics" (Ernest Caulfield, "Some Common Diseases of Colonial Children," *Publications of the Colonial Society of Massachusetts* 35 [1942–46]: 13); idem, "A History of the Terrible Epidemic, Vulgarly Called the Throat Distemper, as It Occurred in His Majesty's New England Colonies between 1735 and 1740," *Yale Journal of Biology and Medicine* 11 (1938–39): 334.

dover despite the existence of certain demographic similarities. The maturing of a money economy, itself an index of cumulative economic development, had disrupted the character of the old subsistence-oriented agricultural communities. When Kent was founded in 1738, it took the proprietors only two years to distribute the greater part of the town's land, and ownership of property was not restricted to those who intended to migrate to the new settlement. Only 60 percent of the men who owned land in Kent during the subsequent twenty-five years ever became members of the community; the rest preferred to speculate with their holdings, hoping to profit from the steadily rising land values in the frontier town. This was a far cry from the close communal consciousness that had prevailed when Dedham had been settled in 1636, when residents sought land as much for the sake of community as for the love of money. As Bushman has shown in his study of Connecticut, the New England towns had not been able completely to withstand the processes of historical change.

It is with this point firmly in mind that we must now turn to Zuckerman's contention that the basic values and behavior of the inhabitants of those towns did not change significantly between 1691 and 1776. On the basis of a close reading of the reports of hundreds of town meetings, Zuckerman concludes that "the consciousness of community, in Massachusetts, continued at least three quarters of the way through the eighteenth century as a prime value of public life, an abiding core of provincial culture."[18]

There is much to be said in support of that

---

18. Zuckerman, *Peaceable Kingdoms*, vii.

interpretation. When New Englanders of the colonial period reflected on the nature of the social order, they did not espouse the ethic of individualism and its attendant values of pluralism, toleration, and majority rule. Rather, they emphasized the harmful effects of political factionalism and of religious and cultural diversity. Simultaneously, people of the eighteenth century exalted the virtues of harmony, conformity, and consensus. Real freedom (though they would not have formulated it precisely in this way) was possible only within a community of like-minded individuals. Time after time, the secession of a dissident group inevitably resulted in the creation of a new and more acceptable form of social authority. Men and women continued to define themselves and their goals in terms of the community rather than in opposition to it.

Zuckerman is therefore on strong grounds when he points to the persistence of the values of uniformity and consensus in eighteenth-century New England. As he is careful to point out, the methods used to achieve those social ends shifted gradually from physical coercion to moral persuasion. There was little alternative. Lacking a powerful constabulary and a highly developed legal system, the towns had to rely on the goodwill and internal discipline of the inhabitants to secure the implementation of legislation and the payment of taxes. The function of the town meeting was not to determine the will of the majority but to ascertain the General Will, the verdict that would be accepted as law by all members of the community. Consciously using the consensus approach to American history as an analytical tool, Zuckerman points out that only in terms of this larger context can the de facto acceptance of universal male suffrage in town affairs be understood, for unless a man participated in the formulation of law, he could not be expected to obey it. "Whatever the stated business written in the warrant," Zuckerman claims at one point, "the real business of a public meeting was always the consolidation of the community."[19]

That statement, like Zuckerman's general argument, must be qualified in several important respects. The purpose of the town meeting was, in fact, the transaction of substantive business, although the conditions demanded that this be done in a manner acceptable to the group as a whole and not merely to a bare majority. Only when a particular measure threatened the internal cohesion of the community were the inhabitants forced to articulate the principles on which their society was based. Only then did the enterprise take on the explicitly self-conscious communality that Zuckerman has detected.

A further point may be made in this regard. The system of values on which this communal culture rested was enunciated most clearly and most frequently when its ethical norms were most under attack, precisely at the moment at which they were not accepted as binding by a significant number of the inhabitants. It is not accidental, therefore, that most of the affirmations of consensus and community that Zuckerman cites come from the 1750s or later, for it was then that the changed economic and religious conditions of New England had undermined the traditional foundations of town life. An increasingly diverse and rapidly growing society needed a new ethic; until this new system of values was found, political and religious leaders would continue to invoke the old precepts of uniformity, harmony, and community. By the eve of the revolution, however, those

19. Ibid., 184.

invocations were little more than futile calls to a vanished past or the first adumbrations of the new sense of community that would appear at the beginning of the nineteenth century.

This interpretation is supported by Zuckerman's own evidence, but his sources and his methodology—the stress placed on values and goals rather than on behavior and events—have prevented him from developing it fully. In his third appendix, for example, Zuckerman provides a chronological analysis of those local disputes that came to the attention of the Massachusetts legislature. The results are revealing. Only 32 disputes were referred to the authorities in Boston for discussion and resolution in the four decades between 1691 and 1732, but there were 36 such referrals between 1730 and 1742, and at least 44 in the nine subsequent years. The peak came between 1751 and 1755, when more than 70 local disputes were transmitted to the central government for adjudication.

The change in the nature of the disputes that defied a local solution was equally significant. The data in the appendix indicate that 18 of the 32 controversies that came to the attention of the legislature before 1732 related to "disputes within the town," and only 5 to the "rearrangement of the community." This latter category would become the obsessive concern of the next generation. The dispersion of settlement as a result of the growth of population caused an impressive increase in the number of political struggles in the town meetings, as outlying groups of settlers sought to form new churches and new communities. Of the 64 disputes relating to the fragmentation of existing settlements, 51 arose in the period after 1742. Likewise, 50 of the 57 battles between local town meetings and absentee proprietors occurred after this date, a revealing testimony to the increase in land speculation and absentee ownership. Because of Zuckerman's concern with values and with rhetoric, he is blind to the changing social reality that was gradually emerging behind the facade of the traditional clichés.

Yet Zuckerman's tightly woven argument does point to the essence of the evolution of colonial New England society, an essence that does not correspond to the image of declension and disintegration. Even in the new and unfamiliar circumstances brought about by a decline in religious cohesiveness and by an increase in the extent of the market economy, land speculation, and geographic mobility, men and women continued to define themselves as members of a harmonious community and sought a new and more acceptable definition of commonwealth. The substance of community had changed, but not the value of its existence in the minds of New England's inhabitants.

There was a concrete index to this quest for community. The new settlements of eighteenth-century New England were not formed, on the whole, by individuals moving off into the wilderness; rather, they were the result of the coalescence of "fragments" of several existing communities. Nearly 60 percent of the original settlers of Concord, New Hampshire, in the 1720s came from the towns of Andover and Haverhill. At the same time, at least twenty-one members of five Andover families were migrating to Windham County in Connecticut. In Kent during the period from 1738 to 1760 there were eight Beemans, ten Fullers, fourteen Rowlees, and over twenty other families with four or more adult male members. When the pressure of population on resources came to be felt at Kent, no fewer than ten different families moved across the border to the frontier town of Amenia, New York. Like their parents and grandparents before them, these migrants resettled in communities in which the ties of friendship and personal relation mitigated the psychological strains of geographic mobility.

In short, the decline in community was paralleled and to some extent offset by the rise of the family. During the eighteenth century the basic social unit took on more of the tasks of socialization and acculturalization. Between the time of the waning of the influence of the church and the emergence of the public school, the family unit assumed the burden of the education of the young. It was the family, likewise, that became the prime economic institution in the society. With the town lands distributed among the proprietors, it was up to the family to provide for its numerous members. Greven has shown with considerable skill and sensitivity how the traditional structure of the colonial family—nuclear household units with an extended kinship group residing in the community—adapted itself to deal with these new conditions. Instead of settling all their sons in separate households on family land, the members of the third generation of fathers in Andover bought land for some of their male heirs in other communities, defrayed the cost of education or apprenticeship for others, and bestowed small but useful sums of money upon those sons who wished to migrate. The structure of the colonial American family thus facilitated geographic mobility and economic expansion. Patriarchy had given way to parental solicitude and aid by the eighteenth century, but the ties of family and kinship remained as stable, organic, and positive factors in the lives of the colonists, smoothing the passage from one generation and one community to the next.[20]

---

20. This interpretation was derived from a review by David Rothman ("A Note on the Study of the Colonial Family," *William and Mary Quarterly*, 3d ser., 23 [1966]: 627–34) of two important works on the American colonial family: Edmund S. Morgan, *The Puritan Family: Religion and Domestic Relations in Seventeenth-Century New England* (1944; rev. ed., New York, 1966), and Bernard Bailyn, *Education in the Forming of American Society: Needs and Opportunities for Study* (Chapel Hill, N.C., 1960).

The elements of orderly, coherent growth were even more evident in those towns that had reached the "static" phase of their social development. About 1720, five members of the third generation of the Abbot family of Andover—three brothers and two sisters—left the town of their birth to resettle together in Brookfield, Massachusetts. But in 1775 there were still thirty-one adult male members of the family in the old town, all descendants of the first George Abbot. Intermarried into a dozen different Andover families, those men could count as kin a significant portion of the town's population. That interlocking web of family and kinship gave the community a strong sense of unity and cohesiveness, and it presents us with a picture of social reality that belies the traditional image of disintegration and decay. There was a strong element of organic growth and rebirth in the society of colonial New England, and it is time that we began to write its history in the positive terms that its substance demands.

2

The Weber Thesis
Revisited:

The Protestant Ethic and the
Reality of Capitalism
in
Early America

I

"We not only have Liberty to labour in Moderation,"
Thomas Chalkley (1675–1741) of Philadelphia wrote
in his journal, "but . . . it is our Duty so to do." "The
Farmer, the Tradesman, and the Merchant," this devout Quaker continued, "do not understand by our
Lord's doctrine, that they must neglect their Calling,
or grow idle in their Business, but must certainly
work, and be industrious in their Callings. I . . .
followed my Business with Diligence and Industry,"
Chalkley testified, and consequently "throve in the

Things of the World, the Lord adding a Blessing to my Labour."[1]

Chalkley worked with equal diligence for things of the spirit. He sought converts while on business in Bermuda in 1716; warned his son-in-law, an avid reader, to be certain "that thy chief Study in Books may be the holy Scriptures"; and, at his death in 1741, bequeathed 111 religious books to the lending library of the Philadelphia Monthly Meeting. But Chalkley's major contribution to Quakerism was his journal. Like the journals kept by many other "public friends," his *Historical Account of the Life, Travels, and Christian Experiences, of that Antient, Faithful Servant of Jesus Christ, Thomas Chalkley* (1749) was published to set an example for posterity and to further the progress of the truth.[2]

A century before, in the 1630s, Joshua Scottow had migrated to New England. A devout Puritan and the author of passionate moral tracts, he was quickly accepted into the First Church of Boston. An astute trader, Scottow became a prominent merchant, trading with Newfoundland and speculating in land. In 1670 he moved to Scarborough, Maine, invested in the fishing industry, and, like Chalkley, became a public figure and moral preceptor to future generations. "*New-England* is not to be found in *New-England*, nor *Boston* in *Boston*; it has become a lost Town," he lamented in a vividly named tract of 1691, *Old Men's Tears for Their Own Declension Mixed with Fears of Their and Posterities Falling Off from New England's Primitive Constitution.* "We must now cry out," Scottow warned

---

1. Frederick B. Tolles, *Meeting House and Counting House: The Quaker Merchants of Colonial Philadelphia, 1682–1763* (1948; reprint, New York, 1963), 56.
2. Ibid., 90, 146, 154, 166.

his readers, and admit "our *Leanness*, our *Leanness*, our *Apostasy*, . . . *Formality in Worship*, *carnal and vain Confidence* in Church-Privileges, forgetting of GOD our Rock, and Multitude of other Abominations."[3]

Chalkley and Scottow stand forth as exemplars of Max Weber's "Protestant ethic." The Reformed churches and particularly the radical sects, Weber argued, created a new "conception of the state of religious grace." Their members could no longer seek salvation "by any magical sacraments, by relief in the confession, nor by individual good works." Rather, they were driven, both by religious doctrine and a psychological need for assurance of salvation, to pursue their divinely ordained "calling." The result was an unremitting and disciplined "rational planning of the whole of one's life in accordance with God's will."[4] "I followed my Calling; and kept to Meetings diligently," Chalkley asserted, "for I was not easy to be idle; either in my spiritual or temporal callings."

Nor was he alone among the early migrants to British North America. Scottow undoubtedly read John Cotton's *The Way of Life* (1641), the classic exposition of the doctrine of the calling in the literature of New England. "How shall I know that I have that life, in having of which, I may know I have Christ?" Cotton asked his readers (and undoubtedly the members of his Boston congregation). "Art thou diligent in thy

---

3. Bernard Bailyn, *The New England Merchants in the Seventeenth Century* (1955; reprint, New York, 1964): 122–23.

4. Max Weber, *The Protestant Ethic and the Spirit of Capitalism*, trans. Talcott Parsons (London, 1930), 153. "This rationalization of conduct within the world, but for the sake of the world beyond," Weber concluded, "was the consequence of the concept of calling of ascetic Protestantism" (154). See also pp. 80–81, 120–21.

calling, it is well," he answered in part, for *"cursed is He that doth the worke of the Lord negligently,* and the work of his calling is the worke of the Lorde." Spiritual directives in early Pennsylvania were nearly identical. "The perfection of Christian life," declared William Penn, the founder of the Quaker colony, "extends to every honest labour or traffic used among men."[5]

The lives of such Puritans and Quakers were not easy, for this religious doctrine created a major tension in their lives. On the one hand, it directed them to immerse themselves in the things of this world without, on the other hand, lavishing their affections on earthy pursuits. The contradiction was palpable. How many men and women could avoid the sin of covetousness, could pursue profits without succumbing to the temptations of profit? Their numbers were few, but their names were famous. One exemplar was the Boston merchant John Hull, who, it was said, walked constantly in the fear of God. "The loss of my estate will be nothing," Hull consoled himself when the Dutch captured his ships, "if the Lord please to join my soul nearer to himself, and loose it more from creature comforts." He "was a Saint upon Earth," Samuel Willard declared in his funeral sermon for Hull, a man who lived "above the World" with "his heart disentangled" even as he was caught up "in the midst of all outward occasions and urgency of Business."[6]

---

5. Frederick B. Tolles, *Quakers and the Atlantic Culture* (New York, 1960), 61; Perry Miller, *The New England Mind: From Colony to Province* (Boston, 1953), 41; Stephen Foster, *Their Solitary Way: The Puritan Social Ethic in the First Century of Settlement in New England* (New Haven, Conn., 1971), 104; Tolles, *Meeting House,* 55.
6. Foster, *Their Solitary Way,* 120, neatly states this "flaw" in Puritan economics, while Hull's solution is outlined in Miller, *New England Mind: From Colony to Province,* 42–43.

The death of Robert Keayne, another Boston merchant, laid bare the psychological tensions inherent in the Calvinists' conception of the calling. A London tradesman, Keayne migrated to Boston in 1635, joined Joshua Scottow as a member of the First Church, and prospered as an import merchant—at least in part because of his inner discipline and purpose. He had never indulged in "an idle, lazie, or dronish life," Keayne protested in his last will and testament, a 50,000-word apologia for the conduct of his life. Not only had he diligently pursued his business (leaving the substantial estate of four thousand pounds on his death in 1656), but he also made time to compose "3 great writing bookes which are intended as an Exposition or Interpretation of the whole Bible." Nonetheless, Keayne went astray, at least in the eyes of the world. In 1639 the colony's government charged the Boston merchant, to his lasting shame, with a series of economic crimes: "taking above six-pence in the shilling profit; in some above eight-pence; and in some small things, above two for one."[7]

Feelings against Keayne ran high in the Massachusetts Bay, fueled by a decade of scarce goods and inflationary prices. When Keayne's trial began, Reverend Ezekiel Rogers wrote to Governor John Winthrop advocating "a Law to hang up some [of the merchants] before the Lord, they deserve it, and it would to him be a sacrifice most acceptable." As minister in the country town of Rowley, Rogers spoke for many hard-pressed farmers and tradesmen. His advice also reflected his own earlier experiences, and those of many

---

7. Bailyn, *New England Merchants*, 41–42; Miller, *New England Mind: From Colony to Province*, 45.

Rowley residents, in England. They had migrated, in response to severe ecclesiastical persecution and financial distress, from the East Riding of Yorkshire, one of those "drowsy corners of the north" with a traditional open-field system of farming, little agricultural innovation, and manorial courts that strictly regulated economic life. "Shall the already persecuted and impoverished members of Christ," Rogers demanded of Winthrop, "be made a prey to Cormorants?"[8] Responding to such "well guided zeale" (as Keayne called it), the General Court imposed a hefty fine of two hundred pounds. Equally seriously, the elders of the church nearly excommunicated Keayne. After an "exquisite search" of his conduct, they severely admonished him "in the Name of the Church for selling his wares at excessive Rates, to the Dishonor of Gods name," and exacted a public "penetentiall acknowledgement" of his sin.[9]

The lives of Chalkley and Scottow, Hull and Keayne, lend support to various aspects of the Weber thesis. The Calvinist doctrine of the calling obviously did place psychological pressures on a devout laity that could be assuaged only by an outpouring of worldly energy—in their business affairs and, no less importantly, in church concerns and religious tracts.

---

8. Foster, *Their Solitary Way*, 166. David Grayson Allen, *In English Ways: The Movement of Societies and the Transferal of English Local Law and Custom to Massachusetts Bay in the Seventeenth Century* (Chapel Hill, N.C., 1981), chapter 2 and pp. 165–67, describes the Old World origins of Rowley's residents and minister.

9. Bailyn, *New England Merchants*, 42. See also Bernard Bailyn's exegesis of Keayne's last will and testament, "The Apologia of Robert Keayne," *William and Mary Quarterly*, 3d ser., 7 (1950): 568–87, and the complete document in Bailyn, ed., *The Apologia of Robert Keayne: The Self Portrait of a Puritan Merchant* (New York, 1965).

This "Protestant ethic" produced not only disciplined and rationalized lives that embodied the "spirit" of capitalism but also the actual expansion of capitalist economic activity. The enterprise of Quaker merchants helped to make Philadelphia the largest colonial port (and one of the larger towns in the entire British world) by the eve of the American Revolution. Members of the sect constituted about 15 percent of the city's population in 1769, yet they accounted for more than one-half of those paying taxes of one hundred pounds or more. When Jacques-Pierre Brissot de Warville visited Philadelphia a decade and a half later, he ascribed that success, in part, to "the order which Quakers are accustomed from childhood to apply to the distribution of their tasks, their thoughts, and every moment of their lives." "They carry this spirit of order everywhere," he noted; "it economizes time, activity, and money."[10]

Moreover, the lives of these Quaker and Puritan merchants (reconstructed in substantial works of modern scholarship) lend support to Weber's understanding of early America. There were indeed, as he claimed, "complaints of a peculiarly calculating sort of profit seeking in New England" in the 1630s.[11] Moreover, Weber did not err in using Benjamin Franklin's moral precepts to demonstrate the importance of the Protestant ethic in British America. To be sure, Franklin's utilitarian tracts reflected the influence of secular Enlightenment rationalism. But they also stemmed from a still-vital tradition of ascetic religion in Quaker Philadelphia. Franklin wrote *Advice to a*

---

10. Tolles, *Meeting House*, 49, 61.
11. Weber, *Protestant Ethic*, 55–56.

Young Tradesman, the tract used so extensively by Weber, in 1748, at the same time as his printing firm of Franklin and Hall was preparing Thomas Chalkley's journal for publication (in 1749).[12] Moreover, Keayne's painful apologia demonstrated the power of Weber's analysis of lay-controlled church discipline. As the great German sociologist argued in a companion article, entitled "The Protestant Sects and the Spirit of Capitalism," the "tremendous social significance of admission to full enjoyment of the rights of the sectarian congregation" acted as a harsh ethical "premium," encouraging potential members to lead disciplined lives. Whether through the logic of Puritan predestination, Quaker conscientiousness, or sectarian discipline, the lives of some American colonists—perhaps many—embodied "the 'spirit' of modern capitalism, its specific ethos: the ethos of the modern bourgeois middle classes."[13]

---

12. Ibid., 50, 180, 192–98; Tolles, *Meeting House*, 166. Thus in 1719 the Quaker merchant Isaac Norris advised his son to "Come back plain" from his first business trip to London. "This will be a reputation to thee and recommend thee to the best and most Sensible people." Franklin probably imbibed similar precepts from Thomas Denham, another Philadelphia Quaker. "In order to secure my credit and character as a tradesman," he wrote upon leaving Denham's employ, "I took care not only to be in *reality* industrious and frugal, but to avoid all appearance to the contrary. I drest plainly." See ibid., 63.

13. Max Weber, "The Protestant Sects and the Spirit of Capitalism," in *From Max Weber: Essays in Sociology*, ed. H. H. Gerth and C. Wright Mills (New York, 1946), 312, 321, and passim. "It is not the ethical *doctrine* of a religion," Weber pointed out in this restatement and revision of his earlier interpretation, "but that form of ethical conduct upon which *premiums* are placed that matters." "It has been the fundamental mistake of my critics not to have taken notice of this very fact" (321, 459n). See also Benton Johnson, "Max Weber and American Protestantism," *The Sociological Quarterly* 12 (1971): 473–85.

II

Whatever its many insights and merits, Weber's explo-
ration of Protestantism and capitalism failed to comprehend crucial facets of early American religious and
economic history. For example, it did not explain the
strong anticommercial and anticapitalist elements in
seventeenth-century Puritanism. Nor did Weber ade-
quately explain why colonial New England was the
poorest region of British America at the end of the
colonial period, given the alleged predominance of a
procapitalist Protestant Ethic.

These deficiencies of the Weber thesis were not
restricted to the American case, but reflect more general shortcomings. As R. H. Tawney and other scholars of early modern England have demonstrated, most
early English Puritans condemned the pursuit of
economic gain; they sought to control, not unleash,
capitalist enterprise.[14] Moreover, the economic backwardness of seventeenth-century Scotland, the quint-
essential Calvinist society, negates any easy corre-
spondence between sectarian reformed religion and
capitalist development. Weber's narrow focus on the
religious doctrine of the calling and its psychological
implications neglected the role of material conditions
and historical circumstances in the development of
capitalism.

These shortcomings in Weber's thesis had two
causes, both ideological. First, Weber's *Protestant Ethic*
mirrored the sharp religious and political conflicts in
late nineteenth-century Germany. His argument im-

---

14. See R. H. Tawney, *Religion and the Rise of Capitalism* (London,
1926); H. M. Robertson, *Aspects of the Rise of Economic Individualism*
(Cambridge, England, 1933).

plicitly attacked Catholicism by linking its religious and ethical values with economic backwardness. Seen in this light, Weber's thesis was part of the *Kulturekampf*, the generation-long battle between Catholics and Protestants for cultural supremacy in the new German empire. It was also a manifesto by a classical liberal (and an active member of the National Liberal party) against Lutheranism and the German tradition of submissiveness to the authority of church and state. Throughout *The Protestant Ethic* Weber contrasts Luther's conception of a person's calling, "a fate to which he must submit," with that of Calvin: "God's commandment to the individual to work for the divine glory."[15] His heroes are English Calvinists, men and women who not only forged a progressive economic ethic but also challenged the authority of kings and bishops. By depicting the Puritans as protoclassical liberals (and thus minimizing the medieval aspects of their social ethics), Weber sought to link his political cause with the triumph of industrial capitalism.

German liberalism was besieged both by Bismarkian conservatives on the right and Marxian socialists on the left. Consequently, Weber directed a second ideological attack against Karl Marx's interpretation of history. "Marx had run the causal sequence in one direction, i.e., from economic to spiritual fac-

---

15. Weber, *Protestant Ethic*, 160. On Weber's anti-Lutheran bias, see Friedrich Wilhelm Graf, "Weber's Theological Sources" (Paper presented at a symposium on *The Protestant Ethic*, German Historical Institute, Washington, D.C., May 1990). In *The Social Sources of Denominationalism* (1929; reprint, New York, 1957), 94–95, H. Richard Niebuhr posits "the harmony of the Calvinist conception of individual rights and responsibilities with the interests of the middle class." Following Weber's agenda, he suggests: "*Laissez-faire* and the spirit of political liberalism have flourished most in countries where the influence of Calvinism was greatest."

tors," H. Stuart Hughes has suggested, "Weber wanted to run it in the reverse order as a complement to what Marx had done."[16] This interpretation is too benign. Weber wanted not to complement the Marxist theory of historical change but to refute it. In *The Protestant Ethic* he explicitly addressed the "doctrine of the more naive historical materialism, that . . . ideas originate as a reflection or superstructure of economic situations" and found it wanting. "In the country of Benjamin Franklin's birth (Massachusetts)," Weber argued, "the spirit of capitalism (in the sense we have attached to it) was present before the capitalistic order." Likewise, "in the backwoods small bourgeois circumstances of Pennsylvania in the eighteenth century, where business threatened for lack of money to fall into barter, where there was hardly a sign of large enterprise . . . [the pursuit of profit] was considered the essence of moral conduct, even commanded in the name of duty. . . . To speak here of a reflection of material circumstances in the ideal superstructure," Weber concluded with a rhetorical flourish, "would be patent nonsense."[17]

Perhaps so. But Weber himself failed to specify the actual relationship between religion and society, either in Europe or America. Consequently, he raised more questions than he answered. In particular, did the Protestant ethic contribute, in a causal manner, to the rise of capitalism? Some of Weber's defenders deny the relevance of this question, asserting that "his purpose had *not* been to explain the origin or the expan-

---

16. H. Stuart Hughes, quoted in *Protestantism, Capitalism, and Social Science; The Weber Thesis Controversy*, ed. Robert W. Green, 2d ed. (Lexington, Mass., 1973), 166.
17. Weber, *Protestant Ethic*, 55–56, 74–75.

sion of capitalism." But that answer will not do, for two reasons. First, Weber himself linked the activist Protestants of early modern Europe to the expansion of capitalism: "those self-confident saints whom we can rediscover in the hard Puritan merchants of the heroic age of capitalism."[18] Second, what other framework can encompass the lives of men like Chalkley, Scottow, Hull, and Keayne? Did not their ascetic energies push forward the historical evolution of capitalism?

These questions expose a fundamental ambiguity in Weber's definition of capitalism and in its history. In *The Protestant Ethic* Weber defined modern Western capitalism in clear but narrow terms: "the rational capitalistic organization of (formally) free labor." He explicitly distinguished this form of enterprise from a universal "greed for gain" and from the activities of "the capitalistic adventurer [who] has existed everywhere." "The impulse to acquisition, pursuit of gain, of money, of the greatest possible amount of money," he argued, "has in itself nothing to do with capitalism." Nor did the "irrational and speculative" activities of "promoters, large-scale speculators, concession hunters" or those of men who sought "acquisition by force, above all the acquisition of booty, whether directly in war or in the form of continuous fiscal booty by exploitation of subjects." Thus "colonial entrepreneurs, as planters with slaves, or directly or indirectly forced labor" were likewise outside the capitalist fold. All these activities or systems of production lacked "what was characteristic of Occidental

---

18. Reinhard Bendix, *Max Weber: An Intellectual Portrait* (New York, 1960), 50n; Weber, *Protestant Ethic*, 112.

capitalism: the middle-class organization of industrial labour on the basis of private property."[19]

When did this capitalist system develop? In England after 1750 and in Europe and North America after 1800? If so, what of the Puritans and Quakers of the previous two centuries? Could they embody the "spirit" of capitalism without actually *being* capitalists? If they organized their businesses for "the pursuit of profit, and forever *renewed* profit, by means of continuous, rational, capitalistic enterprise," then, one might suppose, they acted as causal agents in the creation of modern capitalism.[20]

Weber's failure to demonstrate the influence of ascetic Protestantism on the actual historical evolution of capitalism stemmed in part from his research strategy. "His employment of the ideal-type method," Ephraim Fischoff argued in an important review and restatement of the Weber thesis, "necessarily leads to oversimplification of a complex historical entity through the accentuation and isolation of a particular component factor."[21] Defending Weber's "construc-

---

19. Weber, *Protestant Ethic*, 17, 20–21, also, 111–12, 279–80. As Sidney A. Burrell has noted, Werner Sombart stated the "well known fact" that Protestantism was the ideological manifestation of the nascent capitalism of the sixteenth century. Weber disputed this causal connection, but "by suggesting that the rise of capitalism was influenced by Calvinist thought he . . . strengthened the assumption . . . that the two were somehow necessarily and intimately linked together" ("Calvinism, Capitalism, and the Middle Classes: Some Afterthoughts on an Old Problem," *Journal of Modern History* 32 [1960]: 132, 133).

20. Weber, *Protestant Ethic*, 17.

21. Ephraim Fischoff, "The Protestant Ethic and the Spirit of Capitalism: The History of a Controversy," *Social Research* 11 (1944): 61–77. As Herbert Leuthy put it, Weber's "great and questioning mind was never particularly interested in the facts of history. . . . What he analyzed were not the hybrid and wretched

tion of historical types," Reinhard Bendix and Guenther Roth have argued that such comparative and configurative analysis was "a logical prerequisite for their elucidation." Clearly specified ideal types, they maintained, "suggest specific historical explanations" or "secular theories." As Weber himself put it in 1914, explaining his analytic methods to a medieval historian, "I am dealing with the structure of the political organizations in a comparative and systematic manner. . . . It is the subsequent task of history to find a causal explanation . . . [and to] establish what is specific to, say, the medieval city. . . . Sociology as I understand it can perform this very modest preparatory work."[22]

With Weber's imprimatur to "establish what is specific," let us explore in some detail the history of early America. Our goal will not be to uphold or deny the validity of *The Protestant Ethic* but rather to use Weber's categories of analysis to explore the causal relationship between Protestantism and capitalism and, more broadly, the interaction of ideas and interests in the historical process.

III

Robert Keayne's difficulties reflected a larger conflict within Massachusetts Bay. The issues at stake were

---

forms of an historically realized society. . . but rather the abstract and chemically pure 'ideal types' which should provide the essences of a civilization" ("Once Again: Calvinism and Capitalism," *Encounter* 22 [January 1964]: 26–38).

22. Reinhard Bendix and Guenther Roth, *Scholarship and Partisanship: Essays on Max Weber* (Berkeley, Calif., 1971), 307, 119, 38, 39. See also R. Stephen Warner, "Weber's Sociology of Nonwestern Religions," in Green, *Protestantism*, esp. 47–51.

both philosophical and practical; they involved contradictory visions of the religious and economic order.
On the one side stood a fledgling group of traders,
linked by kinship and interest to the Puritan merchant
community of London. Their presence reflected the
colony's origins as a mercantile venture. On the other
side were the farmers and artisans, powerful in both
numbers and institutional strength. Their leaders
were also the chief men of the colony, Puritan ministers and devout laymen drawn from the ranks of the
lesser English gentry.

The key figure was John Winthrop, the colony's
governor for nearly two decades. A landed gentleman
from the sheep-raising county of Suffolk, Winthrop
suffered financially during the woolen textile depression of the 1620s. Equally important, he came to view
England as a corrupted society, where "all arts and
trades are carried on in a deceitful manner and un-
righteous course." Winthrop's "Model of Christian
Charity," completed during the voyage across the
Atlantic, recalled the virtues of traditional landed
society. It celebrated stable class divisions, condemned calculating economic practices and competitive self-seeking, and reaffirmed the responsibility of
the rich for the poor. "If thy brother be in want," he
wrote, "if thou lovest god, thou *must* help him."[23]

Winthrop sought to recreate a purified social
hierarchy in America, a genuinely "new" England.
"Thus stands the cause between God and us," he
concluded his manifesto. "We are entered into covenant with him for this work . . . if we shall . . . fall to

---

23. Stephen Nissenbaum, "John Winthrop, 'A Model of Christian
Charity,' " in *The Course of United States History*, ed. David Nasaw
(Chicago, 1987), 35.

embrace this present world and prosecute our carnal intentions, seeking great things for ourselves and our posterity, the Lord will surely break out in wrath against us. . . . Now the only way to avoid this shipwreck," Winthrop warned, is to "be knit together in this work as one man . . . in brotherly affection, . . . willing to abridge ourselves of our superfluities, for the supply of other's necessities." In defining ethical conduct in communal terms, Winthrop's social philosophy stood in tension with the Calvinist doctrine of the calling, with its focus on the duties of the individual. Whatever their personal goals, he told his fellow passengers, we must have "always before our eyes . . . our community as members of the same body."[24]

Winthrop's communitarian ethic quickly found expression in Massachusetts Bay. In the so-called Antinomian Controversy, he and the other magistrates banished Anne Hutchinson from the colony. The wife of a prominent merchant, Hutchinson challenged the established ministry. She accused them of preaching a "covenant of works" that emphasized the performance of prescribed duties. In its place she proposed the doctrine of free grace, a mystical ethic that stressed the immediate tie between God and individual men and women. Most merchants supported Hutchinson, probably because they feared close communal regulation of their economic as well as their spiritual lives.[25]

The suppression of Hutchinson, Larzer Ziff has suggested, "put an end to the essential similarity between American Puritanism and sectarianism."

---

24. Ibid., 35–36, 50.
25. Emery Battis, *Saints and Sectaries* (Chapel Hill, N.C., 1962).

While individuals and congregations continued to practice diverse brands of Calvinist thought and practice, Massachusetts Bay became an authoritarian state, a holy commonwealth on the model of Calvin's Geneva. The laymen of the General Court curbed public religious dissent and sought to impose order on the new society. When the economy faltered in 1640, the court intervened vigorously to protect the interests of debtors from their merchant creditors. One law stipulated that property seized for debts must be "valued by 3 understanding and indifferent men." This provision reflected the legislators' hope that most settlers would "have sufficient upon an equal [just] valuation to pay all, and live comfortably upon the rest." A second statute required that all future debts could be paid in "corne, cattle, fish, or other commodities." Significantly, these commodities were not to be valued at market prices, but "at such rates as this Courte shall set downe from time to time." Finally, the magistrates passed a far-reaching measure (defeated in the lower house of deputies) that would have made the commonwealth liable for legally established debts that private individuals lacked the resources to pay.[26]

These measures embodied Winthrop's economic philosophy and that of many migrants from rural England. In cases of conflict, the interests of debtors overrode those of creditors. "What rule must we observe in forgiving [debts]?" Winthrop had asked rhetorically in "A Model of Christian Charity." "If he have nothing to pay thee[, thou] must forgive him," he answered, citing "Deuteronomy, 15, 2: Every seventh

---

26. Larzer Ziff, *Puritanism in America: New Culture in a New World* (New York, 1973), 79–80; Bailyn, *New England Merchants*, 49–50.

year the creditor was to quit that which he lent to his brother if he were poor." Moreover, the welfare of the community was to take precedence over that of entrepreneurs. The General Court bestowed generous privileges on the newly formed Saugus Ironworks in 1644, but it also established a maximum price for its bar iron and prohibited exports until local needs were met. These restrictions, combined with high production costs, forced the Ironworks into bankruptcy by 1652.[27]

Like Winthrop, William Bradford, the governor of the separatist Puritan settlement in Plymouth Colony, sought social justice within a broader regime of authoritarian control and economic inequality. Fee simple landowning was nearly universal in the new settlement, for the migrants consciously sought to avoid the most oppressive features of English landed society. However, the leading men in Plymouth colony gave strong preference to their own families in allocating choice farming lands and meadows, and in awarding exclusive rights to the Indian fur trade. Church members—"visible saints"—likewise received ample land, in the location of their choice, while the nonelect had to settle for smaller plots on marginal soils. The allocation of property rights conformed to the gradations of the hierarchy of social status and religious identity.

Once assigned their place in the social order, members were expected to conform to traditional communal notions of the "just price." The Plymouth authorities called church member Stephen Hopkins

---

27. Nissenbaum, "John Winthrop," 44; Bailyn, *New England Merchants*, 63–64, 69.

into court in 1639 "for selling a looking glass for 16d, the like whereof was bought in the Bay [Colony] for 9d." On the same day it fined Thomas Clark 30 shillings for "buying a pair of boots and spurs for 10s. and selling them again for 15s."[28] The *character* of Plymouth Colony—an isolated agricultural community, dominated by devout landed gentlemen, with political power in the hands of the Puritan congregation—insured the triumph of Winthrop's communal ethic.

The circumstances of life—spiritual and material—in early New England militated against the expansion of capitalist enterprise. The political franchise rested in the hands of church members, poor as well as propertied. Moreover, rural towns dominated the house of deputies; their representatives outvoted the merchants from the commercial centers of Boston and Salem and refused to elect them to the upper house of magistrates in the General Court. Only two of the twenty-two magistrates elected before 1640 were merchants. The court vigorously defended the church-based political order, levying severe fines on the non-Puritan merchants who demanded the broadening of church membership and the franchise in a "Remonstrance and Petition" of 1646. The improvement of economic conditions prompted the court to repeal some prodebtor laws in 1650, but popular opposition

---

28. Rex A. Lucas, "A Specification of the Weber Thesis: Plymouth Colony," *History and Theory* 10 (1971): 330. "When the Protestant ethic exists [where] . . . the congregational church dominates a small and isolated society," Lucas concluded, "the hard work encouraged by the ethic is maintained, but the individual's efforts are channelled largely to the maintenance of social control [and] . . . constant supervision by all within the social group severely restrict[s] the behavioral leeway of the individual" (344).

to merchants and their free-trade policies continued.[29]
Merchants were "so taken up with the income of a
large profit," declared Edward Johnson in *Wonder-
Working Providence of Sions Saviour in New England*, "that
they would willingly have had the Commonwealth
tolerate diverse kinds of sinful opinions to intice men
to come and sit downe with us, that their purses might
be filled with coyn, the civil Government with contention, and the Churches of our Lord Christ with errors."[30]

The first generation of New England merchants
thus pursued their "personal" economic calling in a
restrictive intellectual and social context. They won
respect only insofar as they assumed a public *religious*
role, writing moral tracts like Joshua Scottow or, like
John Hull, dispensing philanthropy in a generous but
humble manner. To demonstrate their elect status,
merchants had to serve God directly, through public
affirmations of their "general" calling and not simply
through the diligent pursuit of their business activities.

Subsequent generations of Boston merchants operated within a more open environment. The Resto-
ration brought new merchants—Anglicans and royal-
ists like Richard Wharton—to New England, and
imperial officials such as Edward Randolph gradually
curbed the autonomy of its holy commonwealths.
Equally significant, many second-generation Puritan
merchants were themselves the offspring of ministers
and landed gentlemen. In his powerful election day
sermon of 1663, *The Cause of God and His People in New*

---

29. Bailyn, *New England Merchants*, 103–4, 38–39, 107.
30. Ibid., 109.

England, the Reverend John Higginson of Salem de-
nounced "the getting of this World's good[s]." It is
"never to be forgotten," he reminded the populace,
"that *New-England is originally a plantation of Religion,
not a Plantation of Trade*." Yet Higginson's daughter
Sarah married Anglican Richard Wharton and two of
Higginson's sons became prominent merchants.[31]
Moreover, pious Puritan merchants—Samuel Sewall,
Anthony Stoddard, and Thomas Brattle, among others—sent some of their sons into the ministry. By
1673 Governor John Leverett and half of the other
twelve magistrates had some connection with mercantile enterprise. Increasingly, the leadership of New
England was drawn from an interrelated group of
merchants, magistrates, and ministers.[32]

The growing wealth of the merchant community
was one factor in its rise in power. As early as 1670,
thirty Boston merchants had estates of ten thousand
to thirty thousand pounds. By the end of the century,
a contemporary observed, many of them had constructed "stately Edifices, some of which cost the
owners two or three Thousand Pounds." Merchants
also had increasing access to political power. When
King James II revoked the Massachusetts Charter in
1686, merchants seized control of the government,
awarding vast tracts of frontier lands and dozens of
governmental offices to themselves and their support-
ers. Two years later, they joined in the overthrow of
the new Dominion of New England in part to protect
their new (and old) land titles against the rapacity of
Royal Governor Edmund Andros. Merchants pros-

---

31. Ibid., 140. For the subsequent activities of the Higginson
family, see the end of this chapter.
32. Foster, *Their Solitary Way*, 120.

pered under the new charter of 1692, using their influence in London to secure appointments as royal governors.[33]

Above all, Boston merchants now lived in a more hospitable religious world. Increasingly, they worshiped in congregations of their own, served by ministers who respected their vocations and ambitions. In 1701 Cotton Mather's *A Christian at His Calling* reaffirmed the Calvinist precept that "a man *Slothful in Business*, is not a man *serving the Lord*." The eminent Puritan minister also advised that "a principle of *Honesty* [should] keep you from every *Fraudulent*, or *Oppressive* Action," but he refused to give practical effect to his system of ethics. When debtors and creditors clashed in Massachusetts Bay during the 1710s, Mather refused to take a political stand, alleging that he was "not versed in the Niceties and Mysteries of the Marketplace." The contrast with John Cotton, Mather's namesake and fellow authority on the calling, was striking. Writing in the 1630s, Cotton had cited various biblical passages in support of the simple principle: "Noe increase to be taken of a poore brother or neighboure for anything lent to him."[34] In Boston, the communal ethic of John Winthrop had yielded to the Protestant ethic of his merchant antagonists.

---

33. Miller, *New England Mind: From Colony to Province*, 45; Bailyn, *New England Merchants*, 175, 191.

34. Cotton Mather, "A Christian at His Calling . . ." in *Puritanism and the American Experience*, ed. Michael McGiffert (Reading, Mass., 1969), 122–26; Bailyn, *New England Merchants*, 21–22. See also Foster, *Their Solitary Way*, 112–13. The subtlety of Cotton's economic ethics appeared in his discussion of prices. He distinguished between ordinary times when "a man may not sell above the current [or customary] price" and times when "there is a scarcity of the commodity." Then the seller could charge more, "for it is a hand of God upon the commodity, and not the person's" (Bailyn, *New England Merchants*, 21).

But not in the countryside. The predominant rural sector of New England created a distinct system of social behavior and values, yielding a continuing controversy with commercial towns. Notions of "fair dealing" formed one aspect of its ethical outlook. In 1639 Ezekiel Rogers had condemned Robert Keayne on behalf of the farmers of Rowley. Two decades later, a traveler in Maine reflected local sentiment in condemning the trade monopoly of the "damnable rich" Boston merchants who "set excessive prices" and who "if they do not gain Cent per Cent they cry out that they are losers." Local fishermen and planters, he explained, "enter into the Merchants books for such things as they stand in need off, becoming thereby the Merchants slaves, and when it riseth to a big sum are constrained to mortgage their plantation."[35] Samuel Stoddard, the evangelically inclined minister of Northampton, in western Massachusetts, took up the rural cry against "oppression" of traders early in the eighteenth century. In country areas "where there is no Market, particular persons may be in great necessity," he noted. "If they go to another Town to buy, the charge will be considerable; the man is also in a strait because strangers will not trust him, and the Seller takes that advantage to oppress him."[36] Old beliefs died slowly in the countryside. Even at the time of the American Revolution, many New England villagers "thought of the great world beyond their borders in religious terms," Christopher Jedrey has concluded, "an archaic geopolitical world view rooted in the England of Elizabeth's time and Foxe's Book of Martyrs."[37]

---

35. Bailyn, *New England Merchants*, 98, 99.

36. Foster, *Their Solitary Way*, 119.

37. Christopher M. Jedrey, *The World of John Cleaveland: Family and Community in Eighteenth-Century New England* (New York, 1979), xii–xiii.

The protests of rural folk against mercantile capitalism took on additional motive force from the peculiar character of New England agricultural society. On the eve of the American Revolution, the fifth generation of settlers was coming to maturity. Their numbers had grown dramatically, primarily from natural increase, from 20,000 in 1640 to 600,000 in 1770. Their living standards had increased as well, but in a much less impressive fashion. Merchants and landed gentlemen lived well in New England (the top 10 percent of the families controlling 57 percent of the wealth), but ordinary farmers and artisans just scraped by. In fact, they had the most spartan lives of all the whites in British America. Wealth holdings per free white person ranged from £1,200 in the rich sugar island of Jamaica, to a substantial £132 in the tobacco and rice settlements on the southern mainland, and to £51 in the wheat-exporting Middle Colonies of New York and Pennsylvania. New England trailed behind, with only £33 per free white person.[38]

The causes of New England's economic backwardness were as obvious to contemporaries as they are to historians. A harsh climate, hilly terrain, and poor soil limited the production of valuable staple crops, while its ever-growing population pressed constantly on living standards. Indeed, fully one-half of the nineteen thousand farms listed on the Massachusetts valuation list for 1772 lacked plows or oxen; 40 percent were not self-sufficient in grain; and two-thirds did not have enough pasture for their livestock. Despite these unfavorable geographic and demo-

---

38. John J. McCusker and Russell R. Menard, *The Economy of British North America, 1607–1789* (Chapel Hill, N.C., 1985), table 3.3.

graphic conditions, New England had avoided a Malthusian crisis. There was never a significant shortage of food. Beyond that, New England families actively sought to maintain the freehold tradition established by the original settlers. Parents carefully arranged the marriages of their sons and daughters, devised ingenious inheritance strategies to preserve viable farmsteads, and bartered goods and labor with their kin and neighbors. Even in the fifth generation, 80 percent of the adult white males would own some land during their lifetimes.[39]

Were these backcountry folk also exemplars of the Protestant ethic, pursuing their "personal" calling as farmers in a diligent, rational fashion? In one sense, the answer must be yes. All were Protestant sectarians, most were Calvinists; their spiritual discipline and purpose obviously assisted them to sustain such a stable European society in this difficult corner of the American wilderness. But strong communal institutions, political as well as religious, and the dominance of a community-based exchange system dampened the individualistic aspects of the ethic. Most towns assigned seats in the meetinghouse according to a communal valuation of age, wealth, and status; people learned their "place" in the community every time they went to church. Rural town meetings sought consensus; the vote of a mere majority lacked moral

---

39. Bettye Hobbs Pruitt, "Self-Sufficiency and the Agricultural Economy of Eighteenth-Century Massachusetts," *William and Mary Quarterly*, 3d ser., 41 (1984): 338–40. See also Robert A. Gross, *The Minutemen and Their World* (New York, 1976), chapter 4; Jedrey, *World of John Cleaveland*, chapter 3; and, in general, James A. Henretta and Gregory H. Nobles, *Evolution and Revolution: American Society, 1600–1820* (Lexington, Mass., 1987), chapters 1–5.

legitimacy and practical effect—for only a nearly unanimous vote was self-executing. Traders in commercial towns recognized the force of communal ideology and, as circumstances demanded, turned it to their own advantage. "The major part of those who were present were [farmers]," merchants in Salem, Massachusetts, argued while seeking to revoke a new tax schedule, "and the vote then passed was properly their vote and not the vote of the whole body of the town."[40] As Winthrop had hoped, these rural communities were "knit together . . . as one man."

The yeoman family's pursuit of a "comfortable subsistence" required access to the resources of the community. At the time of the American Revolution the family of Caleb Jackson, Sr., of Rowley, Massachusetts, could trace its American ancestry back to the Nicholas Jackson who settled on the ample lands of the town in the seventeenth century, perhaps in the company led by Ezekiel Rogers. But now these Jacksons were land poor. Each year the family cultivated its few acres, picked cherries for "ready cash," and pressed its neighbors' cider for sale in Ipswich and Salem. In addition, Caleb Sr. had his two teenage sons cultivate "Mr. Jonathan Wood's Planting land . . . and have half the crop for our labour," plant "our field of potatoes at Capt. D['s]," and pasture their cattle on other families' meadows.[41] These exchanges of goods and labor were often valued at "set" prices; when

---

40. Michael Zuckerman, "The Social Context of Democracy in Massachusetts," *William and Mary Quarterly*, 3d ser., 25 (1968): 542. See also Zuckerman's *Peaceable Kingdoms: Massachusetts Towns in the Eighteenth Century* (New York, 1970).

41. Daniel Vickers, "Competency and Competition: Economic Culture in Early America," *William and Mary Quarterly*, 3d ser., 47 (1990): 4–12.

market rates were used, no interest was charged on any resulting debts. The continued goodwill of a neighbor or kinsman was more valuable, in this inter-dependent subsistence-plus economy, than a few shillings in interest. The rational pursuit of "business" advantage yielded to the imperatives of communal existence.

Thus, the rural world of New England embodied many aspects of "traditionalism," as Weber defined it.[42] Farm families determined the pace of their own work lives, working intensely to complete the crucial "tasks" of planting and harvesting, but otherwise following a leisurely pace. Their economic goals were limited: economic autonomy, a comfortable subsistence for themselves, and a freehold legacy for their children. As Gary Nash has suggested, "a peculiar Puritan blend of participatory involvement within a hierarchically structured society of lineal families on small community-oriented farms" produced "the least dynamic region of the British mainland colonies."[43] Subsequently, it was less the imperatives of the Calvinistic calling than the pressure of population on

---

42. Weber, *Protestant Ethic*, 60–61; Reinhard Bendix, *Max Weber*, 52–54. As Joyce Appleby has noted, Weber rejected "the universal economic impulse of liberal theories . . . [that] had assumed that human beings were inherently geared to the strenuous pursuit of profit." He thereby "made social change a truly historical phenomenon to be understood on its own terms" ("Value and Society," in *Colonial British America: Essays in the New History of the Early Modern Era*, ed. Jack P. Greene and J. R. Pole (Baltimore, Md., 1984), 291.

43. Gary Nash, "Social Development," in Greene and Pole, *Colonial British America*, 237, 236. "For most men in Chebacco," Jedrey has concluded, "time and inheritance, not entrepreneurial ability, was the key to advancement. . . . It was a stable world of finite resources, and . . . most men would not ever own much more than they inherited" (*World of John Cleaveland*, 94).

resources that prompted an intensification of labor
and the emergence of capitalist-financed domestic industry. By 1800 the two teenage boys in the Jackson
family made shoes during the winter months, under a
contract between their father and a local merchant.[44]

In fact, the most dynamic religious impulses in
eighteenth-century New England society were Calvinist and anticapitalist. In the "Model of Christian Charity" Winthrop had urged the Puritan migrants to fulfill
the "covenant" with God that set them apart from
other men and women. Whenever they sensed failure,
Puritans sought ritual assurance in a public "fast day":
"all persons are hereby required to abstain from bodily
labor that day, & to resort to the publike meetings, to
seeke the Lord, as become Christians in a day of
humiliation."[45] Subsequently, ministers and devout
laymen composed "jeremiads," sermons or tracts that
berated Puritans for their sins, recalled their duties
under the covenant, and proposed a scheme of refor-
mation. Then, in the early eighteenth century, ministers sought to combat worldliness through church
"revivals." In these collective outbursts of piety, saints
reaffirmed their identity and converts rejoiced in the
gift of God's grace. Changing forms obscured an
underlying continuity; the demands of the Calvinist
ethos periodically engendered a sense of emotional
crisis that mere pursuit of the calling could not as-
suage.

The Great Awakening of the 1740s was one of

---

44. Vickers, "Competency," 9–10.
45. Miller, *New England Mind: From Colony to Province*, 27. The
Puritans' use of ritual is explored in David D. Hall, "Religion and
Society: Problems and Reconsiderations," in Greene and Pole,
Colonial British America, 336 and passim.

those outbursts. The revival had strong regional roots and characteristics, for it flowed out of and embraced the Calvinist tradition in New England and German pietism in the Middle Colonies of Pennsylvania and New Jersey. But the charismatic preaching of George Whitefield, John Wesley's compatriot in English Methodism, transformed those regions' revivals into a continent-wide Great Awakening. Initially, the revival appealed to all classes and regions; Whitefield found himself welcome in urban as well as rural churches, in the congregations of rich merchants as well as those of poor artisans and farmers. Soon conservative ministers and laymen sensed a danger to social order and their religious outlook. "None can be long a stranger to George Whitefield," James Logan told a friend. "His preaching has a good effect in reclaiming many dissolute people," the Philadelphia merchant and politician admitted, "but from his countenancing so very much the most hotheaded predestinarians, . . . he and they have actually driven divers [people] into despair, and some into perfect madness. . . . His doctrine," Logan explained, stressed "the danger of good works without such a degree of sanctifying faith as come up to his gauge."[46]

Neither predestination nor a rigid "covenant of grace" appealed to well-to-do urban congregations or their ministers by the middle of the eighteenth century. "The optimistic, energetic 'merchant princes' of Boston," Daniel Walker Howe has pointed out, "did not take it kindly when Calvinist clergymen informed them they were miserable sinners, worms, or spiders kept from dropping into the fires of Hell only by the

---

46. Tolles, *Quakers*, 100, 105–6.

whim of an inscrutable God." Nor did Quaker merchants in Pennsylvania welcome the admonitions of "primitive" Friends who recalled the radical aspects of early Quakerism. They ignored John Woolman's injunctions to free their slaves and Anthony Benezet's insistence on "the necessity for the followers of Christ absolutely to refuse the accumulation of wealth."[47]

Believing that "salvation, like earthly prosperity, must be a reward for those ambitious enough to earn it," many merchants had become Arminian or Latitudinarian in outlook. Their ministers—such as Charles Chauncy and Jonathan Mayhew in Boston—emphasized the benevolence of God, not His omnipotence; in the theology of salvation preached by these ministers, human moral responsibility played almost as important a role as God's grace. Devotion to a calling lost its close association with God's grace and religious zeal. "There are Duties to be attended," Chauncy solemnly declared, "as well as religious meetings; But haven't the Zeal of People to attend the latter been so great as to leave little Room for the observable Practise of the former?" In the thought of these nonevangelical Arminians, the tension between the personal and the general calling had been resolved through benevolence. "One natural Benefit of Trade and Commerce," wrote Rev. Benjamin Colman, was that "it enlarges Peoples' hearts to do generous things . . . by means whereof a great Part of the World has been gospelized."[48]

---

47. Daniel Walker Howe, "The Decline of Calvinism: An Approach to Its Study," *Comparative Studies in Society and History* 14 (1972): 317; Tolles, *Meeting House*, 84, 80–84.

48. J. E. Crowley, *This Sheba Self: The Conceptualization of Economic Life in Eighteenth-Century America* (Baltimore, Md., 1974), 74, 112.

Evangelical preachers questioned the link between divine grace and worldly activity in an even more radical manner. "Wicked debauched men" used trade, Jonathan Edwards declared, as a means "to favor men's covetousness and pride." The true business of Christ's disciples, another evangelical minister proclaimed, "is not to hunt for Riches, and Honours, and Pleasures in this World, but to despise them, and deny themselves, and be ready to part with even all the lawful Pleasures and Comforts of the World at any Time." The dramatic gesture of James Davenport, the radical minister of New Haven, Connecticut, symbolized the rejection of the Calvinist doctrine of the calling by many evangelicals and their followers. Placing his followers' prized worldly possessions—their wigs and gowns, rings and necklaces—in a heap, Davenport burned them to ashes.[49]

Like all great social movements, the Great Awakening had diverse and contradictory effects. Most importantly for our purposes, it dissolved the affinity between Calvinism and capitalism postulated by the Weber thesis. "Where capitalism most flourished," among the merchants of the American seaports and in European cities, as Daniel Walker Howe has noted, "Calvinism declined." And, where Calvinism flourished, in the New Light Congregationalist, Presbyterian, and Baptist congregations in the rural hamlets of New England and Virginia, capitalism was viewed with suspicion, if not distaste. Howe has resolved this paradox by suggesting that Calvinism was (and is) intrinsically "an ideology of small property-owners,

---

49. Ibid., 67; Bushman, *From Puritan to Yankee: Character and the Social Order in Connecticut, 1690–1765* (New York, 1970), pp. 192–93.

provincial folk . . . small farmers, and artisans, the lower middle class," those men and women "who feel threatened . . . and who find reassurance in the strength of their God and their own ultimate vindication in His election." Its appeal to merchants and religious intellectuals in the seventeenth century was a historical aberration, prompted by the lack of religious and social order. By the following century Calvinism was in decline, particularly "among those people who were most socially and economically comfortable"— merchants, professional men, and other agents of the new capitalist order. "Religion must necessarily produce both industry and frugality, and these cannot but produce riches," lamented John Wesley, "but as riches increase, so will pride, anger, and love of the world in all its branches." Calvinism had pushed capitalism forward, only to be devoured by its creation.[50]

IV

The triumph of capitalism in British America was a long and slow process. It took decades—indeed, more than a century—to translate the capitalist "spirit" of Puritan and Quaker merchants into concrete economic practices and legal institutions. Only in the early eighteenth century did a rational and routinized capitalist legal system extend its reach into the countryside; and only toward the end of the century had merchants amassed sufficient financial resources and

---

50. Howe, "Decline of Calvinism," 321, 323; Wesley quoted in Weber, *Protestant Ethic*, 175.

organizational skills to initiate the American transition to a capitalist and industrializing society.

The dynamics of legal change emerged in striking form in early eighteenth-century Connecticut. In 1700 Connecticut was a colony of subsistence farmers. Most exchanges of goods or services were local, and so were most of the resulting debts. Between 70 and 80 percent of all debt actions in Hartford and New Haven counties were based on account books (and not signed obligations such as legal bonds or promissory notes), and virtually all book debts were local. Moreover, all actions for debts based on account books in Hartford County pitted one county resident against another; both parties lived in the same town in 60 percent of the cases. Even debt actions based on signed obligations were predominately local, involving ligitants from Hartford in more than 60 percent of the cases.[51]

The character of book debts—and the litigation they spawned—was equally significant. Account books were based on credit and trust. They formed a running account of exchanges among neighbors that did not bear interest. Moreover, their form encouraged what Bruce H. Mann has called a "communal model of disputing." "Books were not conclusive evidence of the debts they recorded," Mann points out, but "merely a starting point for discussing the range of dealings between debtor and creditor in open court." Before 1710 most debtors pled the "general issue." This plea permitted juries to scrutinize the entire economic relationship between defendants and credi-

---

51. Bruce H. Mann, "Rationality, Legal Change, and Community in Connecticut, 1690–1740," *Law and Society Review* 14 (1980): 196–98.

tors and to decide cases according to community norms of equity.[52]

The demise of actions for book debts occurred rapidly in Connecticut, denoting a new social and legal regime. By the 1730s only 30 percent of the debt litigation in Hartford County was based on account books. Instead, actions on written instruments (bonds, bills obligatory, and especially promissory notes) dominated court dockets. Debt actions now had greater definition and legal predictability; all that mattered to the court was the piece of paper signed by the debtor. Consequently, debtors did not contest actions they seemed certain to lose. And judges—not juries—decided 80–90 percent of all contested civil actions, disposing of them not on their factual merits but according to abstract principles of law.[53]

This fundamental transformation in debt relations and legal procedure reflected the commercialization of the Connecticut economy. As paper money appeared and agricultural markets expanded in the early eighteenth century, many farmers took out bonds and notes to buy land and livestock. Subsequently, periodic declines in farm prices extended the use of written instruments, as cautious merchants forced credit-hungry farmers to secure existing book debts with promissory notes. Connecticut had developed a "dual" economic and legal system, with small book debts remaining common among farmers and artisans while promissory notes expressed their economic relations with merchants and traders.

The new legal regime represented the triumph of

---

52. Bruce H. Mann, *Neighbors and Strangers: Law and Community in Early Connecticut* (Chapel Hill, N.C., 1987), 9–22.
53. Ibid., 35, 75–76.

a rational, capitalist economic order enforced by the power of the state. The fate of arbitration conveyed the impact of this new legal consciousness. Before 1700 Connecticut residents resolved many disputes through arbitration. Compliance with the terms of a reward was voluntary, enforced only by community pressure. By the 1730s, however, parties commonly wrote arbitration *contracts* that imposed financial penalties for noncompliance. Finally, a merchant-sponsored statute completed the transition to a coercive and monetized arbitration system. In 1753 the Connecticut assembly empowered courts to enforce monetary awards and penalties through writs of execution, making arbitration simply another mode of legal ajudication. A distinctly "modern" legal culture—what John Adams would call "a government of laws and not of men"—had come into being, laying the foundation for the triumph of capitalist enterprise.[54]

By this time as well, New England merchants had accumulated sufficient capital to finance domestic manufacturing as well as foreign trade. At first merchants and shopkeepers invested in the putting-out system for the production of shoes, cloth, and nails. But by the early nineteenth century, more adventurous capitalists invested in textile factories and hired wage laborers. Appropriately enough, this appearance of a full-fledged Weberian capitalist system was financed, in part, by wealth created initially by seventeenth-century Puritan merchants.

The Higginson family is a case in point. In 1663 the Reverend John Higginson of Salem, in the election

---

54. Ibid., 130–36.

day sermon cited earlier, had warned "merchants and such as are increasing *Cent per Cent*" to remember "that worldly gain was not the end and designe of the people of *New England*." Nonetheless, two of his sons and a daughter prospered as members of merchant families, and the Higginsons became one of the premier mercantile clans in Salem. Many Higginsons moved to Boston during the American Revolution, and there intermarried with the Cabot, Perkins, Jackson, and Sturges families. Those families loomed large in the ranks of the Boston Associates, the capitalist entrepreneurs who financed the textile industry of early nineteenth-century Massachusetts.[55] The ambiguities of the "Protestant ethic" carried to New England by John Hull, Joshua Scottow, and John Higginson had achieved a clear definition in the "capitalist spirit" of the founders of Waltham and Lowell, their religious and biological descendants.

55. Bailyn, *New England Merchants*, 140. On the Higginsons, see Peter Dobkin Hall, *The Organization of American Culture, 1700–1900: Private Institutions, Elites, and the Origins of American Nationality* (New York, 1984), 66–68, 71, and passim, and Robert F. Dalzell, Jr., *Enterprising Elite: The Boston Associates and the World They Made* (Cambridge, Mass., 1987), appendix.

3

Families and Farms:
Mentalité
in
Preindustrial America

The history of the agricultural population of preindustrial America remains to be written. As a result of
quantitative investigations of wealth distribution and
social mobility; of rates of birth, marriage, and death;
and of patterns of inheritance, officeholding, and
church membership, there is an ever-growing mass of
data that delineates the *structures* of social existence in
the small rural communities that constituted the core
of American agricultural society in the North before
1830. But what of the *consciousness* of the inhabitants,
the mental or emotional or ideological aspects of their
lives? And what of the relationship between the two?
Can a careful statistical analysis of people's lives—a
precise description of their patterns of social action—

substantiate at least limited statements about their motivations, values, and goals?

I

A number of historians have attempted to establish a connection between the subsistence activities of the agricultural population and its institutional, ideological, and cultural existence. Consider, for example, the entrepreneurial interpretation implicit in James T. Lemon's highly regarded quantitative analysis of the eighteenth-century agricultural society of southeastern Pennsylvania:

> A basic stress in these essays is on the "liberal" middle-class orientation of many of the settlers. . . . "Liberal" I use in the classic sense, meaning placing individual freedom and material gain over that of public interest. Put another way, the people planned for themselves much more than they did for their communities. . . . This is not to say that the settlers were "economic men," single-minded maximizing materialists. Few could, or even wanted to be. Nevertheless, they defended their liberal propensities in a tenacious manner. . . . Undoubtedly their view was fostered by a sense that the environment was "open." As individualists, they were ready in spirit to conquer the limitless continent, to subdue the land.[1]

However overburdened with reservations and qualifications, the general thrust of this depiction of values

---

1. James T. Lemon, *The Best Poor Man's Country: A Geographical Study of Early Southeastern Pennsylvania* (Baltimore, Md., 1972), xv.

and aspirations is clear enough. Lemon's settlers were individualists, enterprising men and women intent upon the pursuit of material advantage at the expense of communal and noneconomic goals.

Can the "consciousness" with which Lemon has endowed these early Pennsylvanians be verified by historical evidence? The question is important, for many of the statistical data presented by Lemon do not support his description of the inhabitants' "orientation," "spirit," or "propensities." Take the pattern of residence. It is true that the predominance of isolated farmsteads—rather than nucleated villages—suggests that these men and women were planning "for themselves much more than . . . for their communities." But what of the presence of clusters of ethnic and religious groups? Such voluntary concentrations of like-minded settlers indicate the importance of communal values, of people who preferred to share a religious or ethnic identity. Here the author's evidence contradicts his conclusion. "Most of the people who came during this period," Lemon writes of the years between 1700 and 1730, "settled together in areas and communities defined by nationality or denomination. . . . Language and creed thus exerted considerable influence on the whereabouts of people. Yet groups were mixed in several areas, for example on the Lancaster Plain."[2]

This exception only confirms the rule. Nearly every historian who has studied ethnic settlement patterns in the colonial period has stressed the existence of communal concentrations. In the Middle Colonies, for example, patterns of spatial segregation

---

2. Ibid., 221.

appeared among the Dutch in Newark, New Jersey, and to some extent among Quakers and Seventh Day Baptists in the same area. Most of the German immigrants who arrived in Lancaster, Pennsylvania, in 1774 settled on the lots laid out by Dr. Adam Kuhn, the leading German resident, rather than on land offered by the English proprietor, Alexander Hamilton. These linguistic and religious ties extended beyond settlement patterns to encompass economic relationships. Every one of the one hundred names inscribed in the account book of Henry King—shoemaker, butcher, and currier of Second River, New Jersey, in 1775—was of Dutch origin; and the main business connections of the merchants of Lancaster, whether they were Jewish or Quaker or German, were with their coreligionists in Philadelphia.[3]

Is an individualist spirit fully compatible with these communal settlement patterns and this religiously determined economic activity? It is possible, of course, that these ethnic or linguistic preferences facilitated the pursuit of individual economic gain, and that the patronage of the shop of a fellow church member brought preferred treatment and lower prices. But the weight of the evidence indicates that these decisions were not made for narrowly economic or strictly utilitarian reasons: the felt need to maintain a linguistic or religious identity was as important a consideration as the fertility of the soil or the price of the land in determining where a family would settle.

---

3. Dennis P. Ryan, "Six Towns: Continuity and Change in Revolutionary New Jersey, 1770–1792" (Ph.D. diss., New York University, 1974), 57–71; Jerome H. Wood, Jr., "Conestoga Crossroads: The Rise of Lancaster, Pennsylvania, 1730–1789" (Ph.D. diss., Brown University, 1969), 53, 114–15, 129–31.

The "calculus of advantage" for these men and women was not mere pecuniary gain, but encompassed a much wider range of social and cultural goals.[4]

These ethnic, linguistic, or religious ties did not reflect a coherent ideological system, a planned communitarian culture similar to the highly organized Moravian settlement at Bethlehem, Pennsylvania.[5] These bonds among families, neighbors, and fellow church members were informal; nonetheless, they circumscribed the range of individual action among the inhabitants of Pennsylvania and laid the foundations for a rich and diverse cultural existence. These community-oriented patterns of social interaction emerge clearly from Lemon's quantitative data, yet they do not figure prominently in his conclusion. He has not explained the complexity of the settler's existence but has forced their lives into the mold of a timeless, placeless concept of "liberal individualism."

A similar discrepancy between data and interpretation appears in Lemon's analysis of the economic goals and achievements of the inhabitants of eighteenth-century Pennsylvania. What becomes of the open environment and the conquering spirit when "tenant farming was much more frequent than we might expect. . . . [I]n 1760 and 1782 about 30 percent of Lancaster's and Chester's married taxpayers were landless" and an additional 15 percent of the total

---

4. Nor, in E. A. Wrigley's definition, was their society modern—one in which "the unit is the individual or, at the widest, the nuclear family" and "the utilities to be maximized are concentrated in a narrower band and are pursued with a new urgency" ("The Process of Modernization and the Industrial Revolution in England," *Journal of Interdisciplinary History* 3 [1972]: 233, 229).

5. Gillian Lindt Gollin, *Moravians in Two Worlds: A Study of Changing Communities* (New York, 1967).

number of taxpayers in Chester County were single freemen—mostly young men without landed property. With nearly 45 percent of the members of the adult white male population without land of their own, the gap between evidence and conclusion is so obvious that it must be confronted; and what better way than by evoking the spirit of Frederick Jackson Turner? "As long as the frontier was open," Lemon writes, "many people were able to move, and as a result frustrations were dampened and the liberal values of the original inhabitants of the colony were upheld."[6]

This is an appealing interpretation, especially since it admits the necessary connection between the structure of opportunity offered by a given environment and the consciousness of the inhabitants, but it is not completely satisfactory. It assumes that the migrants came with "liberal" values, with an expectation that most adult males would own a freehold estate and that anything less would generate anger and frustration. Neither the basic proposition nor its corollary is acceptable, for both fail to convey the settlers' conception of social reality, their understanding of the structural components of age and wealth.

To be "young" in this agricultural society (as in most) was either to be landless or without sufficient land to support a family. As Philip J. Greven, Daniel Scott Smith, and Robert A. Gross have shown, male

---

6. Lemon, *Best Poor Man's Country*, 94–97; James T. Lemon and Gary B. Nash, "The Distribution of Wealth in Eighteenth-Century America: A Century of Change in Chester County, Pennsylvania, 1693–1802," *Journal of Social History* 2 (1968): table I. Since indentured and hired servants are not included in the categories of married freeholder or single freeman, the proportion of landless males may be greater than 45 percent.

parents normally retained legal control of a sizable portion of the family estate until death, in order to ensure their financial well-being in old age, and the economic security of their widows was carefully protected by dower rights.[7] Nor were these cultural restraints on the transmission of improved property the only, or even the main, obstacle to the economic prospects of the next generation. For the high rate of natural increase constantly threatened to overwhelm the accumulated capital resources of many of these northern farm families. There was never sufficient cleared and improved property, or livestock, or farm equipment, or adequate housing to permit most young men and women to own a farm. In five small agricultural towns in New Jersey in the 1770s, for example, one-half of all white males aged eighteen to twenty-five were without land, while another 29 percent of this age group owned fifty acres or less. And in Concord, Massachusetts, the percentage of landless males (many of whom were young) grew from about

---

7. Philip J. Greven, Jr., "Family Structure in Seventeenth-Century Andover, Massachusetts," *William and Mary Quarterly*, 3d ser., 23 (1966): 234–56, and idem, *Four Generations: Population, Land, and Family in Colonial Andover, Massachusetts* (Ithaca, N.Y., 1970); Daniel Scott Smith, "Parental Power and Marriage Patterns: An Analysis of Historical Trends in Massachusetts," *Journal of Marriage and the Family* 35 (1973): 419–28; Robert A. Gross, *The Minutemen and Their World* (New York, 1976), 210 n. 22. These authors interpret this use of economic power as an attempt by parents to control the marriage age and the subsequent family life of their children. This may have been the *effect* of delayed transmission; the prime *cause*, however, was probably the parents' concern with financial security during their old age. The exercise of parental authority (with the resulting generational conflict) was not an end in itself but simply the by-product of the prudent fiscal management of productive property. Some of the difficulties in interpreting these data are explored in Maris Vinovskis, "American Historical Demography Review Essay," *Historical Methods Newsletter* 4 (1971): 141–48.

30 percent in 1750 to 40 percent in 1800. This correlation between age and wealth persisted throughout the life cycle; all of the males in the lowest quintile of the taxable population in East Guilford, Connecticut, in 1740 were below the age of forty, while every person in the highest quintile was that age or above.[8]

The accumulation of financial resources by aging men brought them higher status and political power. In Concord, between 1745 and 1774, the median age of selectmen at the time of their first election to office was forty-five, a pattern that obtained in Dedham and Watertown as well.[9] Indeed, the correlation among age, wealth, status, and power in these agricultural communities indicates the profound importance of age as a basic principle of social differentiation. And so it appeared to the Reverend William Bentley of Salem on a visit to Andover in 1793; the country people, he noted, assembled to dance "in classes due to their ages, not with any regard to their condition, as in the Seaport Towns."[10] In such an age-stratified society

---

8. Ryan, "Six Towns," 273 (table 61); Robert A. Gross, "Culture and Cultivation: Agriculture and Society in Thoreau's Concord," *Journal of American History* 69 (1982): table 1; John J. Waters, "Patrimony, Succession, and Social Stability: Guilford, Connecticut, in the Eighteenth Century," *Perspectives in American History* 10 (1976): 156–57. The Wisconsin tax lists for 1860 indicate that a man one year older than another had, on the average, 7.8 percent more wealth than his younger counterpart (Lee Soltow, *Patterns of Wealthholding in Wisconsin since 1850* [Madison, Wis., 1971], 8). Soltow finds a "pattern of wealth increase from age 20 to 50 or 55, with a tapering after this age" in rural areas, and that age and nativity account for roughly 60 percent of the inequality in the distribution of wealth (ibid., 46, 42).

9. Gross, *Minutemen*, 196; Kenneth A. Lockridge and Alan Kreider, "The Evolution of Massachusetts Town Government, 1640 to 1740," *William and Mary Quarterly*, 3d ser., 23 (1966): 566.

10. *The Diary of William Bentley, D.D.* . . . (Salem, Mass., 1907), 2:17.

economic "success" was not usual (and not expected) until the age of thirty-five, forty, or even forty-five. Propertied status was the product of one or two decades of work as a laborer or tenant, or of the long-delayed inheritance of the parental farm. The ownership of a freehold estate may have been the goal of young farmers; it was not, even in the best of circumstances, a universal condition among adult males at any time. Age stratification thus constituted an important aspect of what Michael Zuckerman has neatly conceptualized as the "social context" of political activity in these small and ethnically homogeneous agricultural settlements.[11] The economic dependence and powerlessness of young adults was a fact of life, the proper definition of social reality.

If cultural norms legitimated an age-stratified society in the minds of most northern farmers, then the character of social and economic life accustomed them to systematic inequalities in the distribution of wealth. Consider the evidence. In southeastern Pennsylvania in 1760 and again in 1782, the top 40 percent of the taxable population owned 70 percent of the assessed wealth, while the top 10 percent controlled 33 percent. On the 1784 tax list of Newtown, Long Island, the proportions were nearly identical, with the top 40 percent owning 73 percent of the wealth, and the richest 10 percent holding 37 percent. In both places,

---

11. Michael Zuckerman, "The Social Context of Democracy in Massachusetts," *William and Mary Quarterly*, 3d ser., 25 (1968): 523–44. Zuckerman's analysis is not sufficiently critical of Robert E. Brown's work, even as it provides a better conceptual framework for evaluating the importance of a widespread suffrage. Zuckerman ignores not only age stratification but also economic inequality and the increasing appearance of religious conflict. For a more detailed analysis of Zuckerman's work (and that of Philip J. Greven, John Demos, and Kenneth Lockridge) see chapter 1.

inequality increased steadily from the end of the seventeenth century even as the rate of natural population growth declined—a clear indication of advancing social differentiation (and not simply age stratification). And in Newtown, at least, the bulk of the poor population in 1784 was composed not of "younger sons or older men" but of workers in the prime of their productive lives.[12]

The westward migration of this excess farm population was of crucial importance, although not for the precise reasons suggested by Turner and Lemon. Young men and women without a landed inheritance moved to newly settled communities not as yeomen but as aspirants to that status; they hoped to make the difficult climb up the agricultural "ladder" from laborer to tenant to freeholder. This geographical movement in turn helped to maintain social stability in long-settled agricultural towns. One-third of all adult males in Goshen, Connecticut, in 1750 were without land; two decades later a majority of those men had left the town, and 70 percent of those who remained had obtained property through marriage, inheritance, or the savings from their labor. A new landless group of unmarried sons, wage laborers, and tenant farmers had appeared in Goshen by 1771, again encompassing one-third of the adult males. A similar process of outmigration and property accumulation would characterize many of the lives of this landless

---

12. Lemon, *Best Poor Man's Country*, 11 (table I); Jessica Kross Ehrlich, "A Town Study in Colonial New York: Newtown, Queens County (1642–1790)" (Ph.D. diss., University of Michigan, 1974), 178, 164 (table 13). The data for Concord indicate that in 1770–71 the top 20 percent of the population owned 48 percent of the land and 56 percent of the town's wealth but paid only 42 percent of the total tax (Gross, *Minutemen*, 212, 220, 231).

group, but throughout the northern region there was a steady increase in the number of permanent tenant farmers as the century progressed.[13]

The renewed expropriation of aboriginal lands during the early nineteenth century brought a partial reversal of this trend. Massive westward migration enabled a rapidly growing Euro-American population to *preserve* an agricultural society composed primarily of yeoman freeholding families in many eastern areas, and to *extend* those age- and wealth-stratified communities into western regions.[14] This movement did not, however, produce less stratified communities in the Northwest states, nor did it assure the universal ownership of land. Within a few decades of settlement the wealth structure of the frontier states was nearly indistinguishable from that in the agricultural areas of the more densely settled East. In Trempealeau County, Wisconsin, in 1870 the poorest 10 percent of the propertied population owned less than 1 percent of all assessed wealth, while the most affluent 10 percent controlled 39 percent. This distribution was almost precisely the same as that in those regions of Vermont from which many of the inhabitants of this farming county had recently migrated.[15] "On no frontier," Neil

---

13. Jackson Turner Main, *The Social Structure of Revolutionary America* (Princeton, N.J., 1965), 176. For a carefully documented analysis of the agricultural ladder, see Clarence H. Danhof, *Change in Agriculture: The Northern United States, 1820–1870* (Cambridge, Mass., 1969), 78–115.

14. The alternative was a class-stratified society, composed of a few owners of large properties and a mass of wage laborers—an agricultural proletariat. See, for example, J. Harvey Smith, "Work Routine and Social Structure in a French Village: Cruzy in the Nineteenth Century," *Journal of Interdisciplinary History* 5 (1975): 362.

15. Merle Curti et al., *The Making of an American Community: A*

McNall concludes from an intensive study of the settlement of the rich Genesee Valley in upstate New York between 1790 and 1860, "was there an easy avenue to land ownership for the farmer of limited means."[16]

Evidence from a variety of geographic locations indicates, therefore, that Lemon has presented an overly optimistic description of the agricultural economy of early America and has falsely ascribed a "liberal" consciousness to the inhabitants of eighteenth-century Pennsylvania. His analysis is not unique. A number of historians of colonial New England have offered similar interpretations of an entrepreneurial mentality among the majority of the agricultural population. Sometimes the ascription is implicit and perhaps inadvertent, as in the case of Philip Greven's path-breaking analysis of Andover, which focuses attention on the single economic variable of land transmission. Was the preservation of a landed inheritance the concern of most Andover fam-

---

Case Study of Democracy in a Frontier County (Stanford, Calif., 1959), chapter 4. Inequality in the old Northwest was less acute than in Frederick and Berkeley counties in the Shenandoah Valley of Virginia in 1788, where the top 10 percent of the landowners held nearly 50 percent of the land, or in the "cotton South," where the top decile controlled between 50 percent and 55 percent of the total wealth in 1850 and 1860. See Robert D. Mitchell, "Agricultural Change and the American Revolution: A Virginia Case Study," *Agricultural History* 47 (1973): 131, and Gavin Wright, " 'Economic Democracy' and the Concentration of Agricultural Wealth in the Cotton South, 1850–1860," *Agricultural History* 44 (1970): 63–85.

16. Neil Adams McNall, *An Agricultural History of the Genesee Valley, 1790–1860* (Philadelphia, 1952), 240–41. For the rapid and extensive emergence of farm tenancy in Illinois and Iowa see Paul W. Gates, "Frontier Estate Builders and Farm Laborers," in *Turner and the Sociology of the Frontier*, ed. Richard Hofstadter and Seymour Martin Lipset (New York, 1968), 115–16.

ilies, or only that of the very select group of substantially endowed first settlers and their descendants
whom Greven has studied? The pattern of family life,
geographic mobility, and economic values may have
been very different among later arrivals to Andover—
those who had less land to pass on to the next generation—yet that group constituted a majority of the
town's population by the eighteenth century. Or what
of the pervasive entrepreneurial outlook among Connecticut farmers that Richard L. Bushman posits in
From Puritan to Yankee?[17] Bushman's interpretation of
the Great Awakening is predicated upon the emergence of an accumulation-oriented pattern of behavior,
and yet little if any evidence is presented to demonstrate its existence among the mass of the population.

Indeed, the only work that attempts explicitly to
demonstrate the predominance of entrepreneurial values among the farming population of New England is
the small but influential study by Charles S. Grant,
Democracy in the Connecticut Frontier Town of Kent. According to Grant, the one-hundred-odd male settlers
who arrived in Kent during the late 1730s and the
1740s were "remarkably uniform . . . prosperous
enough to buy proprietary shares and to accumulate
large amounts of land." They were "versatile and
ambitious," and the economic opportunity available in
Kent—"fertile (but stony) farming land, . . . deposits
of iron ore, and abundant water power for . . . mills"—
induced in these settlers "not placid contentment, but
an almost frenzied determination to try a hand at

---

17. Richard L. Bushman, *From Puritan to Yankee: Character and the
Social Order in Connecticut, 1690–1765* (Cambridge, Mass., 1967).
The possible bias in Greven's work is suggested in Vinovskis,
"American Historical Demography," 142–45.

everything."[18] Thus "virtually every family settled on a farm which . . . usually produced a salable surplus"; "virtually every family had some member involved as operator or part owner of an ironworks"; and "virtually every early settler was an avid land speculator." By the time of the American Revolution this activity had produced "a population raised on an economic tradition of land speculation and individualistic venturing" that refused to make "economic sacrifices" for the sake of independence.[19] While Grant indicates that there may have been "humble subsistence farmers" and "obscure yeomen" in the town, he "is impressed not so much with the contented subsistence way of life as with the drive for profits." Indeed, he devotes a chapter to "the drive for profits" and concludes it by stressing the acquisitiveness of the economic elite, the "aggressive opportunists" whose ethical standards were "part and parcel of the spirit of Kent." "One sees in certain of the Kent settlers not so much the contented yeoman, certainly not the 'slave' toiling for his master, but perhaps the embryo John D. Rockefeller."[20]

Even when stated in more historically realistic language, Grant's argument is not sustained by his evidence. He begins by distorting much of the allegedly opportunistic and profit-seeking economic activity in Kent by calling it "nonagricultural." In actuality, most of the nonfarm enterprises were sawmills, gristmills, fulling mills, and tanneries. These were profit-seeking businesses, but they were also social

---

18. Charles S. Grant, *Democracy in the Connecticut Frontier Town of Kent* (1961; reprint, New York, 1972), 99, 29, 169–70.
19. Ibid., 170, 42, 53, 171.
20. Ibid., 78, 29, 54, 53.

necessities in a rural community; all were intimately connected to agricultural production. With the exception of the iron industry (the development of which lends some support to Grant's thesis), these enterprises produced primarily for a local market and were so crucial to the welfare of the inhabitants that they were supported by communal action. Following the long New England tradition of material inducements to skilled artisans, the proprietors of the town voted an extra lot in the first division to Ebenezer Barnum "on condition he build a sawmill by the last of December next and also a gristmill in two years."[21] Thus the mere existence of most of these "nonagricultural" enterprises will not substantiate Grant's interpretation. They were traditional, not new, enterprises, practical necessities rather than dramatic innovations, and the product of communal legislation as much as of an adventurous individualism.

A second distortion appears when Grant argues that "the most significant aspect of this enterprise . . . would seem to be the magnitude of profit-seeking activity." "Altogether," he indicates, "209 men were investors in nonagricultural enterprise at Kent between 1739 and 1800."[22] But what is the significance of that number? Neither in his monograph nor in his dissertation does Grant indicate the aggregate number of adult males who lived in Kent during this sixty-year period, yet this total is crucial, for it represents

---

21. This vote (as well as the fact that there was a common field system in Kent in the early 1740s) is mentioned in Charles S. Grant's "A History of Kent, 1738–1796: Democracy on Connecticut's Frontier" (Ph.D. diss., Columbia University, 1957), 43, 57–58, although not in the published version.
22. Grant, *Democracy in Kent*, 44.

the number of *potential* investors. The statistical material that is available suggests that at least 1,000 (and probably 1,500) adult males worked and resided in Kent during this period; thus the 209 resident "profit-seekers" constituted only 15–20 percent of the potential investing population.[23] What Grant has depicted as the activity and the ethos of most of the inhabitants of Kent becomes, at most, the enterprise and outlook of a well-to-do upper class.

In an attempt to demonstrate the pervasiveness of this entrepreneurial outlook in Kent, Grant adduces another type of evidence. His position, based more on assumption than on argument, is that the sale of "surplus" agricultural products on the market constitutes prima facie evidence of a profit-oriented attitude. Considered abstractly, this is a weak line of reasoning, if only because of the word "surplus" itself. This term, as it was widely used in America until the middle of the nineteenth century, clearly indicated that market sales were a secondary rather than a primary consideration: the "surplus" was what was left over after the yearly subsistence requirements of the farm household had been met.[24]

Even if this faulty reasoning is ignored, the factual evidence will not sustain Grant's argument that a majority of these farmsteads produced a surplus that could be sold or exchanged. Grant himself states that

---

23. Grant notes that 474 adult males lived in Kent between 1738 and 1760 and that 525 adult males lived in or moved through Kent in the four years 1774–77. Since some of these 999 men were undoubtedly "double-counted," the total number was somewhat less, but because this calculation pertains only to twenty-six years out of a total of sixty-two, the total number of resident adult males during this period must have been at least 1,000.

24. Danhof, *Change in Agriculture*, 17–18.

40 of the 103 farms in Kent in 1796 could provide only enough foodstuffs for the sustenance of their occupants. And this estimate is undoubtedly too low, since his computations assume a grain harvest of twenty-five bushels per acre for both corn and wheat. Such yields might be attained on the best land (and then only for the first harvests), but reliable data from areas as far apart as Massachusetts, Pennsylvania, Virginia, and North Carolina indicate average yields of fifteen bushels per acre for corn and eight to twelve bushels for wheat.[25] If these yields are assumed, the proportion of Kent farmsteads that produced even a small salable surplus drops from two-thirds to one-third; only the most productive farms—15–20 percent of the total—could have produced enough to engage in extensive market transactions.

Why was this the case? Was the soil too poor? The climate too forbidding? Or were the aspirations of the settlers too limited? What was the economic and cultural consciousness of the mass of the agricultural population? These questions raise fundamental

---

25. Grant, *Democracy in Kent*, 34, n. 3. The computations appear only in Grant, "History of Kent," 67–68, 78–79, where heavy reliance is placed on the yields reported in *American Husbandry*. This anonymous work, published in 1775, is criticized for its inflated estimates of farm yields in Harry Roy Merrens, *Colonial North Carolina in the Eighteenth Century: A Study in Historical Geography* (Chapel Hill, N.C., 1964), chapter 6, n. 11. Merrens provides more reliable estimates (110ff.), as does James T. Lemon, "Household Consumption in Eighteenth-Century America and Its Relationship to Production and Trade: The Situation among Farmers in Southeastern Pennsylvania," *Agricultural History* 41 (1967): 59–70, and *Best Poor Man's Country*, 152–53 (table 27). In Concord, average grain yields—corn and wheat combined—increased from 12.2 to 15 bushels per acre between 1771 and 1801 (Gross, *Minutemen*, 231), while Mitchell reports wheat yields of 10 bushels per acre in the newly settled Shenandoah Valley ("Agricultural Change," 129).

issues pertaining to the nature of social reality and the sources of human motivation, and their resolution must begin with an investigation of the epistemological premises of the entrepreneurial school of agricultural historians. Once again, Charles Grant offers an ideal entrée, this time as he explicitly acknowledges the source of his interpretation: Richard "Hofstadter suggests," Grant explains in a footnote, "that where the yeoman practiced only subsistence farming, he did so out of necessity (lack of transportation and markets) and not because he was enamored of this way of life. The yeoman farmer wanted profits."[26] At issue here is not validity of the argument but the assumptions on which it is based. Following Hofstadter, Grant effects a radical disjunction between the constraints imposed by the material and social environment and the yeoman's consciousness. The "drive for profits" simply exists, even given the "lack of transportation and markets." The subsistence way of life does not seem to affect or alter the sensibility of the farmer; consciousness is divorced from condition.

Contemporary observers who spoke to this issue assumed a rather different relationship between environmental opportunities and human goals. "We know," wrote one migrant to the Genesee Valley in 1810, "that people who live far from markets and cannot sell their produce, naturally become indolent and vicious." "There can be no industry without motive," another migrant warned the readers of *The Plough Boy* in 1820, "and it appears to me [that without markets] there is great danger that our people will

---

26. Grant, *Democracy in Kent*, 191. The reference is to Richard Hofstadter, "The Myth of the Happy Yeoman," *American Heritage* 7 (April 1956): 43–53.

soon limit their exertions to the raising of food for their families."[27] A somewhat similar point had been made in the mid-eighteenth century by William Byrd II when he came upon a fertile allotment that "would be a valuable tract of land in any country but North Carolina, where, for want of navigation and commerce, the best estate affords little more than a coarse subsistence." All were agreed that "convenience and a ready market is the life of a settler—not cheap lands."[28]

Such astute contemporary perceptions constituted the empirical foundations for the argument propounded in 1916 by Percy Bidwell, the leading modern historian of early American agriculture. Why should the farmer specialize, "why should he exert himself to produce a surplus," Bidwell asked in his classic analysis of the rural economy of New England, when there was no market in which to sell it, when "the only return he could expect would be a sort of psychological income?"[29] Bidwell's logic is still compelling, for it is based on epistemological principles that command assent. It recognized, if only implicitly, that there was a considerable diversity of motivation and of economic values among the farm population. In this respect, it echoed the observation of another contemporary. "Farming may be so conducted as to be made profitable, or merely to afford a living or to run out the farm," a Massachusetts writer noted in 1849.

---

27. Quoted in McNall, *Agricultural History*, 104.

28. Louis B. Wright, ed., *The Prose Works of William Byrd of Westover: Narratives of a Colonial Virginian* (Cambridge, Mass., 1966), 184; McNall, *Agricultural History*, 96.

29. Percy W. Bidwell, "Rural Economy in New England at the Beginning of the Nineteenth Century," *Transactions of the Connecticut Academy of Arts and Sciences* 20 (1916): 330.

"Taking the land as it averages in the state, this depends more on the farmer than on the soil." At the same time, Bidwell insisted that everyone was affected by the structural possibilities and limitations of the society, whatever their cultural propensities or economic aspirations. There was a direct relationship between the material environment, on the one hand, and the consciousness and activity of the population on the other. This understanding informs Bidwell's account and renders it far superior to that of the entrepreneurial school of agricultural historians. "Potatoes are very much used and increased attempts are making to raise them for market," Bidwell quotes the Reverend Samuel Goodrich of Ridgefield, Connecticut (c. 1800), "but the distance from the market is so great that it is not expected the practice will be general."[30] Acquisitive hopes had yielded to geographic realities.

II

A convincing interpretation of northern agriculture must begin, therefore, not with an ascribed consciousness but rather with an understanding of the dimensions of economic existence. These varied significantly from one region to another, primarily as a result of differential access to an urban or an international market. Yet in every area similar cultural constraints circumscribed the extent of involvement in the market economy. Indeed, the tension between the demands of the market and the expectations stemming from

---

30. Ibid., 317n; the Massachusetts quotation is from Danhof, *Change in Agriculture*, 134.

traditional social relationships was a fact of crucial significance in the lives of this preindustrial population.

Given the absence of an external market, there was no alternative to subsistence or semisubsistence production.[31] Following the settlement of an inland region, for example, there would be a flurry of barter transactions as established settlers exchanged surplus foodstuffs, seeds, and livestock for the scarce currency and manufactured items brought by newly arrived migrants. Subsequently, the diversification of the local economy created a small demand for farm produce among artisans and traders. Yet neither of these consuming groups was large. Migrants quickly planted their own crops, and most rural artisans cultivated extensive gardens and kept a few head of livestock. The economy had stabilized at a low level of specialization.

This system of local exchange, moreover, did not constitute a market economy in the full sense of the term. Many of these transactions were direct ones—between producers of different types of goods and services—without the involvement of a merchant, broker, or other middlemen. Farm men and women exchanged wheat for tools, meat for furniture, or vegetables for cloth, because their families had a specific personal use for the bartered product. They would

---

31. By these terms I mean limited participation in a commercial market economy. As the preceding quotations suggest, most farm families had enough land, equipment, and labor to raise as much food as they could consume. Thus their living standards (in terms of calories and protein) could rise even if they did not engage in extensive market transactions. The pressure of population on resources inhibited such advances, but there were no near-famines or subsistence crises in the northern colonies, as there were, for instance, in France in the 1690s.

attempt to drive a hard bargain or to make a good deal in their negotiations with the blacksmith, cabinet-maker, or seamstress—to insist, for example, on a carefully crafted, high-quality product. Yet their goal was not profit but the acquisition of a needed item for use. "Robt. Griffins wife got 10 cocks of hay from me which she is to pay in butter," Matthew Patten of Bedford, New Hampshire, noted in his diary in the 1770s; "I asked her 2£ for a cock." Even when an artisan or merchant would "sell" goods to a farmer and record the obligation in monetary terms, it was assumed that the debt would continue (usually without interest) until it was balanced in a subsequent barter transaction of "Country Produce at Market Price."[32]

A market existed, therefore, and it regulated the overall terms of trade among farmers, artisans, and merchants. But this price system was not sovereign; it was often subordinated, in the conduct of daily existence, to barter transactions based on exchange value—what an item was worth to a specific individual. Some goods could not be purchased at any price because they were spoken for by friends, neighbors, or kinfolk. "I went to joseph Farmers and Alexanders to buy some corn," Patten noted in 1770, "but Farmers was all promised and Alexander wood [would] not take 2 pistereens a bushel and I got none."[33] The maximiz-

---

32. Max George Schumacher, *The Northern Farmer and His Markets during the Late Colonial Period*, Dissertations in American Economic History (New York, 1975), 88, 83. For further detail see *The Diary of Mathew Patten of Bedford, N.H., from Seventeen Fifty-Four to Seventeen Eighty-Eight* (Concord, N.H., 1903).

33. Schumacher, *Northern Farmer*, 20. My argument in these two paragraphs is based on Michael Merrill, "Cash Is Good to Eat: Self-Sufficiency and Exchange in the Rural Economy of the United States," *Radical History Review* 7 (1977): 42–69.

ing of profit was less important to these producers
than the meeting of household needs and the maintaining of established social relationships within the community. And it was this "subsistence farm society"
that Jackson T. Main correctly specifies as "the most
common type throughout New England and perhaps
in the entire North" until the end of the eighteenth
century.[34] As Bidwell argued, "the revolution in agriculture, as well as the breaking down of the self-
sufficient village life, awaited the growth of a [large,
urban] non-agricultural population."[35]

A commercially oriented agriculture began to
develop after 1750, in response to lucrative urban and
European markets for American grain. Yet the size of
these new trading networks should not be overesti-
mated. The meat exports of the entire state of Connecticut between 1768 and 1773 would have been
absorbed by an additional urban population of twenty-

---

34. Main, *Social Structure*, 18. Another important characteristic of
many of these communities was an extensive debt structure.
Grant, *Democracy in Kent*, notes a "vast tangle of debts" in Kent,
with each adult male having an average of 20 creditors in the
1770s. There was no concentration of debts in the hands of a
money-lending class; most of the obligations were small, often ran
for years, and frequently canceled each other out. When Elizur
Price died in 1777, he had 20 creditors but was himself owed
money by 17 men. In more commercial settlements there was a
distinct financial elite. When Elisha Hurlbut, a merchant of
Windham, Connecticut, died in 1771, he was owed a total of £590
by no fewer than 77 debtors, and during the preceding 12 years
had initiated 212 debt actions (13 percent of the total) in Windham
County Court (see William F. Willingham, "Windham, Connecticut: Profile of a Revolutionary Community, 1775–1818" [Ph.D.
diss., Northwestern University, 1972], 77–91, 240–61). The debt
structure in Newtown, New York, remained extensive as late as
1790, while that in Lancaster, Pennsylvania, conformed to the
Windham pattern (Ehrlich, "Town Study," 151–54; Wood, "Conestoga Crossroads," 167–68).
35. Bidwell, "Rural Economy," 353.

two thousand—a city the size of New York—and the shipments of grain from Connecticut ports were even smaller. Exports of wheat and flour from the Middle Colonies during those years were far more substantial, with the annual average equivalent to 2.1 million bushels of wheat. Still, the amount of wheat consumed by the residents of those colonies was nearly twice as large (3.8 million bushels per year). And wheat was normally cultivated on only one-third of the acreage devoted to the production of grain, most of which was corn that was consumed by livestock. The "surplus" wheat exported to foreign markets thus remained a relatively small part of total production (15–20 percent), even for commercially minded family farmers.[36] As late as 1820 "the portion of farm products not consumed within the northern rural community" and sold on all outside markets, both foreign and domestic, amounted to only 25 percent of the total.[37]

Given the existence of a growing European market—a demand for wheat that brought a price rise of 100 percent during the second half of the eighteenth century—the slow and limited commercialization of northern agriculture is significant. Far more dramatic changes were occurring in the South, on slave plantations rather than on family farms. During the years from 1768 to 1773 wheat and flour exports from Virginia and Maryland amounted to 25 percent of the

---

36. Schumacher, *Northern Farmer*, 33, 42, 42n for the macro-estimates; Lemon, *Best Man's Poor Country*, tables 27 and 28, pp. 180–81, indicates that 8 of 26 cultivated acres on a typical farm of 125 acres would be planted in wheat and that 50 bushels of grain (out of a total of 295) would be available for sale or exchange.

37. Danhof, *Change in Agriculture*, 11, 2.

total from the breadbasket colonies of New York and Pennsylvania. This "striking expansion of the wheat belt" to the southern colonies after 1750 clearly indicated, as Max Schumacher has argued, "that production on the individual [northern] farms was not elastic enough to cope with the rising wheat market."[38]

The high cost of inland transport was one factor that inhibited the expansion of northern wheat production. A bushel of wheat could be shipped 164 miles on the Hudson River from Albany to New York City in 1769 for fourpence, or 5 percent of its wholesale value, but the proportion rose to 18 percent for a journey of the same distance on the shallow and more difficult waters of the upper Delaware River in Pennsylvania. And the cost of land transportation was much higher. Even in 1816, when the price of grain was high in Philadelphia, the cost of transporting wheat from 50 miles outside the city amounted to one-fourth of the selling price.[39]

Technological restraints and cultural preferences placed even greater limitations on the expansion of wheat production on the family farms of the North. Thomas Jefferson isolated the crucial variable when he noted, in 1793, that planters "allow that every laborer will manage ten acres of wheat, except at harvest." The inefficiency of the sickle, which limited the amount a worker could reap to one-half or three-quarters of an acre per day, placed a severe constraint on the cultivation of wheat. Large-scale production—with annual yields of one thousand bushels from one

---

38. Schumacher, *Northern Farmer*, 142. See also pp. 110, 154, 167.
39. Ibid., 57–59; George Rogers Taylor, *The Transportation Revolution, 1815–1860* (New York, 1951), 133.

hundred acres—was attempted only by those northern producers who were prepared to bid for scarce wage labor during the short harvest season or who controlled a captive labor supply of indentured servants or black slaves. In Somerset County, New Jersey, one farmer relied on the assistance of six blacks to harvest his eighty acres of wheat, while a Trenton proprietor had three blacks to reap twenty acres.[40] Such entrepreneurial farmers were exceptions. They entered the market not only to buy necessities and to sell their surplus but also to buy labor—slaves, servants, wage workers—in order to make a profit. Their farms were "capitalistic" enterprises in the full sense of the term: privately owned productive properties, operated for profit through a series of market-oriented contractual relationships.

Even in the most market-oriented areas of the Middle Colonies, many farmers participated in the commercial capitalist economy in a much more limited way and with rather different goals. Lacking slaves or indentured servants and unwilling to bid for wage labor, they planted only eight to ten acres of wheat each year, a crop that could conveniently be harvested by the farmer, one or two growing sons, and (in some cases) his wife. Of the normal yield of eighty to one hundred bushels, sixty would be consumed by the family or saved for seed; the surplus of twenty to forty bushels would be sold on the Philadelphia market, bringing a cash income in the early 1770s of five to ten pounds sterling. The ordinary male farmer, Lemon concludes, was content to produce "enough for his

---

40. Jefferson to President Washington, 28 June 1793, in *The Writings of Thomas Jefferson*, ed. Andrew A. Lipscomb and Albert E. Bergh (Washington, D.C., 1903), 9:142.

family and . . . to sell a surplus in the market to buy what he deemed necessities."[41] There was little innovative, risk-taking behavior; there was no determined pursuit of profit. Indeed, the account books of these farm families indicate that they invariably chose the security of diversified production rather than hire labor to produce more wheat or to specialize in milk production. Economic gain was important to these men and women, yet it was not their dominant value. It was subordinate to (or encompassed by) two other goals: the yearly subsistence and long-term financial security of the family unit.

Thus the predominance of subsistence or semi-subsistence productive units among the yeoman farming families of the northern colonies was not only the result of geographic or economic factors—the ready access to a reliable, expanding market. These men and women were enmeshed also in a web of social relation-

---

41. Lemon, *Best Poor Man's Country*, 180; see also tables 27 and 28 and pp. 179–83. Was there a "motivationally subsistent agricultural class" in the North similar to that found among the poor white population in the South? "A common practice of [southern white cotton] farmers in plantation areas," Julius Rubin has argued, "was to raise the minimal amount of cash crop needed to buy a narrow and rigid range of necessities: tobacco, lead, powder and sugar." For these men, mere participation in the international economy was neither an indication of nor conducive to the development of an entrepreneurial mentality. See Julius Rubin, "Urban Growth and Regional Development," in *The Growth of the Seaport Cities, 1790–1825: Proceedings of a Conference Sponsored by the Eleutherian Mills-Hagley Foundation, March 17–19, 1966*, ed. David T. Gilchrist (Charlottesville, Va., 1967), 15. Two other works that begin to examine the values, behavior, and life-style of the poor white agricultural population of the South are Rhys Isaac, "Evangelical Revolt: The Nature of the Baptists' Challenge to the Traditional Order in Virginia," *William and Mary Quarterly*, 3d ser., 31 (1974): 345–68, and Aubrey C. Land, "Economic Base and Social Structure: The Northern Chesapeake in the Eighteenth Century," *Journal of Economic History* 25 (1965): 639–54.

ships and cultural expectations that inhibited the free play of market forces. Much of the output of their farms was consumed by the residents, most of whom were biologically or legally related and who were not paid wages for their labor. A secondary group of consumers consisted of the inhabitants of the local area, members of a community often based on ties of kinship, language, religion, or ethnicity. An impersonal price system figured prominently in these transactions, but goods were often bartered for their exchange value or for what was considered a "just price." Finally, a small (but growing) proportion of the total production of these farms was "sold" on an external market through a series of formal commercial transactions.

If freehold ownership and participation in these urban and international markets meant that northern agriculture did not have many of the characteristics of a closed peasant or a precapitalist economy,[42] they do

---

42. There are a number of other reasons for not describing this as a "peasant society," as Kenneth A. Lockridge has done in *A New England Town: The First Hundred Years: Dedham, Massachusetts, 1636–1736* (New York, 1970). Dedham was simply not analogous to the subjugated aboriginal settlements that Eric Wolf depicted as "closed corporate peasant communities" ("Closed Corporate Peasant Communities in Mesoamerica and Central Java," *Southwestern Journal of Anthropology* 10 [1957]: 1–18). A more realistic comparison is with the peasant societies of early modern western Europe, and the differences are sufficiently great as to render use of the term unwise in the American context. There were few landlords and no nobility in the northern colonies; the settlement pattern was diffuse rather than nucleated by the eighteenth century; the central government was weak; the role of the church was limited, and the established Congregational churches of New England were nonhierarchical in structure; and the system of property relationships was contractual and malleable. Finally, these American farming communities constituted the central core of the society; they were not "part-societies" and "part-cultures" (in the definition

not imply that this system of production and exchange was modern or that its members were motivated primarily by liberal, entrepreneurial, individualist, or capitalist values. Nor is it sufficient to describe these farming communities as "transitional" between the ideal-types of traditional and modern or precapitalist and capitalist. To adopt such an idealist approach is to substitute typology for analysis, to suggest a teleological model of historical development, and to ignore the specific features of this social and economic system. Rather, one must point to its central features: the community was distinguished by age and wealth stratification and (usually) by ethnic or religious homogeneity, while on the family level there was freehold property ownership, a household mode of production, limited economic possibilities and aspirations, and a safety-first subsistence agriculture within a commercial capitalist market structure. One must then seek an understanding of the "coping strategies" used by individuals, groups, and governments to reconcile the competing demands, the inherent tensions, and the immanent contradictions posed by this particular configuration of historical institutions and cultural values.

---

of peasant society advanced by Robert Redfield), dependent upon and exploited by a metropolitan elite.

If a historical analogy is required, then the "post-reform" peasant societies of nineteenth-century western Europe are the most appropriate, not those of the *ancien régime*. See, for example, Walter Goldschmidt and Evelyn Jacobson Kunkel, "The Structure of the Peasant Family," *American Anthropologist*, n.s., 73 (1971): 1058–76. Then, too, the pattern of family behavior and values may be similar among small freeholding farmers, whether they live in a yeoman or in a peasant society: compare, for example, Greven's Andover families with those analyzed in Lutz K. Berkner, "The Stem Family and the Development Cycle of the Peasant Household: An Eighteenth-Century Austrian Example," *American Historical Review* 77 (1972): 398–418.

III

It would be premature, at this point, to attempt a complete analysis of the *mentalité* of the preindustrial yeoman population. Yet a preliminary examination may suggest both a conceptual framework for future research and the character of certain widely accepted values, goals, and behavioral norms. An important, and perhaps controversial, premise should be made explicit at the beginning. It is assumed that the behavior of the farm population constitutes a crucial (although not a foolproof) indicator of its values and aspirations. This epistemological assumption has an interpretive implication, for it focuses attention on those activities that dominated the daily lives of the population—in the case of this particular society, on the productive tasks that provided food, clothing, and shelter.

This process of production and capital formation derived much of its emotive and intellectual meaning from the cultural matrix—from the institutional character of the society. Work was arranged along familial lines rather than controlled communally or through a wage system. This apparently simple organizational fact was a crucial determinant of the historical consciousness of this farming population. For even as the family gave symbolic meaning and emotional significance to subsistence activities, its own essence was shaped by the character of the productive system. There was a complex relationship between the agricultural labor and property system of early America and its rural culture; and it is that matrix of productive activities, organizational structures, and social values which the following analysis attempts (in a very preliminary fashion) to reconstruct.[43]

---

43. The exciting work of E. P. Thompson on the agricultural

Because the primary economic unit—the family—was also the main social institution, production activities had a profound effect on the entire character of agrarian life. Family relationships could not be divorced from economic considerations; indeed, the basic question of power and authority within the family hinged primarily on legal control over the land and, indirectly, over the labor needed to work it. The parents (principally the husband) enjoyed legal possession of the property—either as freeholders, tenants, or sharecroppers—but they were dependent on their children for economic support in their old age. Their aim, as Greven has pointed out, was to control the terms and the timing of the transfer of economic resources to the succeeding generation.[44]

The intimate relationship between agricultural production and parental values, between economic history and family history, is best approached through a series of case studies. The first of these small family dramas began in 1739 with the arrival in Kent, Connecticut, of Joseph Fuller. At one time or another Fuller was an investor in an ironworks, a "typical speculative proprietor," and a "rich squatter" who tried to deceive the Connecticut authorities into grant-

---

society of eighteenth-century England, "The Moral Economy of the English Crowd in the Eighteenth Century," *Past and Present* 50 (1971): 76–136, and "Patrician Society, Plebian Culture," *Journal of Social History* 7 (1974): 382–405, focuses on conflicts engendered by consumption shortages and by asymmetrical authority relationships. It assumes, but does not investigate in detail, class- or wealth-related production differences. A similar concentration on authority, especially in its religious aspects, characterizes the excellent work of Rhys Isaac (see n. 41 above). Ultimately, it will be necessary to specify the relationships among productive activity, religious inclination, and the system of authority.

44. Greven, "Family Structure," 234–56, and *Four Generations*.

ing him (and his partner Joshua Lassell) 4,820 acres of provincial land. Fuller's energy, ambition, and activities mark him as an entrepreneur, even a "capitalist." Yet his behavior must be seen in the widest possible context, and the motivation assessed accordingly. When this restless man arrived in Kent at the age of forty (with his second wife), he was the father of seven sons, aged two to sixteen; thirteen years later, when his final petition for a land grant was rejected, he had nine sons, aged eleven to twenty-nine years, and five daughters. With fourteen children to provide with land, dowries, or currency, Fuller had to embark on an active career if he wished to keep his children (and himself and his wife in their old age) from a life of landless poverty.

In the event, fecundity overwhelmed the Fullers' financial ingenuity. None of the children of Joseph Fuller ever attained a rating on the tax list equal to the highest recorded for their father, and a similar pattern prevailed among the sons of the third generation. The total resources of the Fuller "clan" (for such it had become) grew constantly over time—with nine second- and twelve third-generation males appearing on the tax lists of Kent—but their per capita wealth declined steadily.[45] The gains of one generation, the slow accumulation of capital resources through savings and invested labor, had been dispersed among many heirs.

Such divisions of limited resources inevitably roused resentment and engendered bitter disputes within farm families. Ultimately, the delicate recipro-

---

45. Grant, *Democracy in Kent*, 101, table 13. See also pp. 17, 47–50, 67, 71.

cal economic relationship between parents and children might break down completely. Insufficiency of land meant that most children would have to be exiled—apprenticed to wealthier members of the community or sent out on their own as landless laborers—and that parents would have to endure a harsh old age, sharing their small plot with the remaining heir. High fertility and low mortality threatened each generation of children with the loss of class status; the unencumbered inheritance of a freehold estate was the exception, not the rule.

Even in these circumstances, as a second example will suggest, the ideal for many dispossessed children remained property ownership and eventual control of the transfer process with regard to their own offspring. "My parents were poor," an "Honest Farmer" wrote to the *Pennsylvania Packet* in 1786,

> and they put me at twelve years of age to a farmer, with whom I lived til I was twenty one. . . . I married me a wife—and a very working young woman she was—and we took a farm of forty acres on rent. . . . In ten years I was able to buy me a farm of sixty acres on which I became my own tenant. I then, in a manner, grew rich and soon added another sixty acres, with which I am content. My estate increased beyond all account. I bought several lots of out-land for my children, which amounted to seven when I was forty-five years old. About this time I married my oldest daughter to a clever lad, to whom I gave one hundred acres of my out-land.[46]

---

46. Quoted in Stevenson W. Fletcher, *Pennsylvania Agriculture and Country Life, 1640–1840* (Harrisburg, Pa., 1950), 315.

Was this "success story" typical? Did the "Honest Farmer" minimize the difficulties of his own ascent and exaggerate the prospects of his seven children, each of whom would have to be provided with land, livestock, or equipment? It is clear, at any rate, that this Pennsylvanian enjoyed a crucial advantage over Joseph Fuller; he could accumulate capital through the regular sale of his surplus production on the market and offer economic assistance to his children. His grandchildren, moreover, would grow up in the more fully developed commercial economy of the early nineteenth century. Ten years of work as a farm laborer—and an intense commitment to save—would now yield a capital stock of five hundred dollars. With this sum invested in equipment, livestock, and supplies, it would then be feasible to rent a farm, "with the prospect of accumulating money at a rate perhaps double that possible by wage work."[47] To begin with less than five hundred dollars was to increase dependence on the landlord—to accept a half-and-half division of the produce rather than a two-thirds share. In either case, there was a high financial and psychological price to be paid. For many years these young adults would be "dependent," would work as wage laborers without security, as sharecroppers without land, or as mortgagors without full independence; their labor would enrich freeholders, landlords, and bankers even as it moved them closer to real economic freedom.

This process is readily apparent in a third case study, an archetypical example of the slow but successful accumulation of productive agricultural prop-

---

47. Danhof, *Change in Agriculture*, 91, 78–115.

erty in the mid-nineteenth century. In 1843 a young farmer in Massachusetts bought an old farm of eighty-five acres for $4,337; "in order to pay for it, I mortgaged it for $4,100, paying only $237, all that I had, after buying my stock." Nine years later it was clear that some progress had been made, for he had "paid up about $600 on the mortgage, and laid out nearly $2,000 in permanent improvements on my buildings and farm." This hardworking farmer was "a little nearer the harbor than I was when I commenced the voyage," but he was still $3,500 in debt and had interest payments of $250 to make each year.[48] These obligations might be met in ten or fifteen years, but by then new debts would have to be incurred in order to provide working capital for his children. This farmer would die a property owner, but at least some of his offspring would face a similarly time-consuming and difficult climb up the agricultural ladder.

Two features of the long-term process of capital formation through agricultural production revealed by these case studies stand out as particularly important, one static and the other dynamic. The recurrent factor was the continual pressure of population on the existing capital stock; the rate of natural increase constantly threatened to outstrip the creation of new productive resources: cleared land, machinery, housing, and livestock. This danger is demonstrable in the case of the Fuller clan, and its specter lurks in the prose of the "Honest Farmer" and his younger accumulation-oriented counterpart in Massachusetts. Economic prosperity was the result of unremitting labor by each

---

48. Ibid., 112; quotations are from Amasa Walker, ed., *Transactions of the Agricultural Societies in the State of Massachusetts, for 1852* ... (Boston, 1853), 93–94.

generation. Only as farm parents began consciously to limit their fertility were they able to pass on sizable estates to their children—and this occurred primarily after 1830.[49]

What changed from the seventeenth to the early nineteenth century was the increased rate of capital formation stemming from the expansion of the market economy; the growing importance of "unearned" profits because of the rise in the value of land and of other scarce commodities; and the extent to which middlemen dominated the processes of agricultural production and of westward migration. These three developments were interrelated. All were aspects of an increasingly important system of commercial agriculture that generated antagonistic social relationships and incipient class divisions. These alterations brought greater prosperity to those farmers whose geographic locations and cultural values were conducive to market activity. The new structural possibilities undoubtedly induced other producers (who might otherwise have been content with their subsistence existence) to raise their output, perhaps even to alter their mode of production by hiring labor or purchasing farm machinery. Certainly, the boom in land values enabled those settlers with substantial estates to reap windfall profits. They had not always purchased their land with speculative resale in mind, but they benefited nonetheless from social and economic forces beyond their control: the surge in population

---

49. Robert Wells, "Family Size and Fertility Control in Eighteenth-Century America: A Study of Quaker Families," *Population Studies* 25 (1971): 73–82, traces the beginning of this process, while the sequel is explored in Richard A. Easterlin, "Population Change and Farm Settlement in the Northern United States," *Journal of Economic History* 36 (1976): 45–75.

and in agricultural prices both in the American colonies and in western Europe. Finally, there were individuals and groups who sought to manage the new system of production and exchange. By the mideighteenth century merchants and land speculators had appeared as crucial factors in the westward movement of population, and within another fifty years bankers and mortgage companies were also extracting a share of agricultural production. At some times and places the monetary liens imposed by middlemen and substantial landowners were justified; they represented fair returns for services rendered. More often, the farm population—especially those of its members who were young or landless—paid a disproportionate price for access to the productive system because bankers, speculators, and merchants were able to use their political and economic power to set the terms of exchange and to gain a greater share of the growing wealth of the society than was warranted by their entrepreneurial contribution.[50]

Even as this process of economic specialization and structural change was taking place, the family persisted as the basic unit of agricultural production, capital formation, and property transmission. This is a point of some importance, for it suggests that alter-

---

50. On this controversial topic see McNall, *Agricultural History*, 14, 48, 63–64, 240–41, and chapter 4. A favorable view of the tenancy system is offered by Sung Bok Kim, "A New Look at the Great Landlords of Eighteenth-Century New York," *William and Mary Quarterly*, 3d ser., 27 (1970): 581–614. Kim succeeds only in demonstrating that their own financial interests often prompted landlords to offer reasonable terms to their tenants; he demonstrates neither the inherent superiority of the tenancy system nor that it was less exploitative than, for instance, the grants of the New England governments during the seventeenth century or those of the U.S. government under the Homestead Acts.

ations in the macrostructure of a society or an economic system do not inevitably or immediately induce
significant changes in its micro-units. Social or cultural change is not always systemic in nature, and it
proceeds in fits and starts. Old cultural forms persist
(and sometimes flourish) within new economic structures; there are lags, as changes in one sphere of life
are gradually reconciled with established values and
patterns of behavior.

And so it was in the case of the preindustrial
yeoman family. Changes in societal structure did not
alter the basic character of the farm family (although
the proportion of such families in the population
steadily decreased). As the case studies suggest, the
agricultural family remained an extended lineal one;
each generation lived in a separate household, but the
character of production and inheritance linked these
conjugal units through a myriad of legal, moral,
and customary bonds. Rights and responsibilities
stretched across generations. The financial welfare of
both parents and children was rooted in the land and
in the equipment and labor needed to farm it. Parents
therefore influenced their children's choice of marriage
partners. Their welfare, or that of their other children,
might otherwise be compromised by the premature
division of assets that an early marriage entailed.[51]
The line was more important than the individual; the
patrimony was to be conserved for lineal purposes.

IV

The historical significance of those lineal values was
immense. The emphasis on the line or on the welfare

---

51. See the discussion in note 7 of this chapter.

of the entire family, for example, inhibited the emergence of individualism. When the members of this agricultural society traced the contours of their cultural landscape, they began with the assumption, as John Demos has amply demonstrated, that the basic unit was a family, "a little commonwealth," not a man (and still less a woman) "for himself," in their disparaging phrase.[52] This stress on family identity also shaped the character—and often confined the scope— of entrepreneurial activity and capitalist enterprise. Lemon's analysis indicates that most male farmers in Pennsylvania preferred family labor (including the assistance of nearby relatives) to that provided by indentured servants, slaves, or wage laborers. Religious membership was also circumscribed by cultural values, especially in the Congregational churches of New England. As Edmund Morgan argued in the 1940s (in a hypothesis supported with quantitative evidence by Gerald Moran thirty years later), Puritanism quickly became a "tribal" cult, with family lineage the prime determinant of elect status.[53]

Nevertheless, lineal values were not always dominant. And they were often affected by the emergent market economy; indeed, the commercial family-capitalism of the early modern period and the small

---

52. John Demos, *A Little Commonwealth: Family Life in Plymouth Colony* (New York, 1970), 77–78.

53. Edmund S. Morgan, *The Puritan Family: Religion and Domestic Relations in Seventeenth-Century New England* (Boston, 1944), chapter 6; Gerald Francis Moran, "The Puritan Saint: Religious Experience, Church Membership, and Piety in Connecticut, 1736–1776" (Ph.D. diss., Rutgers University, 1974). Moran has analyzed the membership of a number of Congregational churches in Connecticut between the time of their founding (1630s and 1640s) and 1800. He finds that 60 to 70 percent of all members during that period were either the original founders or their descendants.

father-son businesses of the nineteenth century represented striking adaptions of the lineal ideal.[54] Equally
significant alterations took place in rural areas in response to the pressure of population on agricultural
resources. In the seventeenth century many settlers
had attempted to identify the family with a specific
piece of land, to ensure its continued existence by
rooting it firmly in space. Thus in 1673 Ebenezer
Perry of Barnstable, Massachusetts, entailed his land
to his son Ebenezer and to the latter's "eldest son
surviving and so on to the male heirs of his body
lawfully begotten forever."[55] Other early inhabitants
of Massachusetts preferred to bequeath the family
homestead to the youngest son—ultimogeniture—
both because this would allow elder siblings to leave
the farm at an early age and because the youngest son
often came to maturity just as the parents were ready
to retire. In either case, the transmission of property
was designed to link one generation with the next, and
both with "family land."

When the pressure on family resources made it
impossible to provide all surviving sons with a portion
of the original family estate, the settlers devised alternative strategies of heirship. Some parents uprooted
the family and moved to a newly settled area where it
would be possible to maintain traditional lineal ties
between generations. "The Squire's House stands on
the Bank of [the] Susquehanna," Philip Fithian re-

---

54. See, for example, Bernard Bailyn, "Communications and
Trade: The Atlantic in the Seventeenth Century," *Journal of Economic History* 13 (1953): 378–87, esp. 380–82.
55. Quoted in John J. Waters, "The Traditional World of the New
England Peasants: A View from Seventeenth-Century Barnstable," *New England Historical and Genealogical Register* 130 (1976): 4.

ported from the frontier region of northeastern Pennsylvania in 1775. "He tells me . . . he will be able to
settle all his Sons and his fair Daughter *Betsy* on the
Fat of the Earth."[56] Other farmers remained in the old
community and sought desperately to settle their children on nearby lands. The premature death of one
son brought the Reverend Samuel Chandler of Andover, Massachusetts, to remember that he had "been
much distressed for land, for his children," and to
regret that "he took so much care . . . [for] one is taken
away and needs none."[57] From nearby Concord, Benjamin Barrett petitioned the General Court for a grant
of land in New Hampshire, since he and many other
residents were "without land for their posterity"; yet
when this request was granted, none of the petitioners
migrated to the new settlement. When Barrett died in
1728, the income from those western lands helped to
settle two sons on his Concord estate and two younger
sons on farms in nearby Worcester County.[58]

This imaginative use of western land rights to
subsidize the local settlement of offspring may have
been fairly widespread. Of the forty-one original pur-
chasers of proprietary shares in Kent, Connecticut,
twenty-five did not become inhabitants of the town
but sold their rights to residents, relatives, and neighbors. Still, the limited availability of arable land in the
older communities of New England and the Middle

---

56. 26 July 1775. Robert Greenhalgh Albion and Leonidas Dod-
son, eds., *Philip Vickers Fithian: Journal, 1775–1776, Written on the
Virginia-Pennsylvania Frontier* . . . (Princeton, N.J., 1934), 71; Jack
Goody, "Strategies of Heirship," *Comparative Studies in Society and
History* 15 (1973): 3–20.
57. Samuel Chandler, diary entry for 23 December 1745, quoted
in Greven, *Four Generations*, 254.
58. Gross, *Minutemen*, 80.

Colonies ruled out this option for most parents. The best they could do was to finance the migration of some children while keeping intact the original farmstead. Both in Newtown, Long Island, and in German areas of Pennsylvania in the eighteenth century, fathers commonly willed the family farm to the eldest son, requiring him to pay a certain sum of money to his younger brothers and his sisters. In other cases, the farm was "sold" to one son or son-in-law, with the "profits" of the transaction being divided among the other children—daughters usually receiving one-half the amount bestowed on the sons.[59]

These attempts by individual farmers to preserve a viable family estate reflected a set of values that was widespread in the community and that eventually received a formal legal sanction. When the appraisers of intestate property in Concord, Massachusetts, reported that a property could not be divided "without Spoiling the Whole," the probate court granted the farm intact to one heir (usually the eldest son), requiring him to compensate his brothers and sisters for their shares in the estate.[60] Such rulings confirmed the societal norm: even as New England parents wrote wills that divided their lands, they encouraged or directed their children to reconstitute viable economic units, with regard to both size and access. As Mark

---

59. Ehrlich, "Town Study," 123–27; John C. Gagliardo, "Germans and Agriculture in Colonial Pennsylvania," *Pennsylvania Magazine of History and Biography* 83 (1959): 192–98; Greven, *Four Generations*, 234–45. Ryan records a typical intergenerational arrangement: "Samuel Day, having seven sons, could only provide an estate for three sons, leaving them to pay sons David, Robert, Abraham and Jared £100 apiece" ("Six Towns," 85).

60. Gross, "Culture," 44. Of the landed estates settled in probate in Concord between 1738 and 1775, 60 percent were not divided; only 25 percent were divided among three or more heirs.

Hasket of Rochester, Massachusetts, wrote in his will: "my sons shall not any of them debar or hinder one another from having a way over each others Land when and where there may be ocation for it."[61]

There were other respects in which the central position of the lineal family (rather than the conjugal unit or the individual) was reflected in the legal system. On the death of her husband, a wife normally received the "right" to one-third of the real property of the estate. Yet this control was strictly limited: it usually lapsed upon remarriage and, even more significant, did not include the privilege of sale. The widow's "third" had to be preserved intact, so that upon her death the property could revert to the heirs of the estate. More important than the economic freedom of the widow—her rights as an individual—was the protection of the estate and the line of succession. These deeply held values were preserved even in the more diverse, money-oriented economy of eastern Massachusetts in the eighteenth century; the law was changed to permit widows to sell family property, but the court carefully regulated such transactions to ensure that the capital of the estate would be used for the support of the child heirs.[62] Property was "communal" within the family, with the limits of alienation strictly limited by custom or by law. Even as the link to the land was broken, the intimate tie between the estate and the lineal family was reaffirmed.

These traditional notions of family identity were

---

61. Quoted in Waters, "Traditional World," 7; Danhof, *Change in Agriculture*, 80.
62. Alexander Keyssar, "Widowhood in Eighteenth-Century Massachusetts: A Problem in the History of the Family," *Perspectives in American History* 8 (1974): 100–111.

subjected to considerable strain by the mid-nineteenth century. The psychological dimensions of the economic changes that diminished the importance of the family farm as the basic productive unit are revealed, in an oblique fashion, in the naming patterns practiced by parents in Hingham, Massachusetts. During the colonial period, most parents in this agricultural settlement did not perceive their children as unique per se. If a child died, his or her existence was perpetuated indirectly, for the same forename was normally given to the next infant of the same sex, especially when the dead child carried the same name as one of the parents. This necronymic pattern, with its obvious emphasis on the line rather than the individual, persisted in Hingham until the 1840s. So also did the tendency of parents to name their first children after themselves—to entail the parental name, as it were, and thus to stress the continuity between generations.[63] As economic change altered the structure and character of Hingham society, these lineal conceptions of identity gradually yielded to more individualistic ones. After 1800 first sons were given the same forenames as their fathers but a distinctive middle name. This was a subtle and complex compromise, for these middle names were often family names as well (the mother's surname, for example)—yet another manifestation of the persistence of traditional forms in a time of transition.

---

63. Daniel Scott Smith, "Child-Naming Patterns, Kinship Ties, and Change in Family Attitudes in Hingham, Massachusetts, 1641 to 1880," *Journal of Social History* 18 (1985): 541–66. Over 60 percent of first sons and over 70 percent of first daughters bore the same forename as their parents in seventeenth-century Hingham families, and the proportions remained high until the first children of the 1861–80 marriage cohorts, when "the respective fractions are two-fifths and one-sixth."

It is significant that this shift toward a distinctive personal identity—toward individualism—has been traced in Hingham, Massachusetts, one of the oldest English settlements in America, and not on the frontier. A similar development may have resulted from (or accompanied) the westward movement, but it is more likely—Frederick Jackson Turner to the contrary—that lineal family values were *more* important than individualism in the farming communities of the old Northwest. For farm families usually trained and encouraged their children "to succeed *them*, rather than to 'succeed' by rising in the social system."[64] The young adults of thriving farm communities were not forced to confront the difficult problems of occupational choice and psychological identity as were those from depressed and overcrowded rural environments or growing cities. The dimensions of existence had expanded in the East, even as the eighteenth-century patterns of farm life, community stratification, and family identity were being recreated, in a modified form, in the new settlements of the West.

In some of those older and crowded communities in New England and the Middle States, lineal family values remained important well into the nineteenth century because they were consistent, at least temporarily, with rural industrialization and an emergent

---

64. The quotation refers to the socialization process in a "tradition-directed" culture, as described in David Riesman, *The Lonely Crowd: A Study of the Changing American Character* (New Haven, Conn., 1950), 40, 17–18. See also Joseph F. Kett, "Adolescence and Youth in Nineteenth-Century America," *Journal of Interdisciplinary History* 2 (1971): 283–99. As Nancy Cott and R. Jackson Wilson have pointed out to me, the agricultural journals of the 1830s are filled with articles and letters expressing parental concern over the urban migration of farm youth; such sentiments suggest the persistence of lineal, farming-oriented values.

market economy. Fathers and mature sons continued to farm the (now depleted or subdivided) land while mothers, daughters, and younger sons turned their talents and energies to the production of textiles, shoes, and other items. The period between 1775 and 1815 was "the heyday of domestic manufactures" in America.[65]

The family factory assumed major economic importance as a result of the commercial dislocations produced by the American Revolution; household production of linen and woolen cloth was increased to compensate for the lack of English imports. Subsequently, this enlarged productive capacity was systematically organized by American entrepreneurs. In some cases, merchants sought out new markets for household manufactures and then capitalized part of the productive process itself, providing necessary materials and credit through the "putting out" system. Tens of thousands of "Negro shoes" were sold to southern slaveholders by Quaker merchants from Lynn, Massachusetts; and this productive network extended far back into the New England countryside. An even more important product of the rural family factory was wearing apparel. In New York State the production of textiles increased steadily until 1825, when the per capita output of household looms amounted to 8.95 yards.[66]

---

65. Lewis C. Gray, *History of Agriculture in the Southern United States to 1860* (Washington, D.C., 1933), 1:455; Rolla Milton Tryon, *Household Manufactures in the United States, 1640–1860* (1917; reprint, New York, 1966), esp. 243–76.

66. Paul G. Faler, "Workingmen, Mechanics, and Social Change: Lynn, Massachusetts, 1800–1860" (Ph.D. diss., University of Wisconsin, 1971), 41–43; Taylor, *Transportation Revolution*, 212–13; Tryon, *Household Manufactures*, 190, 276–79, 370–71, and tables 12, 16, 18.

This extraordinary household output was made possible not only by the existence of a regional or national market—the product of a mature, merchant-directed commercial capitalism—but also by the peculiar evolution of the factory system. By the late eighteenth century certain operations that were difficult in the home—such as fulling, carding, dyeing, and spinning in the case of textile production—had been assumed, with constantly increasing efficiency, by small mills. This process of specialization was as yet incomplete; eventually the weaving of cloth (as well as the preparation of the yarn) would be removed from the home and placed in the factory. For the moment—indeed, for more than a generation—this final stage in the "evolution of the simple household industry into the . . . factory system" was held in abeyance by technological constraints, and the family factory reigned supreme.[67] Rural industrialization expanded the productive capacity of the society and systematically integrated female labor into the market economy; but it did so without removing the family from the center of economic life.

One result was to perpetuate, for another generation, the delicate and reciprocally beneficial economic relationship between eastern farm parents and their offspring. The intergenerational exchange of youthful labor for an eventual inheritance had been threatened in the mid-eighteenth century by land scarcity, which diminished the financial security of aging parents and their ability or willingness to assist their children. Some young adults implicitly rebuked their parents

---

67. Tryon, *Household Manufactures*, 243–59, 272–76; Danhof, *Change in Agriculture*, 20–21.

by migrating; others stayed and exercised a gentle form of coercion. Nineteen percent of all first births registered in Concord, Massachusetts, in the 1740s were premaritally conceived, and the proportion rose to 40 percent in Concord, Hingham, and many other northern communities by the end of the century. "If they were again in the same circumstances," one observer noted, these young men and women "would do the same again, because otherwise they could not obtain their parents' consent to marry."[68] Once the legal and financial concessions were extracted from reluctant parents, marriage quickly followed. Both parents and children shunned illegitimacy; both accepted the cultural norm of stable family existence.

Whatever their economic weakness and vulnerability to youthful persuasion, parents retained significant power over their offspring. Affective bonds remained strong, and they were augmented by the power of the state. Young men who wished to work outside the household unit before they attained their legal majority were obliged to buy their economic freedom, undertaking in written contracts to pay their parents a certain sum in return for the privilege. Similarly, the first New England mill girls turned at least a portion of their earnings over to their parents; they were working outside the home, but not for themselves as unattached individuals.[69] The lineal

---

68. Quoted in Daniel Scott Smith and Michael S. Hindus, "Premarital Pregnancy in America, 1640–1971: An Overview and Interpretation," *Journal of Interdisciplinary History* 5 (1975): 557; Gross, *Minutemen*, 217–35.

69. Joseph F. Kett, "Growing Up in Rural New England, 1800–1840," in *Anonymous Americans: Explorations in Nineteenth-Century Social History*, ed. Tamara K. Hareven (Englewood Cliffs, N.J., 1971), 1–16; Joan W. Scott and Louise A. Tilly, "Women's Work

family remained predominant, in large part because there were few other institutions in early nineteenth-century America that could assume its social and economic functions—few schools, insurance companies, banks, or industries to provide training and capital for the new generation, and comfort and security for the old. Only a major structural change in the society itself—the widespread appearance of nonfamilial social, economic, and political organizations—would undermine the institutions of lineage; until this occurred there were simply no "alternatives to the family as a source of provision for a number of crucially important needs."[70]

The lineal family—not the conjugal unit and certainly not the unattached individual—thus stood at the center of economic and social existence in northern agricultural society in preindustrial America. The interlocking relationship between the biological life cycle and the system of agricultural (and domestic) production continued to tie the generations together even as the wider economic structure was undergoing a massive transformation and the proportion of farming families in the population was steadily declining. Most men, women, and children in this yeoman society continued to view the world through the prism of family values. This cultural outlook—this inbred pattern of behavior—set certain limits on personal autonomy, entrepreneurial activity, religious membership, and even political imagery.[71] Lineal family values did

---

and the Family in Nineteenth-Century Europe," *Comparative Studies in Society and History* 15 (1975): 36–64.

70. Michael Anderson, *Family Structure in Nineteenth-Century Lancashire* (Cambridge, England, 1971), 96.

71. For an extended discussion of the importance of family im-

not constitute, by any means, the entire worldview—the *mentalité*—of the agricultural population, but they did define a central tendency of that consciousness, an abiding core of symbolic and emotive meaning; and, most important of all, they constituted a significant and reliable guide to behavior amid the uncertainties of the world.

---

agery in eighteenth-century politics and political theory and in the War for Independence, see Edwin G. Burrows and Michael Wallace, "The American Revolution: The Ideology and Psychology of National Liberation," *Perspectives in American History* 6 (1972): 167–306.

4

*Economic Development
and
Social Structure
in
Colonial Boston*

A distinctly urban social structure developed in Boston in the 150 years between the settlement of the town and the American Revolution. The expansion of trade and industry after 1650 unleashed powerful economic forces that first distorted, then destroyed, the social homogeneity and cohesiveness of the early village community. All aspects of town life were affected by Boston's involvement in the dynamic, competitive world of Atlantic commerce. The disruptive pressure of rapid economic growth, sustained for over a century, made the social appearance of the town more diverse, more complex, more modern—increasingly different from that of the rest of New England. The magnitude of the change in Boston's social composition and structure may be deduced from an analysis and comparison of the tax lists for 1687 and 1771. Containing a wealth of information on property ownership in the community, these lists make it possible to block out, in quantitative terms, variations in the size and influence of economic groups and to trace the change in the distribution of the resources of the community among them.[1]

The transformation of Boston from a land-based society to a maritime center was neither sudden nor uniform. In the last decade of the seventeenth century, a large part of the land of its broad peninsula was still cultivated by small farmers. Only a small fraction was laid out in regular streets and even less was densely settled. The north end alone showed considerable change from the middle of the century, when almost every house had a large lot and garden. Here, the later-comers—the mariners, craftsmen, and traders who had raised the population to six thousand by 1690—were crowded together along the waterfront.[2] Here, too, in the series of docks and shipyards that jutted out from the shoreline, were tangible manifestations of the commercial activity that had made the small town the largest owner of shipping and the principal port of the English colonies. Over 40 percent

---

1. "Tax List and Schedules—1687," in *First Report of the Record Commissioners of the City of Boston, 1876* (Boston, 1876), 91–133; "Tax and Valuation Lists—1771," in Massachusetts Archives 132:92–147, State House, Boston.

2. The tax list for 1687 shows eighty polls with holdings of five acres or more within the town limits. For the size and location of most Boston real estate holdings from 1630 to 1645 see the "Book of Possessions" (and appendix), *The Second Report of the Record Commissioners of the City of Boston*, 2d ed. (Boston, 1881), and also the detailed property maps compiled by George Lamb, *Series of Plans of Boston . . . 1630, 1635,1640, 1645* (Boston, 1905).

of the carrying capacity of all colonial-owned shipping was in Boston hands.[3]

Dependence on mercantile endeavor rather than agricultural enterprise had by 1690 greatly affected the extent of property ownership. Boston no longer had the widespread ownership of real estate characteristic of rural Massachusetts to the end of the colonial period. The tax list for 1687 contained the names of 188 polls, 14 percent of the adult male population, who were neither owners of taxable property of any kind nor "dependents" in a household assessed for the property tax.[4] Holding no real estate, owning no merchandise or investments that would yield an income, these men constituted the "propertyless" segment of the community and were liable only for the head tax, which fell equally upon all men above the age of sixteen.[5] Many in this group were young men, laborers and seamen, attracted by the commercial prosperity of the town and hoping to save enough from their wages to buy or rent a shop, to invest in the tools of an artisan, or to find a start in trade. John Erving, a poor Scottish sailor whose grandson in 1771 was one of the richest men in Boston, was one prop-

---

3. Curtis Nettels, "The Economic Relations of Boston, Philadelphia, and New York, 1680–1715," *Journal of Economic and Business History* 3 (1930–31): 185–215.

4. In 1771, in Concord, Middlesex County, only 26 of 396 polls (6.5 percent) were without taxable property; in Easton, Bristol County, 26 of 261 (10 percent); and in Hadley, Hampshire County, 8 of 157 polls (5.1 percent) (Mass. Archives 132:199–210, 269–74, 251–54).

5. William H. Whitmore, ed., *The Colonial Laws of Massachusetts: Reprinted from the Edition of 1672, with the Supplements through 1686* (Boston, 1887), 22–23; Edwin R. A. Seligman, "The Income Tax in the American Colonies and States," *Political Science Quarterly* 10 (1895): 221–47.

ertyless man who rose quickly to a position of wealth and influence.[6]

But many of those 188 men did not acquire either taxable property or an established place in the social order of Boston. Only 64, or 35 percent, were inhabitants of the town eight years later. By way of contrast, 45 percent of the polls assessed from two to seven pounds on the tax list, 65 percent of those with property valued from eight to twenty pounds, and 73 percent of those with estates in excess of twenty pounds were present in 1695. There was a direct relation between permanence of residence and economic condition. Even in an expanding and diversifying economic environment, the best opportunities for advancement rested with those who could draw on long-standing connections, on the credit facilities of friends and neighbors, and on political influence. It was precisely these personal contacts that were denied the propertyless.[7]

A second, distinct element in the social order consisted of the dependents of property owners. Though propertyless themselves, these dependents—grown sons living at home, apprentices, and indentured servants—were linked more closely to the town

6. Clifford K. Shipton, *Sibley's Harvard Graduates* (Boston, 1962), 12:152–56. For other examples of mercantile success, see Bernard Bailyn, *The New England Merchants in the Seventeenth Century* (Cambridge, Mass., 1955), 192–97.

7. Mobility and residence data were determined by comparing the names on the tax list of 1687 with those on a list of the inhabitants of Boston in 1695 in the *First Report of the Record Commissioners*, 158–70. While the death rate was higher among the poorer sections of the population, this alone does not explain the variation in permanence of residence. See John B. Blake, *Public Health in the Town of Boston, 1630–1822* (Cambridge, Mass., 1959), chapter 6.

as members of a tax-paying household unit than were the 188 "unattached" men without taxable estates. Two hundred and twelve men, nearly one-sixth of the adult male population of Boston, were classified as dependents in 1687. The pervasiveness of the dependency relationship attested not only to the cohesiveness of the family unit but also to the continuing vitality of the apprenticeship and indenture system at the close of the seventeenth century.

Yet even the dependency relationship, traditionally an effective means of alleviating unemployment and preventing the appearance of unattached propertyless laborers, was subjected to severe pressure by the expansion of the economy. An urgent demand for labor, itself the cause of short indentures, prompted servants to strike out on their own as soon as possible. They became the laborers or semiskilled craftsmen of the town, while the sons of the family eventually assumed control of their father's business and a share of the economic resources of the community.[8]

The propertied section of the population in 1687 was composed of 1,036 individuals who were taxed on their real estate or their income from trade. The less-skilled craftsmen, 521 men engaged in the rougher trades of a waterfront society, formed the bottom stratum of the taxable population in this preindustrial age. These carpenters, shipwrights, blacksmiths, and shopkeepers owned only 12 percent of the taxable wealth of the town.[9] Few of these artisans and laborers

---

8. See Samuel McKee, Jr., *Labor in Colonial New York, 1664–1776* (New York, 1935), chapters 2, 3; also, Richard B. Morris, *Government and Labor in Early America* (1946; reprint, Boston, 1981), 147–49.
9. The lower 50 percent of the property owners is treated as a

had investments in shipping or in merchandise. A small store or house, or a small farm in the south end of Boston, accounted for their assessment of two to seven pounds on the tax list (see tables 4.1 and 4.2).

Between these craftsmen and shopkeepers and the traders and merchants who constituted the economic elite of the town was a middle group of 275 property owners with taxable assets valued from eight to twenty pounds. Affluent artisans employing two or three workers, ambitious shopkeepers with investments in commerce, and entrepreneurial-minded sea masters with various maritime interests bulked large in this center portion of the economic order. Of the 275, 180 owned real estate assessed at seven pounds or less and were boosted into the third quarter of the distribution of wealth by their holdings of merchandise and shares in shipping (see tables 4.1 and 4.2). The remaining 95 possessed real estate rated at eight pounds or more and, in addition, held various investments in trade. Making up about 25 percent of the propertied population, this middle group controlled 22 percent of the taxable wealth in Boston in 1687. Half as numerous as the lowest group of property owners, these men possessed almost double the amount of taxable assets (see table 4.2).

Merchants with large investments in English and West Indian trade and individuals engaged in the ancillary industries of shipbuilding and distilling made up the top quarter of the taxable population in 1687. With taxable estates ranging from £20 to £170, this commercial group controlled 66 percent of the town's

whole since tables 4.2 and 4.3 and figure 4.1 indicate that the proportion of wealth held by this section of the population was approximately the same in 1687 and 1771.

wealth. But economic development had been too rapid, too uneven and incomplete, to allow the emergence of a well-defined merchant class endowed with a common outlook and clearly distinguished from the rest of the society. Only eighty-five of these men, one-third of the wealthiest group in the community, owned dwellings valued at as much as £20. The majority held landed property valued at £10, only a few pounds greater than that of the middle group of property holders (see table 4.1).[10] The merchants had not shared equally in the accumulated fund of capital and experience which had accrued after fifty years of maritime activity. Profits had flowed to those whose daring initiative and initial resources had begun the exploitation of the lucrative colonial market. By 1687 the upper 15 percent of the property owners held 52 percent of the taxable assets of the town, while the fifty individuals who composed the highest 5 percent of the taxable population accounted for more than 25 percent of the wealth (see table 4.2).

By the end of the seventeenth century widespread involvement in commerce had effected a shift in the locus of social and political respectability in Boston and distinguished it from the surrounding communities. Five of the nine selectmen chosen by the town in 1687 were sea captains.[11] This was more than deference to those accustomed to command. With total estates of £83, £29, £33, £33, and £24 respectively,

---

10. See Edwin L. Bynner, "Topography and Landmarks of the Provincial Period," in *The Memorial History of Boston* . . . , ed. Justin Winsor, (Boston, 1881), vol. 2, chapter 17; Bailyn, *New England Merchants*, chapters 6, 7; Nettels, "Economic Relations," 185–200.

11. Robert Francis Seybolt, *The Town Officials of Colonial Boston, 1634–1775* (Cambridge, Mass., 1939), 74.

Table 4.1   Real Estate Ownership in Boston in 1687 and 1771

	1687	
Assessed Total Value of Real Estate	Number of Owners	Cumulative Total of Owners
£ 1	0	0
2	168	168
3	75	243
4	203	446
5	85	531
6	167	698
7	3	701
8	54	755
9	2	757
10	107	864
11	0	864
12	24	888
13	0	888
14	3	891
15	25	916
16	8	924
17	0	924
18	7	931
19	1	932
20	46	978
21–30	25	1,003
31–40	11	1,014
41–50	2	1,016

*The assessed annual worth of real estate in the 1771 valuation

	1771	
Assessed Annual Worth of Real Estate*	Number of Owners	Cumulative Total of Owners
£ 1	0	0
2	1	1
3	9	10
4	49	59
5	22	81
6	79	160
7	0	160
8	115	275
9	3	278
10	91	369
11	4	373
12	43	416
13	163	579
14	10	589
15	3	592
15	148	740
17	6	746
18	7	753
19	5	758
20	236	994
21–25	41	1.-35
26–30	163	1,198
31–35	93	1,291
36–40	92	1,383
41–45	5	1,388
46–50	42	1,430
51–60	32	1,462
61–70	10	1,472
71–80	9	1,481
81–90	3	1,484
91–100	3	1,487

must be multiplied by six to give the total property value.

Table 4.2   Distribution of Assessed Taxable Wealth in Boston in 1687

Total Value of Taxable Wealth	Number of Taxpayers in Each Wealth Bracket	Total Wealth in Each Wealth Bracket	Cumulative Total of Wealth
£ 1	0	£ 0	£ 0
2	152	304	304
3	51	153	457
4	169	676	1,133
5	33	165	1,298
6	97	582	1,880
7	19	133	2,013
8	43	344	2,357
9	22	198	2,555
10	45	450	3,005
11	17	187	3,192
12	30	360	3,552
13	13	169	3,721
14	12	168	3,889
15	22	330	4,219
16	21	336	4,555
17	1	17	4,572
18	18	324	4,896
19	1	19	4,915
20	30	600	5,515
21–25	41	972	6,487
26–30	48	1,367	7,854
31–35	29	971	8,825
36–30	21	819	9,644
41–45	19	828	10,472
46–50	16	781	11,253
51–60	16	897	12,150
61–70	19	1,245	13,395
71–80	7	509	13,904
81–90	3	253	14,157
91–100	7	670	14,827
101 +	14	1,764	16,591

Note: Money values are those of 1687. Many of the assessments fall at regular five-pound intervals and must be considered an estimate of the economic position of the individual. No attempt was made to compensate for systematic overvaluation or undervaluation inasmuch as the analysis measures relative wealth. The utility of a relative presentation of wealth (or income) is that it can be com-

Cumulative Total of Taxpayers	Cumulative Percentage of Taxpayers	Cumulative Percentage of Wealth
0	0.0%	0.0%
152	14.7	1.8
203	19.6	2.8
372	35.9	6.8
405	39.1	7.8
502	48.5	11.3
521	50.3	12.1
564	54.4	14.2
586	56.6	15.4
631	60.9	18.1
648	62.5	19.2
678	65.4	21.4
691	66.7	22.4
703	67.9	23.4
725	70.0	25.4
746	72.0	27.5
747	72.1	27.6
765	73.8	29.5
766	73.9	29.6
796	76.8	33.2
837	80.0	39.1
885	85.4	47.3
914	88.2	53.2
935	90.3	58.1
954	92.1	63.1
970	93.6	67.8
986	95.2	73.2
1,005	97.0	80.7
1,012	97.7	83.8
1,015	98.0	85.3
1,022	98.6	89.4
1,036	100.0	100.0

pared to another relative distribution without regard to absolute monetary values. See Mary Jean Bowman, "A Graphical Analysis of Personal Income Distribution in the United States," *American Economic Review* (1944–45): 607–28, and Horst Mendershausen, *Changes in Income Distribution during the Great Depression* (New York, 1946).

captains Elisha Hutchinson, John Fairweather, Theophilus Frary, Timothy Prout, and Daniel Turell were among the wealthiest 20 percent of the population (see table 4.2).[12] Still, achievement in trade was not the only index of respectability. Henry Eames, George Cable, Isaac Goose, and Elnathan Lyon, the men appointed by the town to inspect the condition of the streets and roads, had the greater part of their wealth, £105 of £130 all together, invested in land and livestock.[13] And the presence of Deacon Henry Allen among the selectmen provided a tangible indication of the continuing influence of the church.

These legacies of an isolated religious society and a stable agricultural economy disappeared in the wake of the rapid growth that continued unabated until the middle of the eighteenth century. In the fifty years after 1690 the population of the town increased from six thousand to sixteen thousand. The farms of the south end vanished and the central business district became crowded. In the populous north end, buildings that had once housed seven people suddenly began to hold nine or ten.[14] Accompanying this physical expansion of Boston was a diversification of eco-

---

12. *First Report of the Record Commissioners*, 99, 116, 126, 99, 95.

13. Seybolt, *Town Officials*, 74; *First Report of the Record Commissioners*, 98, 109, 127, 109; Bailyn, *New England Merchants*, chapters 6, 7.

14. Clifford K. Shipton, "Immigration to New England, 1680–1740," *Journal of Political Economy* 44 (1936): 225–38; Boston's population was 9,000 in 1710; 13,000 in 1730; 16,382 in 1742; 15,731 in 1752; and 15,520 in 1771 (Lemuel Shattuck, *Report to the Committee of the City Council Appointed to Obtain the Census of Boston for the Year 1845* [Boston, 1846], 3–5). In 1687 there were 850 houses for 6,000 people, or 7.06 persons per house ("Tax Lists and Schedules–1687"). The average number of persons per house in 1742 was 9.53; in 1771, 8.47 (Shattuck, *Report*, 54).

nomic endeavor. By 1742 the town led all the colonial cities in the production of export furniture and shoes, although master craftsmen continued to carry on most industry on a small scale geared to local needs. Prosperity and expansion continued to be rooted not in the productive capacity or geographic position of the town but in the ability of the Boston merchants to compete successfully in the highly competitive mercantile world.[15]

After 1750 the economic health of the Massachusetts seaport was jeopardized as New York and Philadelphia merchants, exploiting the rich productive lands at their backs and capitalizing on their prime geographic position in the West Indian and southern coasting trade, diverted a significant portion of European trade from the New England traders. Without increasing returns from the lucrative "carrying" trade, Boston merchants could no longer subsidize the work of the shopkeepers, craftsmen, and laborers who supplied and maintained the commercial fleet. By 1760 the population of Boston had dropped to fifteen thousand persons, a level it did not exceed until after the revolution.[16]

The essential continuity of maritime enterprise in Boston from the late seventeenth to the mid-eighteenth century concealed the emergence of a new type of social system. After a certain point increases in the scale and extent of commercial endeavor pro-

---

15. Samuel Eliot Morison, "The Commerce of Boston on the Eve of the Revolution," in *Proceedings of the American Antiquarian Society*, n.s., 32 (Worcester, Mass., 1922): 24–51.

16. See the table of entries and clearances in 1773 for the major colonial ports, ibid., 28. By 1760 Philadelphia had 23,750 inhabitants and New York 18,000 (Carl Bridenbaugh, *Cities in Revolt, Urban Life in America, 1743–1776* [New York, 1955], 5).

duced a new and more fluid social order. The development of the economic system subjected the family, the basic social unit, to severe pressures. The fundamental link between one generation and another, the ability of parents to train their offspring for their life's work, was endangered by a process of change that rendered obsolete many of the skills and assumptions of the older, land-oriented generation and opened the prospect of success in new fields and new places. The well-known departure of Benjamin Franklin from his indenture to his brother was but one bright piece in the shifting mosaic of colonial life.

The traditional family unit had lost much of its cohesiveness by the third quarter of the eighteenth century. The Boston tax lists for 1771 indicate that dependents of property owners accounted for only 10 percent of the adult male population as opposed to 16 percent eighty-five years earlier. Increasingly, children left their homes at an earlier age to seek their own way in the world.

A second factor in the trend away from dependency status was the decline in the availability of indentured servants during the eighteenth century. Fewer than 250 of 2,380 persons entering Boston from 1764 to 1768 were classified as indentured servants.[17] These were scarcely enough to replace those whose indentures expired. More and more, the labor force had to be recruited from the ranks of "unattached" workers who bartered their services for wages in a market economy.[18]

---

17. Compiled from "Port Arrivals—Immigrants," in Record Commissioners of the City of Boston, *A Volume of Records Relating to the Early History of Boston* (Boston, 1900), 254–312. See also Mildred Campbell, "English Emigration on the Eve of the American Revolution," *American Historical Review* 61 (1955–56): 1–20.

18. For most of the eighteenth century, black slaves compensated

This laboring force consisted of the nondependent, propertyless workers of the community, now twice as numerous relative to the rest of the population as they had been a century before. In 1687, 14 percent of the total number of adult males were without taxable property; by the eve of the revolution, the propertyless accounted for 29 percent. The social consequences of this increase were manifold. For every wage earner who competed in the economy as an autonomous entity at the end of the seventeenth century, there were four in 1771; for every man who slept in the back of a shop, in a tavern, or in a rented room in 1687, there were four in the later period. The population of Boston had doubled, but the number of propertyless men had increased fourfold.

The adult males without property, however, did not form a single unified class, a monolithic body of landless proletarians. Rather, the bottom of society consisted of a congeries of social and occupational groups with a highly transient maritime element at one end of the spectrum and a more stable and respected artisan segment at the other. Although they held no taxable property, hardworking and reputable

---

for the lack of white servants. From 150 in 1690, the number of blacks rose to 1,100 in a population of 13,000 in 1730. In that year they made up 8.4 percent of the population; in 1742, 8.4 percent; in 1752, 9.7 percent; but only 5.5 percent in 1765 (computed from data in Shattuck, *Report*, 4–5, 43). The 1771 tax list indicates that only 17 of 318 black "servants for life" were held by persons whose property holdings placed them in the lower 50 percent of the distribution of taxable wealth; 70 by individuals in the third quarter of the economic scale; and 231, or 72.6 percent, by the wealthiest 25 percent of the population. A somewhat different picture is presented in Robert E. Brown, *Middle-Class Democracy and the Revolution in Massachusetts, 1691–1780* (Ithaca, N.Y., 1955), 19, and McKee, *Labor*, 171.

craftsmen who had established a permanent residence in Boston participated in the town meeting and were elected to unpaid minor offices. In March 1771, for instance, John Dyer was selected by the people of the town as "fence viewer" for the following year. Yet according to the tax and valuation lists compiled less than six months later, Dyer was without taxable property.[19] At the same town meeting, four carpenters, Joseph Ballard, Joseph Edmunds, Benjamin Page, and Joseph Butler, none of whom was listed as an owner of taxable property on the valuation lists, were chosen as "measurers of boards."[20] That propertyless men should be selected for public office indicates that the concept of a "stake in society," which provided the theoretical underpinning for membership in the community of colonial Boston, was interpreted in the widest possible sense. Yet it was this very conception of the social order that was becoming anachronistic under the pressure of economic development. For how could the growing number of propertyless men be integrated into a social order based in the first instance on the principle that only those having a tangible interest in the town or a definite family link to the society would be truly interested in the welfare of the community?[21]

Changes no less significant had taken place within the ranks of the propertied groups. By the third quarter of the eighteenth century, lines of economic

---

19. Seybolt, *Town Officials*, 341; "Tax and Valuation Lists—1771," ward 1. Dyer apparently paid rent for part of a house assessed at £20.

20. Seybolt, *Town Officials*, 340–41; "Tax and Valuation Lists—1771," wards 1 and 2.

21. For a different view, see Brown, *Middle-Class Democracy*, 28–30, 79–95.

division and marks of social status were crystallizing as Boston approached economic maturity. Present to some degree in all aspects of town life, these distinctions were clearly apparent in dwelling arrangements. In 1687, 85 percent of Boston real estate holdings had been assessed within a narrow range of two to ten pounds; by the seventh decade of the eighteenth century, the same spectrum ran from twelve to two hundred pounds (see table 4.1). Gradations in housing were finer in 1771 and had social connotations that were hardly conceivable in the more primitive and more egalitarian society of the seventeenth century. This sense of distinctiveness was reinforced by geographic distribution. Affluent members of the community who had not transferred their residence to Roxbury, Cambridge, or Milton built in the spacious environs of the south and west ends. A strict segregation of the social groups was lacking; yet the milieu of the previous century, the interaction of merchant, trader, artisan, and laborer in a waterfront community, had all but disappeared.[22]

The increasing differences between the social and economic groups within the New England seaport stemmed in part from the fact that craftsmen, laborers, and small shopkeepers had failed to maintain their relative position in the economic order. From 1687 to 1771 the share of the taxable wealth of the community controlled by the lower half of the propertied population declined from 12 to 10 percent (see table 4.3). If these men lived better at the end of the century than at the beginning, it was not because the economic

---

22. Walter Muir Whitehill, *Boston: A Topographical History* (Cambridge, Mass., 1959), chapters 1–3; Bridenbaugh, *Cities in Revolt*, 25.

Table 4.3   Distribution of Assessed Taxable Wealth in Boston in 1771

Total Value of Taxable Wealth	Number of Taxpayers in Each Wealth Bracket	Total Wealth in Each Wealth Bracket	Cumulative Total of Wealth
£ 3–20	78	£ 1,562	£ 1,562
31–40	86	2,996	4,558
41–50	112	5,378	9,936
51–60	74	4,398	14,334
61–70	33	3,122	17,456
71–80	165	12,864	30,320
81–90	24	2.048	32,368
91–100	142	13,684	46,052
101–10	14	494	46,546
111–20	149	17,844	64,390
121–30	20	2,570	66,960
131–40	26	4,600	71,560
141–50	20	2,698	74,258
151–60	88	14,048	88,306
161–70	11	1,846	90,152
171–80	18	3,128	93,280
181–90	10	1,888	95,168
191–200	47	9,368	104,536
201–300	126	31,097	135,633
301–400	60	21,799	157,432
401–500	58	24,947	182,379
501–600	14	7,841	190,220
601–700	24	15,531	205,751
701–800	26	19,518	225,269
801–900	20	17,020	242,289
901–1,000	16	15,328	257,617
1,001–1,500	41	48,346	305,963
1,501–5,000	37	85,326	391,289
5,001 +	7	69,204	460,493

Note: The extant tax list is not complete. In ward 3 there are two pages and 68 polls missing; in ward 7, one page and 24 polls; in ward 12, an unknown number of pages and 225 polls. Only the total number of polls (224) is known for ward 11. The missing entries amount to 558, or 19.3 percent of the total number of polls on the tax list. Internal evidence (the totals for all wards are known) suggests the absent material is completely random. Nev-

Cumulative Total of Taxpayers	Cumulative Percentage of Taxpayers	Cumulative Percentage of Wealth
78	5.0%	0.3%
164	10.6	1.0
276	17.9	2.2
350	22.6	3.1
383	24.8	3.8
548	35.4	6.6
572	37.0	7.0
714	46.2	10.0
728	47.1	10.1
877	56.7	14.0
897	58.0	14.5
923	59.7	15.5
943	61.0	16.1
1,031	66.7	19.2
1,042	67.4	19.6
1,060	68.6	20.3
1,070	69.2	20.7
1,117	72.3	2.7
1,243	80.4	29.5
1,303	84.3	34.2
1,361	88.0	39.6
1,375	88.9	41.3
1,399	90.5	44.7
1,425	92.2	48.9
1,445	93.5	52.6
1,461	94.5	55.9
1,502	97.1	66.4
1,539	99.5	85.0
1,546	100.0	100.0

ertheless, it should be remembered that this table represents an 80 percent sample.

The value of shipping investments and of "servants for life" was not included in the computation of the table, as it was impossible to determine the assessor's valuation. For the law regulating the assessment, see *The Acts and Resolves, Public and Private, of the Province of the Massachusetts Bay* . . . , vol. 4 (Boston, 1881), 985–87. Money values are those of 1771.

development of Boston had effected a redistribution of wealth in favor of the laboring classes but because the long period of commercial prosperity had raised the purchasing power of every social group.

The decline in the economic distinctiveness of the middle group of property holders, the third quarter of the taxable population in the distribution of wealth, is even more significant. In 1771 these well-to-do artisans, shopkeepers, and traders (rising land values had eliminated the farmers and economic maturity the versatile merchant–sea captain) owned only 12.5 percent of the taxable wealth, a very substantial decrease from the 21 percent held in 1687. These men lived considerably better than their counterparts in the seventeenth century; many owned homes and possessed furnishings rarely matched by the most elegant dwellings of the earlier period. But in relation to the other parts of the social order, their economic position had deteriorated drastically. This smaller middle group had been assessed for taxable estates twice as large as the bottom 50 percent in 1687; by 1771 the assets of the two groups were equal.

On the other hand, the wealthiest 25 percent of the taxable population by 1771 controlled 78 percent of the assessed wealth of Boston. This represented a gain of 12 percent from the end of the seventeenth century. An equally important shift had taken place within this elite portion of the population. In 1687 the richest 15 percent of the taxpayers held 52 percent of the taxable property, while the top 5 percent owned 26.8 percent. Eighty-five years later, the percentages were 65.9 and 44.1 (see tables 4.2 and 4.3 and figure 4.1).

Certain long-term economic developments accounted for the disappearance of a distinct middle group of property owners and the accumulation of wealth among a limited portion of the population. The

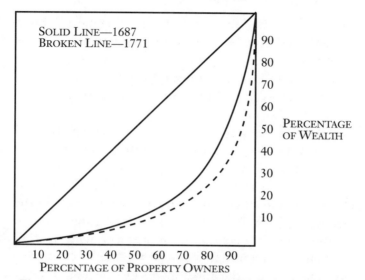

SOLID LINE—1687
BROKEN LINE—1771

PERCENTAGE
OF WEALTH

PERCENTAGE OF PROPERTY OWNERS

*Figure 4.1   Lorenz Curves Showing the Distribution of Wealth
in Boston in 1687 and 1771. (Drawn from data
in tables 4.2 and 4.3.)*

scarcity of capital in a relatively underdeveloped economic system, one in which barter transactions were
often necessary because of the lack of currency, required that the savings of all members of the society
be tapped in the interest of economic expansion. The
prospect of rapid commercial success and the high
return on capital invested in mercantile activity attracted the small investor. During the first decade of
the eighteenth century, nearly one of every three adult
males in Boston was involved directly in trade, owning
at least part of a vessel. In 1698 alone, 261 people held
shares in a seagoing vessel.[23] Trade had become "not

---

23. Bernard Bailyn and Lotte Bailyn, *Massachusetts Shipping, 1697–
1714: A Statistical Study* (Cambridge, Mass., 1959), 56, 79 (table II).

so much a way of life as a way of making money; not a social condition but an economic activity."[24] This widespread ownership of mercantile wealth resulted in the creation of a distinct economic "middle class" by the last decades of the seventeenth century.

A reflection of a discrete stage of economic growth, the involvement of disparate occupational and social groups in commerce was fleeting and transitory. It lasted only as long as the economy of the New England seaport remained underdeveloped, without large amounts of available capital. The increase in the wealth and resources of the town during the first half of the eighteenth century prompted a growing specialization of economic function; it was no longer necessary to rely on the investments of the less affluent members of the community for an expansion of commerce. The change was slow, almost imperceptible; but by 1771 the result was obvious. In that year, less than 5 percent of the taxable population of Boston held shares in shipping of 10 tons or more, even though the tonnage owned by the town was almost double that of 1698. Few men had investments of less than 50 tons; the average owner held 112 tons. By way of contrast, the average holding at the end of the seventeenth century had been about 25 tons.[25] Moreover, on the eve of the revolution ownership of shipping was concentrated among the wealthiest men of the community. Ninety percent of the tonnage of Boston in 1771 was in the hands of those whose other assets placed them in the top quarter of the popula-

---

24. Bailyn, *New England Merchants*, 194.

25. In 1771 Bostonians owned 10,396 tons of taxable shipping; the town's tonnage was 6,443 in 1698 (see Bailyn and Bailyn, *Massachusetts Shipping*, 79 [table II]).

tion.[26] With the increase in the wealth of the town had come a great increase in the number of propertyless men and a bifurcation of the property owners into (1) a large, amorphous body of shopkeepers, artisans, and laborers with holdings primarily in real estate, and (2) a smaller, somewhat more closely defined segment of the population with extensive commercial investments as well as elegant residences and personal possessions.

A similar trend was evident in other phases of town life. In the transitional decades of the late seventeenth and early eighteenth century, the fluidity inherent in the primitive commercial system had produced a certain vagueness in the connotations of social and economic status. Over 10 percent of the adult males in Boston designated themselves as "merchants" on the shipping registers of the period from 1698 to 1714, indicating not only the decline in the distinctiveness of a title traditionally limited to a carefully defined part of the community but also the feeling that any man could easily ascend the mercantile ladder. Economic opportunity was so evident, so promising, that the social demarcations of the more stable maritime communities of England seemed incongruous.[27] By the sixth decade of the eighteenth century, however, rank and order were supplanting the earlier chaos as successful families tightened their control of trade.

---

26. Only 2.3 percent of the 8,898 tons of shipping for which the owners are known was held by individuals in the bottom half of the distribution of wealth (estates of £100 or less in table 4.3); 5.9 percent more by those with estates valued from £100 to £200; and an additional 19 percent by persons with wealth of £200 to £500. Seventy-three percent of Boston's shipping was held by the wealthiest 12 percent of the propertied population, those with estates in excess of £500 (see table 4.3).

27. Bailyn and Bailyn, *Massachusetts Shipping*, 57–58.

The founding in 1763 of a merchants' club with 146 members was a dramatic indication that occupations and titles were regaining some of their traditional distinctiveness and meaning.[28]

An economic profile of the 146 men who composed this self-constituted elite is revealing. Of those whose names appeared on the tax and valuation lists of 1771, only five had estates that placed them in the bottom three-quarters of the distribution of wealth. Twenty-one were assessed for taxable property in excess of £1,500 and were thus in the top 1 percent of the economic scale. The taxable assets of the rest averaged £650, an amount that put them among the wealthiest 15 percent of the population.

That 146 men, 6.5 percent of the adult male population, were considered eligible for membership in a formal society of merchants indicates, however, that mercantile activity was not dominated by a narrow oligarchy. The range of wealth among the members of the top quarter of the propertied population was so great and the difference of social background so large as to preclude the creation of a monolithic class or guild with shared interests and beliefs.

Yet the influence of this segment of society was pervasive. By the third quarter of the eighteenth century, an integrated economic and political hierarchy based on mercantile wealth had emerged in Boston to replace the lack of social stratification of the early part of the century and the archaic distinctions of power

---

28. "Society for the Encouraging of Trade and Commerce Within the Province of Massachusetts Bay," Ezekiel Price Papers, Massachusetts Historical Society, Boston. See also Charles M. Andrews, "The Boston Merchants and the Non-Importation Movement," in *Publications of the Colonial Society of Massachusetts* 19 (Boston, 1918), 159–259.

and prestige of the religious community of the seventeenth century. All of the important offices of the town government, those with functions vital to the existence and prosperity of the town, were lodged firmly in the hands of a broad elite, entry into which was conditioned by commercial achievement and family background. The representatives to the General Court and the selectmen were the leaders of the town in economic endeavor as well as in political acumen. John Hancock's taxable wealth totaled £18,000, James Otis's was assessed at £2,040, while Colonel Joseph Jackson had property valued at £1,288. Other levels of the administrative system were reserved for those whose business skills or reputation provided the necessary qualifications. Samuel Abbot, John Barrett, Benjamin Dolbeare, John Gore, William Phillips, William White, and William Whitewell, overseers of the poor in 1771, had taxable estates of £815, £5,520, £850, £1,747, £5,771, £1,953, and £1,502 respectively. All were among the wealthiest 7 percent of the property owners, and Barrett and Phillips were two of the most respected merchants of the town. John Scollay, a distiller with an estate of £320, and Captain Benjamin Waldo, a shipmaster assessed at £500, who were among those chosen as "firewards" in 1771, might in an earlier period have been dominant in town affairs; by the seventh decade of the century, in a mature economic environment, the merchant prince had replaced the man of action at the apex of the social order.

Gradations continued to the bottom of the scale. Different social and occupational levels of the population were tapped as the dignity and responsibility of the position demanded. It was not by accident that the estates of the town assessors, Jonathan Brown, Moses Deshon, and John Kneeland, were £208, £200, and £342 respectively. Or that those of the "cullers of staves," Henry Lucas, Thomas Knox, and Caleb Hayden, totaled £120, £144, and £156 respectively. The assumption of a graded social, economic, and political scale, neatly calibrated to indicate the relation of each individual to the whole, was the basic principle on which the functioning of town meeting "democracy" depended. William Crafts, with a taxable estate of £80, was elected "fence viewer." Half this amount qualified William Barrett to be "measurer of coal baskets," while Henry Allen and John Bulfinch, "measurers of boards," were assessed at £80 and £48. The design was nearly perfect, the correlation between town office and social and economic position almost exact.[29]

As in 1687, the distribution of political power and influence in Boston conformed to the standards and gradations of a wider, more inclusive hierarchy of status, one that purported to include the entire social order within the bounds of its authority. But the lines of force that had emerged on the eve of the American Revolution radiated from different economic and social groups than those of eighty-five years before and now failed to encompass a significant portion of the population. The weakening of the extended family unit and the appearance of a large body of autonomous wage earners, proletarians in condition if not in consciousness, had introduced elements of mobility and diversity into the bottom part of society. Equally significant had been the growing inequality of the distribution of wealth among the propertied segment of the community, notably the greater exclusiveness and predomi-

---

29. Seybolt, *Town Officials*, 339–43; "Tax and Valuation Lists—1771."

nance of a mercantile "elite." Society had become more stratified and unequal. Influential groups, increasingly different from the small property owners who constituted the center portion of the community, had arisen at either end of the spectrum. Creations of the century-long development of a maritime economy in an urban setting, these merchant princes and proletarians stood out as the salient characteristics of a new social order.

5

Wealth
and
Social Structure

Wealth and social structure is hardly a venerable topic. Indeed, the subject achieved an autonomous status only in 1965, with the publication of Jackson Turner Main's *The Social Structure of Revolutionary America*. Before the appearance of Main's volume, scholars had treated colonial wealth and social structure as subsidiary topics, subordinate to analyses of political events and, to a lesser extent, of the process of social development. This method of treatment constituted the legacy of the great Progressive historians Charles Beard and Frederick Jackson Turner. In his most famous and influential work, *An Economic Interpretation of the Constitution of the United States* (1913), Beard examined the wealth holdings of members of the Constitutional Convention to demonstrate the economic roots of that document and to explain certain of its provisions. He did not attempt a systematic analysis of the social structure. Nor did Frederick Jackson Turner, even though his "frontier thesis" assumed the existence and the evolution of distinct social formations. The concerns of those scholars and of most of their followers rested primarily in the spheres of politics and national character.[1]

Why was this so? Intellectual traditions provide part of the answer. More than most European countries, the United States lacked a radical or socialist tradition of scholarship that fastened attention on social groups and classes. The genteel amateurs and academics who studied the colonial period placed prime emphasis on persons and events. A second reason is equally important: before 1950 there was widespread agreement on the character of prerevolutionary American society. Both Progressive historians of the liberal left and Brahmin authors of the conservative right assumed the existence of class divisions in the colonial period, however much they might argue about their political implications. Indeed, the most class-conscious portraits of early American life were penned by patrician conservatives such as Samuel Eliot Morison and James Truslow Adams. There were "marked social distinctions between the colonists," Adams wrote in *Provincial Society, 1690–1763* (1927), for "economically, societies are always like a pyramid, and the mass of men at the opening of the eighteenth century was composed of those who had made only a moderate success or none at all in the art and practice

---

1. The first detailed analysis of a "frontier" community came only in 1959: Merle Curti et al., *The Making of an American Community: A Case Study of Democracy in a Frontier County* (Stanford, Calif., 1959). See also Charles S. Grant, *Democracy in the Connecticut Frontier Town of Kent* (1961; reprint, New York, 1972).

of living."[2] For these authors the existence of a privileged social and political elite was completely compatible with the relative prosperity of the British mainland colonies in relation to Europe. American "exceptionalism" was a matter of degree, not of kind.

Because of widespread agreement across this narrow ideological spectrum, there were few debates among historians regarding the social structure of early America. Robert E. Brown shattered that complacency in 1955. In his *Middle-Class Democracy and the Revolution in Massachusetts, 1691–1780,* Brown argued that Massachusetts was a "middle class society in which property was easily acquired"; that the "great majority of men" met the franchise requirements; and that poorer backcountry towns were equitably represented in the provincial assembly. Brown's "consensus" interpretation of social stratification and political privilege found few advocates. Indeed, criticism came from three quarters. First, neo-Progressive scholars challenged the accuracy of his data on wealth and the franchise, particularly with respect to Boston and other urban areas. Second, historians with more of a sense of historical complexity accepted his statistics but repudiated his intellectual assumptions. They pointed out that not "democracy" but rather the Whig concept of a "balanced constitution" was the operative political theory of the eighteenth century. Because Whig principles found institutional expression in a bicameral legislature and a royal executive, the effective power of the demos was strictly limited. These critics insisted, moreover, on the existence of a defer-

---

2. James Truslow Adams, *Provincial Society, 1690–1763* (New York, 1927), 85. See also Samuel Eliot Morison, *The Maritime History of Massachusetts, 1783–1860* (1921; reprint, Boston, 1979).

ential polity ruled by the wealthy and well-born, whatever the extent of the franchise.[3] Support for their position came from a third group of critics. Younger scholars used quantitative methods to demonstrate that those with college educations, judicial appointments, and eastern constituencies dominated the leadership positions in the Massachusetts assembly and in other provincial legislatures.[4]

A quarter of a century later, it is clear that Brown's thesis represented a creative failure. Most of its specific propositions have been discredited or modified beyond recognition. And yet his work, and that of B. Katherine Brown, transformed the terms of debate in two major respects. In the first place, *Middle-Class Democracy* (and its less successful sequel, *Virginia, 1705–1786: Democracy or Aristocracy?*) gave importance to the topic of social stratification.[5] Second, the

---

3. Robert E. Brown, *Middle-Class Democracy and the Revolution in Massachusetts, 1691–1780* (Ithaca, N.Y., 1955), 403; John Cary, "Statistical Method and the Brown Thesis on Colonial Democracy," *William and Mary Quarterly*, 3d ser., 20 (1963): 251–76; Richard Buel, Jr., "Democracy and the American Revolution: A Frame of Reference," ibid., 21 (1964): 165–90; J. R. Pole, "Historians and the Problem of Early American Democracy," *American Historical Review* 67 (1962): 626–46.

4. Robert Zemsky, *Merchants, Farmers, and River Gods: An Essay on Eighteenth-Century American Politics* (Boston, 1971), 31–38, 294–99. See also Jack P. Greene, "Foundations of Political Power in the Virginia House of Burgesses, 1720–1776," *William and Mary Quarterly*, 3d ser., 16 (1959): 485–506; and Jackson Turner Main, "Government by the People: The American Revolution and the Democratization of the Legislatures," ibid., 23 (1966): 391–407.

5. Robert E. Brown and B. Katherine Brown, *Virginia, 1705–1786: Democracy or Aristocracy?* (East Lansing, Mich., 1964). The lack of controversy engendered by the Virginia volume reflected its failure to convince rather than its success. Most scholars have preferred the "deferential," or "aristocratic," interpretation offered by Charles S. Sydnor, *Gentlemen Freeholders; Political Practices in Washington's Virginia* (Chapel Hill, N.C., 1952).

Browns' work shifted the attention of social historians to the mass of the adult white male population. Even the best social history written in the 1940s and 1950s had been elitist in orientation and subsidiary to the analyses of political events. The early articles of Jackson Turner Main are a case in point. Through his mentor Merrill Jensen at the University of Wisconsin, Main inherited the intellectual concerns of the great Progressive historians. Following Beard, he studied the Constitution, but he focused on its Antifederalist opponents. Emulating Turner, Main explained its political configurations within the various states. Thus his early articles on Virginia explored the relationships between wealth, social structure, and voting patterns during the Confederation period.[6] Like the Browns', Main's work was as much traditional as innovative. It made use of new records, such as tax lists, and adumbrated a new methodology, but its emphasis remained political. It sought to explain political formations rather than social processes.

A similar purpose informed Bernard Bailyn's influential essay of 1959, "Politics and Social Structure in Virginia." Bailyn's concern was the vicissitudes of the various political elites who ruled the tobacco colony from its founding until the early eighteenth century. He sought both to explain the breakdown of the hierarchical class structure inherited from England—a classic Turnerian question—and to comprehend the logic of Bacon's Rebellion of 1675–76. These tradi-

---

6. Jackson Turner Main, "The Distribution of Property in Post-Revolutionary Virginia," *Mississippi Valley Historical Review* 41 (1954): 241–58; idem, "The One Hundred," *William and Mary Quarterly*, 3d ser., 11 (1954): 354–84; idem, "Sections and Politics in Virginia, 1781–1787," ibid., 12 (1955): 96–112.

tional issues were balanced by two innovative features: the application of Sir Lewis Namier's prosopographic techniques to early American materials and the causal significance accorded to social and economic factors. For Bailyn, the crucial elements determining the political structure of Virginia were not institutional or ideological. Rather, shifts in political power had social, demographic, and economic roots: cycles of elite immigration, high mortality and low fertility, the boom and bust of the tobacco market. If Brown and Main were innovators in methodology, Bailyn led the way conceptually. His work of the late 1950s demonstrated the evolution of basic social formations—the family, the Virginia aristocracy, the New England merchants—and suggested their autonomous treatment through rigorous historical analysis.[7]

Yet it was Jackson Turner Main who established wealth and social structure as independent scholarly topics. His accomplishment was almost accidental. As Main explained in the preface to *The Social Structure of Revolutionary America*, he undertook that study "out of a conviction that an understanding of political history during the revolutionary era depends upon mastery of the underlying social structure." It was only because "the subject proved much too large" and too complex that Main was unable to achieve the desired synthesis: "an essay on the relationship between class and the structure of power." More than chance determined this result. As Main acknowledged, his thinking was

---

7. Bernard Bailyn, "Politics and Social Structure in Virginia" in *Seventeenth-Century America*, ed. James M. Smith (Chapel Hill, N.C., 1960); idem, "Communications and Trade: The Atlantic in the Seventeenth Century," *Journal of Economic History* 12 (1953): 378–88; idem, *The New England Merchants in the Seventeenth Century* (New York, 1955).

deeply influenced by "recent literature on the class structure of contemporary America."[8] In fact, a close analysis of *The Social Structure of Revolutionary America* reveals a significant reorientation of intellectual priorities. Its organization and argument was determined less by the historiographic tradition—or even by Main's previous scholarship—than by two theoretical perspectives derived from the social sciences: the analysis of economic development and the study of social mobility.

These intellectual antecedents were of considerable importance, for they shaped the character of Main's interpretation and much of the subsequent scholarship. Beginning in the mid-1950s, American students wrote extensively on the subject of economic development, especially with respect to the superiority of "capitalist" or "communist" models for the Third World. W. W. Rostow composed the most concise and influential argument in 1960 in *The Stages of Economic Growth: A Non-Communist Manifesto*.[9] The ideological bias of these works is less important for our purposes than the analytic assumptions they fostered. These theories of social development emphasized the primacy of economic forces and market structures in the historical transition to industrial capitalism. Such "economist" assumptions were pervasive in the early

---

8. Jackson Turner Main, *The Social Structure of Revolutionary America* (Princeton, N.J., 1965), vii.

9. W. W. Rostow, *The Stages of Economic Growth: A Non-Communist Manifesto* (Cambridge, 1960); by 1963 Rostow's book was in its ninth printing. Other works include Albert O. Hirschman, *The Strategy of Economic Development* (New Haven, Conn., 1958); Bert F. Hoselitz, ed., *Theories of Economic Growth* (New York, 1960); and Douglass C. North, *The Economic Growth of the United States, 1790–1860* (Englewood Cliffs, N.J., 1961).

1960s. They suffused the work of many historians, cutting across traditional ideological divisions. They informed my treatment of colonial Boston, published in 1965, reprinted here as chapter 4.

Main was equally influenced by these theories of economic development. He detected four "subsocieties," or "class structures," in colonial America, each characterized by a specific stage of commercial development and a distinct distribution of wealth. On the undeveloped frontier the richest 10 percent of the property holders owned 33–40 percent of the wealth. In subsistence farming regions the percentage rose to 35–45 percent, while involvement in commercial farming raised the share of the top 10 percent to 45–65 percent. Finally, the port cities stood at the apex of the commercial system. Their merchant elites controlled 55–65 percent of the total taxable wealth.[10] In this schema social structure became a quantified measure of commercial development.

The research of economic historians shaped the substantive as well as the conceptual understanding of the mainland colonies. Inspired by developmental studies of the U.S. economy in the nineteenth century, George Rogers Taylor published an exploratory essay in 1964, "American Economic Growth before 1840." Taylor knew that the gross national product (GNP) per capita had increased 1.6 percent per year between 1840 and 1960. His review of the available literature produced three hypotheses for the preceding two centuries: first, that "until about 1710 growth was slow, irregular, and not properly measured in percentage terms"; second, that from 1710 to 1775 growth

---

10. J. T. Main, *Social Structure*, 276n and passim.

rates averaged 1 percent per annum, "relatively rapid for a preindustrial economy"; and finally, that there was little increase in per capita output between 1775 and 1840.[11] Like the Brown thesis, Taylor's hypotheses generated an intense debate among historians, especially with respect to the alleged stagnation of the early nineteenth century.

Nonetheless, Taylor's positive evaluation of the eighteenth-century economy provided added support for Main's extremely optimistic interpretation of colonial welfare. If Main turned to economists for causal models of wealth distribution, he sought a sociological explanation of the relationship between wealth and welfare. More precisely, he relied on one particular group of sociologists, American analysts of "social mobility." Once again, the departure from the historiographic tradition was striking. There was no mention of social mobility, not even a separate chapter on social development, in Clarence Ver Steeg's highly regarded survey, *The Formative Years, 1607–1763*, published in 1964. Nor did this concept intrude into the far more innovative study of English preindustrial society by Peter Laslett, *The World We Have Lost* (1965). Yet "social mobility" was very much in the intellectual air in American academic circles in the 1960s. Building on a series of important journal articles and sociological studies, Seymour Martin Lipset and Reinhard

---

11. George Rogers Taylor, "American Economic Growth before 1840," *Journal of Economic History* 24 (1964): 427–44. See also Ralph Andreano, ed., *New Views of American Economic Development: A Selective Anthology of Recent Work* (Cambridge, Mass., 1965), 50–51, and Robert E. Gallman, "The Pace and Pattern of American Economic Growth," in *American Economic Growth: An Economist's History of the United States*, ed. Lance E. Davis et al. (New York, 1972), 17–25.

Bendix attempted a wide-ranging comparative historical analysis in *Social Mobility in Industrial Society* (1963).
In the following year Stephen Thernstrom published
his enormously influential study of the "mobility" of
Irish laborers in Newburyport, Massachusetts, while
in 1966 Lawrence Stone used the concept to analyze
the changing social structure of early modern England.[12]

Main pursued a similar strategy. Indeed, by
stressing mobility, geographic as well as vertical, he
restated the classic Turnerian interpretation of American development. There were marked social divisions
in colonial society, Main suggested, but they were not
fixed. For "westward the land was bright" and "a man's
ability to move to a new location . . . gave him a
chance to rise." In the end the possibilities of American life impressed Main more than did the "long-term
tendency . . . toward greater inequality" revealed by
his research. This positive tone suffused not only his
chapter "Mobility in Early America" but also another,
"Social Classes in the Revolutionary Era," which
closed on a note of romantic optimism: "Since anyone
could acquire property, anyone could rise, and the
poor man could and occasionally did become a
wealthy esquire."[13]

Main's contributions to the social analysis of early

---

12. Clarence L. Ver Steeg, *The Formative Years, 1607–1763* (New
York, 1964); Peter Laslett, *The World We Have Lost* (New York,
1965); Seymour Martin Lipset and Reinhard Bendix, *Social Mobility in Industrial Society* (Berkeley, Calif., 1963); Stephan Thernstrom, *Poverty and Progress: Social Mobility in a Nineteenth-Century
City* (Cambridge, Mass., 1964); and Lawrence Stone, "Social
Mobility in England, 1500–1700," *Past and Present* 33 (1966):
16–55.

13. J. T. Main, *Social Structure*, 287, 164, 286, 220.

America were both substantial and flawed. In retrospect it is clear that *The Social Structure of Revolutionary America* successfully completed the shift in focus begun by Brown; its subject was neither politics nor the wealth of the elite but rather the structure of the entire social order. It demonstrated as well how probate records and tax lists formed the documentary basis for an autonomous social history. Finally, Main's book provided a causative model of commercial development for the "forgotten" period of colonial history—the century separating the end of settlement and the onset of the independence struggle.[14] These accomplishments were undermined, at least in part, by Main's use of two anachronistic models of social change. The theories of economic development and social mobility imply change, movement, transformation. They were originally devised to explain the nineteenth-century transition from agricultural to industrial society. Yet no historian maintained that this process of technological change and urban growth had begun in a significant way in America by 1775. Main's social theories failed to address colonial reality. They could not comprehend the character and pace of life and the intractability of social arrangements in the predominately agricultural society of seventeenth- and eighteenth-century America.

Since 1965 historians have attempted, some more

---

14. It was not accidental that most of the previous work on wealth and social structure traced either the erosion of English status in the American environment or the social conflicts of the Revolutionary era, for these "problems" had been conceptualized by the Progressive historians. See, for example, Norman H. Dawes, "Titles as Symbols of Prestige in Seventeenth-Century New England," *William and Mary Quarterly*, 3d ser., 6 (1949): 69–83, and William A. Reavis, "The Maryland Gentry and Social Mobility, 1637–1676," ibid., 14 (1957): 418–28.

consciously than others, to remedy these interpretive deficiencies. They have proposed various theoretical models to define and elucidate the actual social processes of this historic epoch. The study of colonial demography and the family produced the first major conceptual advance. In work published between 1965 and 1970, the triumvirate of Philip Greven, John Demos, and Kenneth Lockridge offered a new perspective on the study of social change. They demonstrated that men and women in New England married in their mid- to late twenties, bore "completed" families of seven to eight children (declining over time to five to six), and lived, as did most of their offspring, to an advanced age.[15] Their work suggested that the same process of reproduction and family formation held the key to the distribution of wealth in New England's agricultural society.

That exciting conclusion was implicit in Greven's study of the founding families of Andover, Massachusetts. He demonstrated that successive generations had less land to distribute and that patterns of inheritance, property ownership, and migration changed accordingly. It followed that fertility and mortality rates were as influential as market forces in determining patterns of inequality, as Lockridge argued in "Land,

---

15. John Demos, "Notes on Life in Plymouth Colony," *William and Mary Quarterly*, 3d ser., 22 (1965): 264–86; idem, *A Little Commonwealth: Family Life in Plymouth Colony* (New York, 1970); Philip J. Greven, Jr., "Family Structure in Seventeenth-Century Andover, Massachusetts," *William and Mary Quarterly*, 3d ser., 23 (1966): 234–56; idem, *Four Generations: Population, Land, and Family in Colonial Andover, Massachusetts* (Ithaca, N.Y., 1970); Kenneth A. Lockridge, "The Population of Dedham, Massachusetts, 1636–1736," *Economic History Review*, 2d ser., 19 (1966): 318–44; idem, *A New England Town: The First Hundred Years: Dedham, Massachusetts, 1636–1736* (New York, 1970).

Population, and the Evolution of New England Society, 1630–1780."[16] Lockridge posited an agricultural crisis in New England by the third quarter of the eighteenth century: the sustained growth of population through natural increase had overwhelmed the productive capacity of the available land; the result was a classic Malthusian subsistence crisis.

Lockridge's interpretation was derived from Charles S. Grant's *Democracy in the Connecticut Frontier Town of Kent* (1961). Writing in the Turnerian tradition (but with Brown's thesis firmly in mind), Grant had posited an evolutionary pattern of social development for Kent. He argued that Kent's society was "predominately middle class in 1751, [but] included a growing class of propertyless men" by 1796, the result of "the pressure of a population swollen by a fantastic birthrate against a limited amount of land." Lockridge appropriated Grant's argument and applied it to New England as a whole. Then in "Social Change and the Meaning of the American Revolution" Lockridge speculated that those developments had profound, if vaguely specified, political ramifications. "A shortage of land, commercialization, and social differentiation," Lockridge maintained, "must have activated and perhaps strained the political system," undermining the position of the "colonial elite" and perhaps prompting them to undertake a "purgative crusade" against British rule.[17]

---

16. Kenneth A. Lockridge, "Land, Population, and the Evolution of New England Society, 1630–1780," *Past and Present* 39 (1968).

17. Grant quoted in Lockridge, "Evolution of New England Society," in *Colonial America: Essays in Politics and Social Development*, ed. Stanley N. Katz (Boston, 1971), 478; idem, "Social Change and the Meaning of the American Revolution," in Katz, *Colonial America*, 2d ed. (Boston, 1976), 501, 514.

Subsequent research has failed to demonstrate a strong causal relationship between the "agricultural crisis" specified by Lockridge and the independence movement. In *The Minutemen and Their World* (1976), Robert A. Gross confirmed many of Grant's and Lockridge's findings in his empirical analysis of the agricultural system of Concord, Massachusetts. Indeed, Gross argued that mid-eighteenth-century Concord farmers lived in "a world of scarcity." Yet his microanalysis of this commercial farming town failed to detect a dramatic relationship between a declining agricultural economy and the independence movement. The impetus to rebellion came from Boston and from the British challenge to traditional colonial autonomy, Gross concluded, and not from a shortage of prime agricultural land and increasing social stratification. At most, he suggests, "the continuing decay in their fortunes added a special poignancy to their fears." Richard Bushman's astute analysis "Massachusetts Farmers and the Revolution" (1976) substantiates and extends that interpretation. "It is not necessary to posit a social crisis to explain the passionate reaction [of farmers] to parliamentary taxation," Bushman maintains, for their hostility stemmed primarily from a century-long tradition of resistance to the creation of a burdensome political and religious establishment. These abiding fears were only accentuated by agricultural decline, rising debts, and the specter of "slavish tenantry." "The transfer of fear from debt to taxes was nearly automatic," Bushman observed, "because taxes were a form of debt, and were ultimately collected in the same way, by forced land sales." Viewing these economic and political changes from a transatlantic comparative perspective, Hermann Wellenreuther likewise located the resistance of the American freeholder population not in its progressive impoverishment but rather in the British challenge to its "share

in the political decision-making process." These studies posit an indirect relationship between a changing
social structure and the revolutionary impulse. The
independence movement in the countryside was less
the desperate revolt of a recently impoverished agricultural population than the defense of a society of
small freeholders against the twin forces of agricultural stagnation and administrative reform.[18]

If the relationship between economic stagnation
and political rebellion remains problematic, these
studies of families and their farms have revised our
understanding of the character of colonial society. In
the first place, they cast doubt on the Taylor-Main
thesis of considerable per capita economic growth and
social mobility in the eighteenth century. Second,
they provide an appropriate theoretical approach to
the analysis of that agricultural society. As Bailyn
argued in *Education and the Forming of American Society*,
the family was the key institutional unit. It was the
basic property-owning unit among the white population, and the family household was the prime productive unit, except on the larger plantations of the South.
The dynamics of family existence thus form a crucial
aspect of social process, whatever the extent of commercialization or geographic movement. Finally, this

---

18. Robert A. Gross, *The Minutemen and Their World* (New York,
1976), 107; Richard L. Bushman, "Massachusetts Farmers and the
Revolution," in *Society, Freedom, and Conscience: The Coming of the
Revolution in Virginia, Massachusetts, and New York*, ed. Richard M.
Jellison (New York, 1976), 122, 120; Hermann Wellenreuther, "A
View of Socio-Economic Structures of England and the British
Colonies on the Eve of the American Revolution," in *New Wine in
Old Skins: A Comparative View of Socio-Political Structures and Values
Affecting the American Revolution*, ed. Erich Angermann, Marie-
Luise Frings, and Hermann Wellenreuther (Stuttgart, 1976),
14–40.

approach offers a structural framework for analysis. It suggests that the productive system did not change fundamentally between 1650 and 1750 and provides a set of conceptual categories to comprehend those changes that did occur.[19]

II

With this historiography in mind, let us turn to more recent work in the field. My synthesis of this scholarship contains an argument: I will suggest that apart from one exception, changes in the American social structure over the course of the colonial period were primarily *extensive;* that is, they involved the replication and modification of existing patterns rather than their transformation through a process of *intensive* development. This perspective disputes Taylor's interpretation of the growth of wealth during the colonial period, modifies Main's discussion of changes in its distribution, and challenges Lockridge's thesis of the "Europeanization" of the American social order. In the end, my emphasis will fall on the continuous creation and adaption of traditional modes of existence rather than their demise.

---

19. See chapter 3. Too often the analysis of the "early modern period" of European and American history has been undertaken with concepts and theories articulated originally to describe the industrializing society of the nineteenth century. Thus when Gary B. Nash compiled his useful anthology *Class and Society in Early America* (Englewood Cliffs, N.J., 1970), he used Bernard Barber's ahistorical survey "Social Stratification" (originally published in the *International Encyclopedia of Social Sciences*, ed. David L. Sills [New York, 1968], 15:288–95) as his theoretical, or analytic, reading.

THE PRODUCTION OF WEALTH

The Taylor thesis lies in shreds. Not a single one of its hypotheses has survived detailed scholarly analysis. Critics directed their first attacks against Taylor's suggestion that the American economy stagnated, in terms of per capita GNP, between 1775 and 1840. While most analysts agreed that per capita *exports* and perhaps per capita *wealth* declined during the Revolutionary era, they maintained that substantial growth occurred between 1790 and 1840. Douglass North suggested an export-led process of development, beginning with the trade boom between 1792 and 1807. Conversely, Paul David emphasized internal factors: he argued that modest increases in farm productivity and a substantial expansion in the more efficient non-agricultural sector accounted for two surges, between 1790 and 1806 and between 1820 and 1835; these produced a per capita growth rate of 1.3 percent per annum in the half century before 1840. Alice Hanson Jones also disputed the importance of the trade boom of the 1790s. Her data indicated a decline in real wealth per capita until 1805, after which wealth increased at an annual rate of 1.9 percent until 1850. Finally, Robert Gallman proposed an expansion rate for the early nineteenth century somewhat lower than those of David and Jones, but still above 1 percent per annum.[20] Whatever their differences with regard to

20. North, *Economic Growth*; Paul David, "The Growth of Real Product in the United States before 1840: New Evidence, Controlled Conjectures," *Journal of Economic History* 27 (1967): 151–97; Alice Hanson Jones, *Wealth of a Nation to Be: The American Colonies on the Eve of the Revolution* (New York, 1980): 305–7; Gallman, "Pace and Pattern." For an overview see John J. McCusker and Russell R. Menard, *The Economy of British America, 1607–1789* (Chapel Hill, N.C., 1985), chapter 15.

timing and causation, these economic historians rendered a unanimous verdict with respect to the period as a whole. Gross national product per capita in the United States rose at least 50 percent between 1775 and 1840, with the entire increase coming after 1790.

These findings had significant implications. They indicated that over the short term the war for independence retarded American economic growth, and they supported the traditional interpretation of the 1780s as a "critical period." More important for our purposes, they showed that Taylor's estimate of per capita wealth of four hundred dollars for 1775 (in 1840 prices) was too high. This conclusion in turn undermined Taylor's hypothesis of a sustained high rate of growth during the eighteenth century.

A second series of studies yielded a similar result. Research on the seventeenth-century economy demonstrated major increases in productivity and wealth, especially between 1650 and 1680. European demand for Chesapeake tobacco rose until 1680, maintaining profits for producers despite falling commodity prices. More important, tobacco production per worker nearly doubled during the midcentury decades, thus increasing profit margins. Even thirty years of stagnating demand and level prices between 1680 and 1710 did not erode these sizable economic gains.[21] New England experienced a similar pattern of boom and stagnation. During the second generation of settlement, farmers increased their productivity markedly

---

21. Russell R. Menard, "The Tobacco Industry in the Chesapeake Colonies, 1617–1730: An Interpretation," *Research in Economic History* 5 (1980): 109–77; Terry L. Anderson and Robert Paul Thomas, "Economic Growth in the Seventeenth-Century Chesapeake," *Explorations in Economic History* 15 (1978): 368–87.

and began to ship their surplus goods to the sugar islands of the West Indies. As a result, real wealth per capita rose at an annual rate of 1.6 percent between 1650 and 1680. Following that spurt, there was little or no growth for the subsequent three decades. Nevertheless, these mid-seventeenth-century bursts in productivity meant that colonial wealth levels were considerably higher in 1720 than Taylor had specified. Terry Anderson estimated that per capita income for New England was eleven pounds for the period 1700–1709, nearly double the five to six pounds proposed by Taylor.[22] Taken together, these findings were devastating: they indicated that Taylor had exaggerated the extent of colonial prosperity in 1775 and underestimated the level of wealth in 1720.

The implications are readily apparent. Per capita rates of growth during the eighteenth century were considerably below Taylor's proposed 1 percent per annum. Empirical data presented in various local and regional studies confirmed such a deduction. The average wealth of decedents, as measured by probate records, in Hampshire County, Massachusetts, rose from an average of £208 in the first decade of the eighteenth century to £296 in the 1770s, yielding an annual growth rate of 0.54 percent. In Hartford, Connecticut, real wealth stagnated at pre-1675 levels until 1765, while in Guilford, Connecticut, mean ratable wealth per resident male taxpayer did not increase significantly during the first seven decades of the eighteenth century.[23] In sum, this research indi-

---

22. Terry L. Anderson, "Economic Growth in Colonial New England: 'Statistical Renaissance,'" *Journal of Economic History* 39 (1979): 243–58, and Anderson's other work cited therein.
23. Anderson, "Economic Growth," table 1; Jackson Turner

cated a modest growth in per capita wealth in New England of 0.2–0.5 percent per year. (See table 5.1.)

The Middle Colonies expanded output per capita at a much higher rate. The mean inventoried wealth of decedents in Chester County, Pennsylvania, leaped from £126 in 1714–31 to £200 in 1734–45. It then rose more slowly to £270 for those inventories filed in 1775–90. The first spurt reflected the productivity gains accruing to the second generation of farmers and thus resembled the seventeenth-century experience of New England and the Chesapeake. It was the product of decades of patient labor. Fields had been cleared, houses and barns built, and roads constructed. The second rise stemmed from international price movements rather than hard-won increases in domestic farm productivity. In Pennsylvania output per farm worker expanded only at the rate of 0.2–0.3 percent per annum between 1730 and 1770.[24] Yet increases in export prices for wheat created an economic boom. Working from data on imports and exports (rather than probate records), Marc Egnal found a spectacular growth rate of 3 to 5 percent for the northern colonies as a whole between 1745 and 1760. In this propitious set of circumstances wealth grew at a rate of 1.2 percent per year in Chester County between 1715 and 1790. By 1774 the per capita level of physical wealth

Main, "The Distribution of Property in Colonial Connecticut," in *The Human Dimensions of Nation Making: Essays on Colonial and Revolutionary America*, ed. James Kirby Martin (Madison, Wis., 1976), tables 11, 13, and passim; John J. Waters, Jr., "Patrimony, Succession, and Social Stability: Guilford, Connecticut, in the Eighteenth Century," *Perspectives in American History* 10 (1976): 159.

24. Duane E. Ball, "Dynamics of Population and Wealth in Eighteenth-Century Chester County, Pennsylvania," *Journal of Interdisciplinary History* 6 (1976): tables 5 and 6.

Table 5.1 The Growth of Wealth: Selected Statistics (in Pounds)

Hampshire County, Mass., Inventories		Guilford, Conn., Mean Ratable Wealth per Resident Male Taxpayer		Chester County, Pa., Mean Total Wealth Inventories		Prince George's County, Md., Inventories*		
1700–1709	208					1705	26.1	32.0
1710–19	269	1716	66.9	1714–31	126.5			
1720–29	301							
1730–39	391	1732	61.3	1734–45	200.6	1733	23.9	37.3
1740–49	258	1740	72.4					
		1749	62.7					
1750–59	381	1756	61.8	1750–70	240.6	1755	19.3	33.2
1760–69	344	1765	57.6					
1770–79	296			1775–90	270.8	1776	33.7	60.6
Average + 0.54% per annum				Average + 1.2% per annum				

Sources: Terry L. Anderson, "Economic Growth in Colonial New England: 'Statistical Renaissance,'" Journal of Economic History 39 (1979): 243–57; John J. Waters, Jr., "Patrimony, Succession, and Social Stability: Guilford, Connecticut, in the Eighteenth Century," Perspectives in American History 10 (1976): 159; Duane E. Ball, "Dynamics of Population and Wealth in Eighteenth-Century Chester County, Pennsylvania," Journal of Interdisciplinary History 6 (1976): tables 5 and 6; Allan Kulikoff, "The Economic Growth of the Eighteenth-Century Chesapeake Colonies," Journal of Economic History 39 (1979): 275–88.
Note: All values have been deflated by an appropriate price index. Figures are not comparable, since not all were computed in pounds sterling.
*Measured in pounds per capita. The first column indicates the year, the second the value of personal property, and the third the total assessed estate, which includes the value of personal property.

in the Middle Colonies totaled £40.2 sterling, as compared with £36.4 for New England.[25]

How should this economic performance be interpreted? Clearly, regional differences were significant. A buoyant export market for grain quickly raised living standards in the more recently settled Middle Colonies to a high level. Yet the wealth of the New England colonies increased significantly as well. These gains came even as many towns quadrupled their population and as the population of the older region increased by a factor of ten. Thus the strongly negative relationship between wealth and population growth posited by Lockridge no longer remained persuasive. Daniel Scott Smith's "Malthusian-frontier" interpretation was somewhat more convincing. Like Lockridge, Smith began with population growth. Because the northern colonies grew at a rate of 3 percent per annum, new resources had to be brought into production continuously to keep per capita wealth at a constant level. This task was so formidable that it absorbed most of the productive energies of the society. Consequently, Smith argued, there was no sustained increase in per capita output, and urban growth and commerce failed to keep pace with population. Export crops declined constantly as a share of total agricultural output—from 20–30 percent in 1710 to 15–20 percent in 1770 to only 10–15 percent by 1790.

---

25. Marc Egnal, "The Economic Development of the Thirteen Continental Colonies, 1720 to 1775," *William and Mary Quarterly*, 3d ser., 32 (1975): table 2; Ball, "Dynamics," table 6; A. H. Jones, *Wealth*, table 9.3. Studies such as Egnal's, which employed statistical data from exports and imports, tended to exaggerate the importance of overseas trade and the commercial economy. Works based on probate records did not measure the timing of economic change but rather gave a more accurate picture of economic performance.

The absence of intensive development did not imply agricultural decline, a subsistence crisis, or an increase in wealth inequality. Rather, the Malthusian rates of population increase and the availability of an agricultural frontier resulted in an *extensive* pattern of growth. Farms were hacked continually out of the wilderness for an ever-growing population; the result was a static multiplication of productive units rather than a process of economic development and transformation.[26]

Smith's argument was astute but not completely persuasive. Growth was primarily extensive, but the inhabitants of established regions slowly diversified their economies and accumulated greater wealth. Two examples will suffice. In the early eighteenth century, inventoried wealth in Chester County, Pennsylvania, consisted primarily of physical property; financial assets amounted to only 11 percent of the total. By the 1770s, however, bills, bonds, and debts accounted for nearly 50 percent of the inventoried wealth. The composition of diet changed as well. The second generation of settlers in Middlesex County, Massachusetts, shifted from a seasonal pattern of consumption of fresh and stored food to greater reliance on stored grains (corn and rye, replacing wheat) and salt meats. Then, during the eighteenth century, Middlesex residents increased the quantity and variety of their stored provisions and substituted cider for beer. Finally, after 1750 the inhabitants consumed a more varied diet. Potatoes and other vegetables appeared on their

---

26. Daniel Scott Smith, "A Malthusian-Frontier Interpretation of United States Demographic History before c. 1815," in *Urbanization in the Americas: The Background in Comparative Perspective*, ed. Woodrow Borah, Jorge Hardoy, and Gilbert A. Stelter (Ottawa, Ont., 1980), 15–24.

tables, and distinct dietary standards began to develop along class lines.[27] Diet thus became more assured, more sufficient, and more varied even as it reflected difficult agricultural adaptations in the face of population growth. Stored meats replaced fresh game; the planting of orchards allowed barley fields to be used for rye and corn; potatoes provided subsistence on shrinking farms. Interwoven with the pattern of extensive growth in the West was an equally important process of adaptation and modification in the East.

Southern development was also consistent, up to a point, with the Malthusian-frontier interpretation. The sudden introduction of tens of thousands of African slaves in the eighteenth century transformed the social structure, but it did not alter the productive capacity of the tobacco economy. In fact, the new slave regime initially cut agricultural productivity. In Prince George's County, Maryland, for example, per capita wealth declined slowly between 1700 and 1725, and despite the increase in tobacco prices, it decreased at a rate of 1 percent per year during the next quarter century. That decline stemmed from three interrelated causes. First, the "dependency ratio" increased markedly. Because of an outmigration of white freedmen and a rising black birth rate, the number of dependents per worker inflated as the labor force changed in composition. Second, African-born slaves were not initially as adept at tobacco cultivation as native-born blacks, servants, or freemen. Finally, the per capita wealth of the *white* population did increase

---

27. Ball, "Economic Growth," 635; Sarah F. McMahon, "A Comfortable Subsistence: The Changing Composition of Diet in Rural New England, 1620–1840," *William and Mary Quarterly*, 3d ser., 42 (1985): 26–65.

over time: by 0.5 percent per year between 1705 and 1733 and by a roughly equal amount between 1733 and 1755 (if the value of slaves are included in the computation of assets). The capacity of the productive system remained stable, but its rewards were systematically appropriated by the slave-owning population.

The prosperity of whites increased even more dramatically in the subsequent two decades. The price of Chesapeake tobacco rose to 2–2.5 pence per pound (up from 1.25–1.75), and a largely native-born slave population brought higher productivity. In Prince George's County the export of grain generated additional revenue (10 percent of the total), while the ready availability of Scottish credit (£26 per household in 1776) encouraged economic expansion. These favorable developments drove up the price of slaves at a rate of 1.4 percent per annum between 1733 and 1776 and brought a massive increase in land prices—from 6.8 shillings per acre in 1733 to 8.4 shillings in 1755 to 27 shillings in 1776. By 1776 total household wealth for whites in the county averaged £357.[28] During the same years the dramatic growth of rice production brought even greater wealth to the white plantation owners of South Carolina.

A strong export economy and an exploited black labor force made white slave owners the wealthiest group on the mainland. The average free wealth holder in the South had total physical resources of £395 in

---

28. Allan Kulikoff, "The Economic Growth of the Eighteenth-Century Chesapeake Colonies," *Journal of Economic History* 39 (1979): 275–88. In All Hallow's Parish, Maryland, the adult-child ratio among slaves decreased from 3 to 1 in the 1690s, to 2.3 to 1 in the 1720s, to 1.04 to 1 in the 1760s (Carville V. Earle, *The Evolution of a Tidewater Settlement System: All Hallow's Parish, Maryland, 1650–1783* [Chicago, 1975], table II).

1774, as compared with £161 for those in New England and £187 for the Middle Colonies. These regional disparities persisted when slaves and servants were not counted as assets; the totals then became £161 for New England, £180 for the Middle Colonies, and £262 for the South. Yet the economy of the South was not more productive than the economies of other regions. For as line (8) of table 5.2 indicates, per capita wealth—land, livestock, producer and consumer goods—was almost exactly the same in 1774 in every region of the mainland.[29] White southerners had more wealth than white northerners only because black southerners had none.

Regional similarities in per capita wealth indicate that Smith's Malthusian-frontier thesis of extensive growth applied to the South as well as to the North. Once again, however, that thesis fails to capture important alterations in the economic and social structure. First, as Aubrey Land and Edmund Morgan have demonstrated, thousands of whites bolstered their economic and social positions by becoming slave owners. By 1745 all householders in Talbot County, Maryland, except tenants and small landowners, owned slaves. Indeed, by 1774, 59 percent of all wealth holders in the South owned a slave (or a white indentured servant).[30] Second, the economy of the Chesapeake gradually diversified. As Carville Earle and Paul Clemens have shown, during the first four decades of

---

29. Jones, *Wealth*, table 9.3.
30. Edmund S. Morgan, *American Slavery, American Freedom: The Ordeal of Colonial Virginia* (New York, 1975), chapter 17; Aubrey C. Land, "Economic Base and Social Structure: The Northern Chesapeake in the Eighteenth Century," *Journal of Economic History* 25 (1965): 639–54; A. H. Jones, *Wealth*, table 7.9.

Table 5.2 Regional Wealth Composition, 1774: Average per Free Wealth Holder, and per Capita (in Pounds Sterling)

	New England	Middle Colonies	South
Per free wealth holder:			
(1) Total physical wealth (2 + 3)	161.2	186.8	394.7
(2) Slaves and servants	0.7	7.2	132.6
(3) Total nonhuman wealth (4 + 5 + 6 + 7)	160.5	179.6	262.1
(4) Land (real estate)	115.1	115.5	181.1
(5) Livestock	12.3	21.3	34.9
(6) Other producers' goods	13.9	24.7	23.7
(7) Consumer's goods	19.2	18.0	22.4
Per capita:			
(8) Total nonhuman wealth (9 + 10 + 11 + 12)	36.4	40.2	36.4
(9) Land (real estate)	26.1	25.9	25.1
(10) Livestock	2.8	4.8	4.8
(11) Other producers' goods	3.1	5.5	3.3
(12) Consumers' goods	4.4	4.0	3.1

Source: Alice Hanson Jones, Wealth of a Nation to Be: The American Colonies on the Eve of the Revolution. (New York, 1980), table 9.3.

the eighteenth century wealthy planters became self-sufficient in food, clothing, and producer goods in order to weather cyclical fluctuations in the tobacco market. Subsequently they produced wheat and corn for export. By the 1760s at least two-thirds of gross agricultural income received by slave owners in Talbot and Kent counties, Maryland, came from wheat and corn; only tenant farmers and small landowners remained tied to the traditional tobacco economy. Finally, much of the increased wealth in the South (as in parts of Connecticut) resulted from a dramatic increase in land prices. In Talbot County, for example, the average price of land jumped from £0.46 per acre in the 1730s to £1.22 per acre in the 1760s. As a result, the number of landless laborers and tenants grew substantially. In All Hallow's Parish, Maryland, 33 percent of the adult white males did not own land in the 1710s, and nearly 50 percent were landless by the 1770s. Despite migration to the frontier, a substantial white underclass of tenant farmers appeared in most settled regions of the Chesapeake.[31]

Thus economic change in all mainland regions consisted of both the extensive growth of frontier regions and the intensive development of settled areas. Older settlements grew wealthier even as they diverted accumulated capital resources to open up new communities. The existence of an untapped agricultural frontier in turn relieved the strain on landed resources in eastern settlements while affording an adequate if hard-won livelihood for the migrant population. The net result was a modest increase in per capita wealth

---

31. Paul G. E. Clemens, *The Atlantic Economy and Colonial Maryland's Eastern Shore: From Tobacco to Grain* (Ithaca, N.Y., 1980), 160–64; Earle, *Evolution,* 209.

during the eighteenth century. This amounted to 0.5 percent per annum, roughly half of Taylor's optimistic estimate of 1 percent but considerably more than that allowed by Smith's hypothesis of a static economy. Growth was slow but sure.

THE DISTRIBUTION OF WEALTH

Initial studies of the distribution of wealth posited increasing concentrations over time and specified commercialization as the causal mechanism. Most analyses published during the following decade accepted that conceptualization. Even if the empirical data were not entirely congruent with those hypotheses, the fit was close enough to discourage reformulation.[32] In 1976 three articles took issue with the evolutionary, mercantile framework propounded by Main and me. After a close analysis of assessment practices and other technical issues, G. B. Warden argued that the distribution of wealth in Boston did not change between 1687 and 1772. Main himself arrived at a similar

---

32. See, for example, James T. Lemon and Gary B. Nash, "The Distribution of Wealth in Eighteenth-Century America: A Century of Change in Chester County, Pennsylvania, 1693–1802," *Journal of Social History* 2 (1968): 1–24. The authors found a "blurred, inconsistent, and often confusing picture" and suggested caution in generalizing about wealth distributions, but in the end confirmed a "gradually increasing differentiation." In fact, Ball, "Dynamics," 636–38, supported the conclusion of increasing inequality, so the most recent evidence from Chester County remained consistent with the Main-Henretta model. Bruce C. Daniels, "Long-Range Trends of Wealth Distribution in Eighteenth-Century New England," *Explorations in Economic History* 2, (1973–74): 123–35, found considerable evidence of stability but used Main's evolutionary model to interpret the data. See also Donald W. Koch, "Income Distribution and Political Structure in Seventeenth-Century Salem, Massachusetts," *Essex Institute Historical Collections* 105 (1969), 50–69.

conclusion with respect to Connecticut: he found cyclical fluctuations but no overall trend. Finally, Gloria Main's examination of probate records from Maryland and Massachusetts pointed toward a new interpretative framework: she argued that gross inequality became a permanent feature of southern life in the late seventeenth century and that a similar structural transformation occurred in the northern states in the early nineteenth century.[33]

This revisionist view was given coherent form by two economic historians, Peter Lindert and Jeffrey Williamson. Their analysis, "Long Term Trends in American Wealth Inequality," revealed no significant changes in wealth distribution before 1800, followed by two major periods of transformation. First, there was a "marked rise" in economic stratification during the first half of the nineteenth century. Then, in the second quarter of the twentieth century, there was a "pronounced decline" in wealth concentrations, following "six decades of persistent and extensive inequality." These findings were significant, pinpointing the period between 1860 and 1930 as the most unequal in all of American history. Most important for our purposes, Lindert and Williamson argued that inequality in the nineteenth century was not the result of trends begun in the colonial period; rather, it was the sudden and unanticipated product of early industrialization. Empirical data provided graphic evidence for their interpretation. In 1774 the top 1 percent of the

---

33. G. B. Warden, "Inequality and Instability in Eighteenth-Century Boston: A Reappraisal," *Journal of Interdisciplinary History* 6 (1976): 49–84; J. T. Main, "Distribution in Connecticut," 54–104; Gloria L. Main, "Inequality in Early America: The Evidence from Probate Records of Massachusetts and Maryland," *Journal of Interdisciplinary History* 7 (1977): 559–82.

free wealth holders held 12.6 percent of total assets, and the wealthiest 10 percent owned about 50 percent. By 1860, however, the richest 1 percent held 29 percent, and the top 10 percent owned 73 percent.[34]

This revisionist perspective has considerable force, for it is stated with considerable care and complexity. Lindert and Williamson granted that wealth concentrations increased over time in settled areas and eventually in each frontier region. They pointed out, however, that new frontier communities (with low levels of per capita wealth and relatively low inequality) were "being added at a very rapid rate"; hence, "in the *aggregate* colonial inequality was stable at low levels." Along with other commentators, these authors also stressed the extent of age-related inequality, which took two forms. First, the major colonial cities attracted a larger proportion of young men and women after 1750. That demographic phenomenon explains, at least in part, the apparent increase in urban inequality in the late colonial period, for few individuals have accumulated wealth in this phase of their life. Life cycle analysis also accounted for a second pattern of inequality. Frontier agricultural communities became more stratified "naturally" as young parents aged and their propertyless sons appeared on the tax lists. As John Waters discovered in the long-settled town of Guilford, Connecticut, "age distribution was the most important factor in explaining both property distribution and officeholding." In Guilford (and also in the agricultural community of Wenham, Massachusetts,

---

34. Peter H. Lindert and Jeffrey Williamson, "Long-Term Trends in American Wealth Inequality," in *Modeling the Distribution and Intergenerational Transmission of Wealth*, ed. James D. Smith (Chicago, 1980), 10, table 1.3, and 12–37.

between 1731 and 1771) not a single father fell in the lowest 40 percent of the wealth distribution; conversely, only a few young men ranked in the top 20 percent.[35] Lines of economic status existed in these communities, for some families had consistently more land and personal property over several generations, but inequality was often age related. Taken together, the phenomena of age stratification and frontier migration provided considerable empirical support for an interpretation that emphasized the long-term stability of the distribution of colonial wealth.

Other scholars questioned the relationship between commercialization and inequality. The connections between the two turned out to be complex and ambiguous. The commercial tobacco economy of the Chesapeake certainly encouraged the early emergence of inequality. By 1700 the top 10 percent of the Virginia population owned one-half to two-thirds of the available acreage and 65 percent of the personal wealth. Most members of this elite owed their fortunes as much to mercantile activity as to tobacco cultivation,[36] yet their economic success reflected the initial

---

35. Lindert and Williamson, "Long-Term Trends," 14, 26–36; Waters, "Patrimony." For Wenham see Douglas L. Jones, *Village and Seaport: Migration and Society in Eighteenth-Century Massachusetts* (Hanover, N.H., 1981), chapter 1, n. 14. Jones found a different pattern in the adjoining seaport of Beverly: there 25 percent of the fathers were in the lowest 40 percent of the wealth distribution. On the basis of seventeenth-century English probate records, Carole Shammas argued that occupation, age, and education taken together explain 32 percent of the variance in personal wealth and, further, that the decline in wealth after age sixty was most apparent among middling farmers and artisans but was not present among wealthy decedents and poor laborers ("The Determinants of Personal Wealth in Seventeenth-Century England and America," *Journal of Economic History* 37 [1977], 675–89).
36. G. L. Main, "Inequality," 570–72. In her "Maryland and the

advantages resulting from their control of land and labor. These planters had imported indentured servants and received head right land allotments. Subsequently they sold or leased that land to new freemen, from whom they also extracted wealth by serving as storekeepers, tobacco merchants, and creditors.

Thus it was not "mere" commercialization or the cultivation of a staple crop that generated extreme inequality in the Chesapeake but rather the social context in which it occurred. Indeed, the market often worked to lessen inequality. Small planters prospered when the tobacco market was good, for that was their only form of cash income. Conversely, wealthy planters did relatively better in times of depression. Their control of labor permitted them to diversify agricultural and craft production, while their control of credit increased their leverage over small planters.[37] During the depressions in the tobacco trade of 1680–97 and 1727–33 the largest 10 percent of the plantations in All Hallow's Parish, Maryland, accounted for over 60 percent of the value of all plantations; during the boom of 1698–1704 that proportion fell to 32 percent.

Chesapeake Economy, 1670–1720," in *Law, Society, and Politics in Early Maryland*, ed. Aubrey C. Land, Lois Green Carr, and Edward C. Papenfuse (Baltimore, Md., 1977), 134–52, Main confirmed Aubrey Land's "mercantile" interpretation of wealth accumulation in the Chesapeake. See Land, "Economic Behavior in a Planting Society: The Eighteenth-Century Chesapeake," *Journal of Southern History* 33 (1967): 469–85, but see also Morgan, *American Slavery, American Freedom*, chapter 10, which considered the effect of political profiteering, and Russell R. Menard, "From Servant to Freeholder: Status, Mobility, and Property Accumulation in Seventeenth-Century Maryland," *William and Mary Quarterly*, 3d ser., 30 (1973): 37–64, which noted the decline in economic opportunity for former servants after 1660.

37. Earle, *Evolution*, 115, 128–32; G. L. Main, "Maryland," 145–47.

Commercial expansion often produced greater equality in the northern colonies as well. In the heavily market-oriented colonies of New Jersey, Pennsylvania, and Delaware the top 10 percent of the free wealth holders owned 35 percent of the physical assets in 1774. By contrast, in subsistence-oriented New England the richest decile owned 47 percent of the wealth. Through an intensive analysis of the 1771 valuation list, Bettye Pruitt demonstrated that the same pattern appeared within Massachusetts. Many towns were both "poor" and unequal. The "poor" agricultural communities had low living standards and considerable inequality, with the wealthiest 10 percent owning 34 percent of the valued assets. Other towns had exactly the same distribution of wealth but a median level of individual wealth that was 50 percent higher. Moreover, in Sunderland, one of six "rich" agricultural communities in Massachusetts in 1771, the top decile owned only 24 percent of the total wealth.[38] In these farming regions market involvement did not automatically or inevitably produce greater inequality. Other factors were equally important: the quality of the soil, the structure of property ownership, the system of credit, and the fortuitous conjuncture of commodity price rises with community or regional development.

Taken together, these findings force major modifications in the evolutionary commercial model of wealth distribution suggested by Jackson Turner Main in *The Social Structure of Revolutionary America*. Both in

---

38. A. H. Jones, *Wealth*, table 6.2; Bettye Hobbs Pruitt, "Agriculture and Society in the Towns of Massachusetts, 1771: A Statistical Analysis" (Ph.D. diss., Boston University, 1981), table 27 and pp. 172–79.

the countryside and in the cities the extent of inequality remained relatively stable. The share of wealth held by the top 30 percent of probated estates in Boston remained steady at 85 percent from 1700 to 1775; the percentage of wealth owned by the top 10 percent of taxpayers in New York stayed constant at 45 percent from 1695 to 1789; and there was a definite "ceiling" to wealth inequality in these preindustrial mercantile centers. Nowhere did the top 10 percent of the free population own more than 60–65 percent of the assessed wealth; nowhere did the Gini coefficient of inequality rise above 0.68. Yet by 1860 the Gini coefficients for Boston, New York, and Philadelphia were 0.93, and the top 5 percent of the taxable population owned at least 70 percent of all urban resources.[39] In the cities, as in the larger society, early industrialization brought a major structural transformation.

Class formation did take place during the colonial period, but it was different in degree and in kind from that of the early nineteenth century. Within the colonial cities three important alterations took place. First,

---

39. Daniels, "Long-Range Trends," 127; Gary B. Nash, "Urban Wealth and Poverty in Pre-Revolutionary America," *Journal of Interdisciplinary History* 6 (1976): table 1; Lindert and Williamson "Long-Term Trends," tables 1.A.3, 1.A.7, and 1.3; A. H. Jones, *Wealth*, tables 8.6, 8.4, and 9.5. The only exception was the South, and then only when all slaves were counted as potential wealth holders and given a wealth of zero; if slaves were counted only as property, the Gini coefficient for free wealth holders fell to 0.67 (ibid., table 9.4). By way of comparison, the Gini coefficient for Massachusetts rose from 0.55–0.62 in the late eighteenth century to 0.77 by 1830 and 0.825 in 1860. For all adult males in the South in 1870 the coefficient was 0.87. Clearly the industrialization of the North created a degree of wealth inequality comparable to that in the slave society of the South (see G. L. Main, "Inequality," 575).

as Gary Nash has demonstrated, a class of genuinely poor people numbering between 10 and 20 percent of the population appeared in Boston in the 1740s and in New York and Philadelphia by the 1760s. Second, wealth became increasingly concentrated at the very top of the social scale as a few merchants amassed huge fortunes. By the end of the colonial period the top 5 percent of inventoried estates in Boston contained 46 percent of probated wealth, while in Philadelphia the proportion soared to 55 percent. This incipient polarization of the social order prompted institutional innovation. Wealthy merchants established a variety of public asylums—almshouses, bettering houses, and workhouses—to care for the poor and to supervise their economic lives. These formal organizations both reflected and encouraged the formation of class consciousness at each end of the social scale. Third, urban artisans established craft lodges and mutual benefit societies and, during the independence crisis, articulated a distinct artisan ideology. Whatever the distribution of urban wealth, class differences obviously were felt with greater intensity and received more institutional expression as the eighteenth century advanced.

Yet these changes did not constitute a basic economic and social transformation. The augmented wealth of the merchant elite was derived from commercial enterprise, not industrial investments. Its new sense of cohesiveness was striking, but mainly in relation to the previous lack of class identity. The new artisan groups likewise merely resembled traditional craft organizations in European preindustrial cities. Finally, many of the poor in the colonial ports consisted, as in the past, of the old, the young, and the widowed. A new and substantial group of propertyless wage-earning families appeared in these urban areas, but its absolute size was small and its influence slight.[40]

In the predominant agricultural economy, there were two major structural changes during the colonial period, one sudden, the other gradual. The abrupt creation of a slave-based economy at the end of the seventeenth century increased inequality and quickly changed the racial composition and character of southern society. Beyond this, there was a slow but eventually significant change in the scale of existence. The multiplication of farms, craft shops, and merchant houses produced, especially in the northern colonies, a more complex and diverse society. The greater density of population facilitated the formation of group identity and increased the prospect of organized political and social conflicts. If these changes in scale and density posed a threat to the dominance of established social and political elites, the cause was not "economic" in the narrow sense of the term, for the per capita wealth of the white population was growing and stratification was not dramatically increasing. Rather, these conflicts stemmed from greater ethnic, occupational, or religious cohesiveness among disadvantaged groups—frontier Scotch-Irish farmers, austere Virginia Baptists, and self-conscious urban artisans.

THE STRUCTURE OF SOCIETY

How, then, was the social history of colonial America to be conceptualized? Two models stressed the impor-

---

40. Nash, "Urban Wealth," tables 3, 4, 5, and 7. Nash provides a detailed treatment of the development of Boston, New York, and Philadelphia in *The Urban Crucible: Social Change, Political Consciousness, and the Origins of the American Revolution* (Cambridge, Mass., 1979).

tance of European antecedents or influence. The first of these examined the English roots of seventeenth-century American society and the alterations induced by the conditions of life in the New World. Scholars treated this topic in three detailed studies. In his wide-ranging and important analysis *American Slavery, American Freedom*, Edmund Morgan underlined the exploitation of white indentured servants in the Chesapeake, thereby pointing to the English origins of the oppressive labor systems of the South. Seen from this perspective, racial slavery became less an anomalous American phenomenon than the logical culmination of upper-class behavior toward indentured servants and the poor in seventeenth-century England. David Grayson Allen posited an even more direct connection between the characters of the two cultures in his *In English Ways: The Movement of Societies and the Transferal of English Local Law and Custom to Massachusetts Bay in the Seventeenth Century*. Allen's portrait of New England resembled a complex mosaic composed of a diverse assemblage of distinct regional and local social practices and institutions transplanted by cohesive groups of migrants. In his view, a common "New England" pattern of political leadership, wealth distribution, agricultural practice, and land allocation emerged only at the end of the seventeenth century.[41]

Morgan and Allen thus stressed the continuities as much as the differences between the European and the colonial American social orders. Their work, like that of many demographers and social historians,

---

41. Morgan, *American Slavery, American Freedom*, esp. 320–26; David Grayson Allen, *In English Ways: The Movement of Societies and the Transferral of English Local Law and Custom to Massachusetts Bay in the Seventeenth Century* (Chapel Hill, N.C., 1981).

demonstrated that the claim for American "exceptionalism" advanced by Louis Hartz, Daniel Boorstin, and other scholars during the 1950s rested on tenuous ground. Other scholars emphasized the complexity of the interaction between transplanted customs and new environmental conditions. Lois Green Carr and Lorena Walsh studied women's lives in relation to the demographic disasters that occurred in the seventeenth-century Chesapeake. High mortality, a skewed sex ratio, and low fertility prevented growth from natural increase. Early deaths disrupted most marriages, and few parents survived to see their children become adults. This fragmented family system undermined traditional patriarchal relationships with respect to the ownership and transmission of property. With no male kin on whom to rely, husbands bestowed greater legal authority on their wives by naming them to execute their wills. They also preferred their wives to their children in the distribution of property. Chesapeake widows commonly received more than their "dower rights" and a life interest in the estate that did not lapse upon remarriage. The appearance of more "normal" demographic patterns permitted the reintroduction of English inheritance customs. By the mid-eighteenth century most Chesapeake males wrote wills that named a male relative as their executor and as the guardian of their children; that restricted their wife's inheritance to the "widow's third" and limited its duration; and that systematically favored their male children at the expense of their marital partners.[42]

---

42. Lois Green Carr and Lorena S. Walsh, "The Planter's Wife: The Experience of White Women in Seventeenth-Century Maryland," *William and Mary Quarterly*, 3d ser., 34 (1977): 542–71;

If these scholars suggested the slow or inconclusive Americanization of transplanted English customs and institutions, other historians proposed an increasing Anglicization of American provincial society during the eighteenth century. Jack P. Greene and Bernard Bailyn demonstrated the profound effect of English practices and ideology on the colonial political leadership with respect to both legislative prerogatives and constitutional thought.[43] Lockridge suggested that much of New England was "rapidly becoming more and more an old world society" characterized by small farms, an articulated social hierarchy, and a substantial poor population. John Murrin and Rowland Berthoff likewise hypothesized a "feudal revival" in the middle and southern colonies in the late colonial period. They pointed out that between 1730 and 1745 the descendents of seventeenth-century proprietors successfully revived long-dormant claims to land and to quitrents. "By the 1760s," Murrin and Berthoff concluded, "the largest proprietors—and no one else in all of English America—were receiving colonial revenues comparable to the incomes of the greatest English noblemen and larger than those of the richest London merchants."[44]

---

idem, "Women's Role in the Eighteenth-Century Chesapeake" (paper presented at the Conference on Women in Early America, Williamsburg, Va., November 1981).

43. Jack P. Greene, *The Quest for Power: The Lower Houses of Assembly in the Southern Royal Colonies, 1680–1776* (Chapel Hill, N.C., 1963); Bernard Bailyn, *The Ideological Origins of the American Revolution* (Cambridge, Mass., 1967).

44. John M. Murrin and Rowland Berthoff, "Feudalism, Communalism, and the Yeoman Freeholder: The American Revolution Considered as a Social Accident," in *Essays on the American Revolution*, ed. Stephen G. Kurtz and James H. Hutson (Chapel Hill, N.C., 1973), 267; Lockridge, "Evolution," passim.

Taken together, these formulations underlined the continuities and similarities between the metropolitan British experience and that of its American colonies. They related these histories to one another in two distinct ways, however. Some authors—Morgan, Allen, Bailyn, and Greene—demonstrated the direct impact of English values, ideas, and behavior patterns on American life. Others—Lockridge and Murrin and Berthoff—employed more problematic arguments by analogy. Just as Main's use of the modern concepts of social mobility and economic development failed to depict the character of preindustrial experience, so terms such as "Europeanization" or "feudal revival" distorted the dimensions of the American colonial existence. Unlike more detailed, more specific comparisons, they implied an unwarranted similarity between colonial and metropolitan life. Moreover, like all broad generalizations, these analogies reified the process of American social development and exaggerated the extent of our understanding of its logic.

In fact, two decades of research had not produced an accepted interpretation of the character of the colonial social structure. Tremendous—even outstanding—progress had been made. Historians could now specify, with considerably accuracy, the shape of the economic hierarchy in scores of towns and villages. Yet the surfeit of empirical data yielded confusion rather than certainty, for this material lacked a set of organizing principles. Commercialization and class stratification served to elucidate aspects of urban development but failed to depict the nature of social change in the dominant agricultural sector. The analysis of rural existence from the perspective of the family revealed the character of inheritance practices, farm life, and economic strategies but could not address important questions of change in the society as a whole. In these circumstances, a definitive synthesis is as impossible as it is unwise. A rapid survey of the literature on landholding and tenancy at the middle of the eighteenth century, however, can clarify the relationship between the production and the distribution of wealth on the one hand and the character of social structure and cultural values on the other.

Landlessness and tenant farming were everywhere on the increase in America in 1750, but nowhere did they approach English levels. In England freeholders personally worked 30 percent of the land, and the nobility and gentry leased the remaining 70 percent to tenants. On the mainland of North America, by contrast, the proportions were reversed. Freeholding families controlled 70 percent of the land and except in the South represented a similar percentage of the total population. Marked differences in wealth holdings and life-styles existed among freeholders, but poor farmers were not in a position of abject dependence.[45] Unlike wage laborers or slaves, they were not directly dependent on the wealthy for their subsistence. In addition, the numerical dominance of freeholders gave normative status to their social values and economic goals. Thus in New England most tenants were either young men or families who needed (or wished) to augment their own holdings. Many owned their own tools or livestock; most would eventually acquire a small estate of their own by migration, savings, or inheritance. Tenancy assumed a more permanent form for many German and Dutch farmers in New York, for the manorial proprietors of the Hudson River valley refused to subdivide their lands for sale. Yet the competition for agricultural labor remained

---

45. Wellenreuther, "View," 15–21.

keen until the end of the colonial period; as a result, most tenants received long leases and the right to sell their "improvements." Like their counterparts in New England, they "owned" productive property and shared many of the economic values of freehold farmers.[46] Even in the South tenancy varied widely. German tenants on the manor of Lord Baltimore in Frederick County, Maryland, had good land, long leases, and profitable wheat crops. Yet propertyless farmers in tobacco areas barely scraped by. In All Hallow's Parish in the 1740s the rental fee for one hundred acres was five hundred to eight hundred pounds of tobacco, while annual production of first-quality leaf (using household labor) was one thousand pounds. Given this narrow margin, few tenant families could live well or acquire property of their own. In the mid-1760s five out of six tenants on one of Baltimore's long-settled tobacco estates were either the original leaseholders or their direct descendents.[47]

If tenancy was ubiquitous, its causes were different and its effects were not equally onerous. As Richard Dunn has argued, patterns of propertylessness reflected regional systems of land use and agricultural production.[48] From the very beginning the Chesapeake

---

46. See the concise argument in Patricia U. Bonomi, *A Factious People: Politics and Society in Colonial New York* (New York, 1971) or the more detailed but sometimes confusing analysis by Sung Bok Kim, *Landlord and Tenant in Colonial New York: Manorial Society, 1667–1775* (Chapel Hill, N.C., 1978).

47. Gregory A. Stiverson, "Landless Husbandmen: Proprietary Tenants in Maryland in the Late Colonial Period," in Land, Carr, and Papenfuse, *Law*, 197–211; Earle, *Evolution*, 207–13.

48. Richard S. Dunn, "Servants and Slaves: The Recruitment and Employment of Labor," in *Colonial British America: Essays in the New History of the Early Modern Era*, ed. Jack P. Greene and J. R. Pole (Baltimore, Md., 1983), 157–94.

colonies used the bound labor of indentured servants. Many rose to freeholder status before the collapse of the tobacco boom in 1670; thereafter most white freedmen clustered in the ranks of the propertyless, working as tenants, laborers, or overseers on the tobacco plantations of the wealthy. They constituted a permanent underclass of families divorced in condition and consciousness from the freeholding population. The legacy of indentured servitude in the Chesapeake was slavery for blacks and a grinding tenancy for many whites.

In the Middle Colonies tenancy took on an ethnic coloration as thousands of eighteenth-century German and Scotch-Irish immigrants worked on properties owned by their well-established countrymen or by those of English ancestry. Many of these indentured servants and redemptioners came with greater material resources than had their seventeenth-century counterparts and after a short period of service became tenants and then small landowners. They benefited as well from the greater availability of freehold land, especially in Pennsylvania, and from the profitable transatlantic trade in grain. This fortunate combination of circumstances—their European background, liberal land policies, and international grain prices—made tenancy in the Middle Colonies less a treacherous dead-end path than a way station on the road to property ownership.

In long-settled regions of New England tenancy had unique causes and characteristics. For generations New England parents had routinely appropriated the youthful labor of their offspring. Throughout the seventeenth century the age at marriage for males was twenty-seven years in the small agricultural village of Wenham, in coastal Essex County, Massachusetts, and it remained high (26.2) until 1750 for nonmigrant males. These young men delayed marriage until they gained access to land, usually through inheritance. By this time Wenham and many other older towns had allocated all their land; generations of use had sapped the fertility of rich bottom land, and continued subdivision was economically unwise. The inability of parents to compensate their children with substantial inheritances slowly eroded the cultural pattern of family labor and prompted various creative adaptions. In Guilford, Connecticut, many families adopted (or maintained) the "stem family" system of residence and inheritance. A married son or son-in-law lived in his parents' household and inherited the farm upon the death of the father; other siblings were given money, apprenticeship contracts, or encouragement to migrate to other communities. As a result, the town's population increased relatively slowly in the eighteenth century (1.4 percent per annum), and the level of assessed wealth per taxable resident remained stable.[49] In Wenham many males married early (age twenty-three) and migrated out of the community. Movement to interior hill towns or to the New Hampshire frontier, rather than family limitation or male celibacy, thus ensured social stability. As Darrett Rutman has shown, there was a direct relationship between the age of New Hampshire towns and their rate of growth; young towns expanded at more than 6 percent per annum, while older communities grew at the barely discernible rate of 0.03 percent.[50] The "safety valve" of the

---

49. Waters, "Patrimony." See also Lutz K. Berkner, "The Stem Family and the Development Cycle of the Peasant Household: An Eighteenth-Century Austrian Example," *American Historical Review* 77 (1972): 398–418.

50. Jones, *Village*, chapter 5; Darrett B. Rutman, "The Social Web: A Prospectus for the Study of the Early American Community," in *Insights and Parallels: Problems and Issues of American Social History*, ed. William L. O'Neill (Minneapolis, 1973), 76n.

frontier limited the incidence of tenancy and the growth of an agricultural proletariat.

In much of New England, migration conflicted with a cultural preference for partible inheritance of land. In Chebacco (near Ipswich), Massachusetts, parents stretched limited resources to the limits of economic feasibility; 90 percent of all decedents with more than one son divided their land rather than bequeath the farm to a single heir. However unpromising at first sight, this strategy seems also to have allowed young families to preserve financial independence. Bettye Pruitt found that communities in Massachusetts remained viable productive units even as the size of individual farms decreased. An analysis of fourteen hundred farms on the 1771 valuation list indicated that only 47 percent had the exact number of acres of pasture, tons of hay, and bushels of grain needed to feed their livestock, but 90 percent of all towns matched forage resources with livestock holdings. "Many farmers kept more cattle than their land could hold, and many kept fewer," Pruitt concludes, "and only in the town as a whole did it all balance out."[51] In dividing their land among their male offspring, Chebacco fathers were buying their sons in to an interdependent economic community.

This rapid survey of the contrasting patterns of landlessness and tenancy suggests the extent to which a common nomenclature obscures a diverse reality and underlines the significance of region in early America. Finally, it suggests that wealth distribution and social structure are not autonomous subjects. Rather, they

---

51. Christopher M. Jedrey, *The World of John Cleaveland: Family and Community in Eighteenth-Century New England* (New York, 1979), 80–83; Pruitt, "Agriculture," 35.

must be understood as part of a wider system of economic, social and, ultimately, political relationships in a given community. In New England, for example, the exchange of economic goods—labor, land, and capital—took place according to three different types of cultural interactions. First, members of kinship groups cooperated with one another. Diaries document an elaborate exchange of female labor among kin-related households, especially with respect to textile production, and male exchange of tools and draft animals followed similar lines. In addition, there were "shucking bees" and other joint economic activities, based on kin or neighborhood connections and the principle of labor reciprocity. Money values figured more prominently in a second series of transactions. Hundreds of formal account books that survive for the period 1750–1820 detail an elaborate system of local exchange among farmers, artisans, and storekeepers. Fields were plowed in return for grazing rights or the repair of a tin pot; purchases of cloth and tools were repaid by labor or the delivery of produce. Each of these transactions received a monetary value, sometimes customary and sometimes reflecting current prices, but accounts were settled only after a year or two, usually with the transfer of a few pounds. The rest had canceled out. Finally, there were "commercial" transactions in the full sense of the term: the sale of surplus grain or livestock by farmers in return for cash or store goods.[52]

---

52. For a fine theoretical statement see Michael Merrill, "Cash Is Good to Eat: Self-Sufficiency and Exchange in the Rural Economy of the United States," *Radical History Review* 4 (1977): 42–69; see also Susan Geib, " 'Changing Works': Agriculture and Society in Brookfield, Massachusetts, 1780–1835" (Ph.D. diss., Boston University, 1981).

Some of these patterns of exchange militated against wealth inequality, while others facilitated it; some tied the lives of the inhabitants together, while others accentuated religious and political divisions. Seen in this light, the prime task is not to analyze the production and distribution of wealth in quantitative terms but rather to comprehend the various sets of cultural interactions that constituted the social structure of the community. Thus the autonomous treatment of the subjects of wealth and social structure inaugurated in the mid-1960s by Taylor and Main should cease. These topics should become important but subordinate parts of a wider social and political history based on the dynamic interaction of individuals and social groups.

The framework within which these actors operated is clear in outline if not in detail. Even at the end of the colonial period the economy of British North America remained agricultural. Unlike England, the mainland colonies boasted a strong class of freeholding farmers and were not burdened by a numerous group of underemployed farmer-artisans or landless laborers. Indeed, the "proto-industrial" cottage system of manufacturing, a longstanding and growing feature of English economic life, began to develop in America only during and after the War for Independence.[53] That timing was not accidental. Freed from the com-

---

53. See, for example, Hans Medick, "The Proto-Industrial Family Economy: The Structural Function of Household and Family during the Transition from Peasant Society to Industrial Capitalism," *Social History* 3 (1976): 291–316; Joan Thirsk, "Industries in the Countryside," in *Essays in the Economic and Social History of Tudor and Stuart England*, ed. F. J. Fisher (Cambridge, England, 1961), 70–88; and A. Soboul, "The French Rural Community in the Eighteenth and Nineteenth Centuries," *Past and Present* 10 (1956): 78–95.

petition posed by highly stratified and impoverished "proto-industrialized" areas of England, New England merchants found it profitable to organize the back-country production of shoes, cloth, and processed foods. Hence the rise of cottage manufacturing in the United States occurred primarily after 1790, almost concurrently with the mechanization of production and the factory system. By the 1830s in New England twenty thousand women and children labored full-time in textile factories, while some forty thousand rural women and children worked part-time making four million palm hats each year. Four decades earlier, neither system of production had been in existence.[54]

The timing of American proto-industrialization addresses the major issues raised in this chapter. First, it explains the relative stability of the per capita *production* of wealth in the colonial period: resources remained in the farming sector and were not diverted to more productive nonagricultural industries. Second, this chronology accounts for the comparative stability in the *distribution* of wealth in the northern colonies. The new social system of slavery brought an increase in inequality to the South after 1690, but a comparable shift occurred in the North only a century later as merchants and industrialists mobilized the rural labor force in a new productive system. Third, the discontinuity between the pre-1775 freeholder-dominated *social structure* of New England and other long-established northern regions and their rapid post-1790 development as proto-industrial areas raises important and as yet unanswered questions regarding

---

54. Thomas Dublin, "Women and the Dimensions of Outwork in Nineteenth-Century New England" (paper presented at the Berkshire Conference on Women's History, June 1981), 10.

the relationship between cultural values and economic development. The task before us is to explicate the distinct structures and patterns of existence in these preindustrial societies and thus to comprehend the logic and dynamic of the lives of their inhabitants.

PART

II

Toward a New Order, 1775–1800

What was the American Revolution? For two centuries historians have addressed this question, but very few have given sustained attention to its economic aspects. Did the revolution begin a new economic era in the United States? Or did the War for Independence merely constitute a temporary disruption in production and finance, leaving unchanged the basic export-oriented commercial economy?

The two concluding essays focus on these questions in part because of their intrinsic importance. It is important to know how the revolution affected American economic life. Beyond that, my interpretation of the colonial economy lends particular importance to these issues. The essays in part 1 emphasize the *continuities* in economic behavior and values before 1775 and suggest the importance of population growth and the diversification of the domestic economy as the prime causal factors in the process of economic growth. My perspective on the colonial economy takes issue with the "staple thesis" advanced by various historians.[1] That interpretation attaches fundamental importance to the export of primary products, such as tobacco and rice, in determining the nature and the rate of economic change. The wartime experience offers a testing ground for the relative merits of my "internalist" and their "externalist" interpretations of the colonial economy. How did Americans survive during eight years of war when the export economy virtually ceased to function? And what role did changes in the domestic economy during the Revolutionary era play in the subsequent development of the American productive system?

These essays also continue the discussion of historical discourse and methodology. In particular, they translate traditional descriptions of domestic manufacturing into the theoretical language of modern social science. Thus the production of homespun cloth before and during the War for Independence is treated not simply as an outburst of female patriotic enthusiasm. Rather, it is seen as a phase of a worldwide process of proto-industrialization that systematically integrated the labor of women (and children and men) into a developing capitalist economic system.

The concept of proto-industrialization has various theoretical weaknesses but also great strengths. It adds rigor and precision to the analysis of the rise of manufacturing in the period before the industrial revolution of the nineteenth century. Moreover, the concept both encourages and facilitates a cross-national

---

1. See, for example, John J. McCusker and Russell R. Menard, *The Economy of British America, 1607–1789* (Chapel Hill, N.C., 1985), especially 10–13 and chapter 1.

comparative approach to the economic history of the early modern world. Finally, proto-industrialization represents a much needed alternative to the theories of "mercantilism" and "staple exports" that have long informed scholarly interpretations of the eighteenth-century American economy.

My concern with the discourse of history writing appears in the final essay, "The Transition to Capitalism." That study includes a series of personal stories that seek to capture the human dynamics of this economic transformation. Such an approach is only appropriate, since most historical change is the result—sometimes intended, sometimes not—of human action. This focus on individual lives is hardly innovative, since storytelling is a most traditional form of historical discourse. Yet the "new social history" (including my own essays) often lost sight of the personal dimension of economic and social life, preferring instead to offer conceptual pictures and theoretical portraits of historical change. As Lawrence Stone has argued,[2] the task is now to write a "new narrative history," one that depicts patterns of social change through the lives of the women and men who made it happen.

---

2. Lawrence Stone, "The Revival of Narrative: Reflections on a New Old History," *Past and Present* 86 (1980): 3–24.

6

The War for Independence
and
American Economic Development

In 1960 Thomas C. Cochran advanced the provocative thesis that the Civil War retarded the industrialization of the United States. Cochran based his argument on statistical indexes of total commodity output—the production of coal, pig iron, textiles, and farm machinery, as well as the rate of construction of new railroad lines. His analysis of these key economic

The first version of this paper was presented at the Shelby Cullom Davis Center at Princeton University. Lawrence Stone, John Murrin, and Paul Clemens offered useful criticisms and suggestions, as did participants in the 1984 United States Capitol Historical Society Symposium—notably James Walsh, Jacob Price, and Franklin Mendels. I am especially grateful to Lois Green Carr for providing me with unpublished materials, to Stanley Engerman for a perceptive critique of my manuscript, and to Michael Merrill for showing me the inner logic of my interpretation.

indicators demonstrated that the pace of economic growth slowed during the 1860s. Cochran's short paper forced a revaluation of the traditional thesis that the war, as Harold U. Faulkner had phrased it, "speeded the Industrial Revolution and the development of capitalism."[1]

Ultimately most scholars agreed with Cochran that wartime economic growth fell below that of the preceding period. At the same time they argued that the war shifted the pattern of economic development in significant ways and, equally important, that it bolstered the financial resources and the political power of industrial capitalists. Seen from the widest perspective, therefore, the Civil War had a much greater total economic impact than Cochran had allowed.

Cochran's argument also turned the attention of historians to the initial decades of American economic growth. During the past twenty years, various scholars—Douglass North, Paul David, Robert E. Gallman, George Rogers Taylor, and, most recently, Diane Lindstrom—have advanced stimulating hypotheses to explain the expansion of the per capita gross national product between 1790 and 1840.

Historians of the Revolutionary era have largely ignored this debate over the timing of the American economic "take-off." With a few exceptions, they have not directly addressed the economic impact of the War for Independence. Our understanding of the wartime

---

1. Thomas C. Cochran, "Did the Civil War Retard Industrialization?" *Mississippi Valley Historical Review* 48 (1961): 197–210. The Faulkner quotation is on p. 197. For a review of the subsequent debate see Ralph Andreano, *The Economic Impact of the American Civil War* (Cambridge, Mass., 1962).

economy rests largely on four books written a generation ago. Robert A. East published his study of entrepreneurial activity, *Business Enterprise in the American
Revolutionary Era,* in 1938. Richard B. Morris added a
detailed examination of workers' occupations and lives
in *Government and Labor in Early America* in 1946.
Then, in 1947, Oscar Handlin and Mary Handlin
provided an institutional synthesis in *Commonwealth:
A Study of the Role of Government in the American Economy: Massachusetts, 1774–1861.* These studies fleshed
out the valuable statistical analyses offered by Anne
Bezanson beginning in 1935 and culminating in *Prices
and Inflation during the American Revolution: Pennsylvania, 1770–1790,* published in 1951.

Subsequent biographies of individual merchants,
such as the Beekmans of New York and the Browns of
Providence, did not attempt an overview of the wartime economy. Nor did they ground their narratives
in a set of theoretical statements. Rather, they described how merchants and other social groups suffered, gained, or simply coped during the war and the
economically difficult decade of the 1780s.[2]

Even as this picture of the war economy remained
fragmentary, important scholarly works revised our
understanding of colonial society. First, quantitatively

---

2. Robert A. East, *Business Enterprise in the American Revolutionary
Era* (1938; reprint, Gloucester, Mass., 1964); Richard B. Morris,
Government and Labor in Early America (1946; reprint, Boston,
1981); Oscar Handlin and Mary Handlin, *Commonwealth: A Study
of the Role of Government in the American Economy: Massachusetts,
1774–1861* (Cambridge, Mass., 1947); Anne Bezanson, *Prices and
Inflation during the American Revolution: Pennsylvania, 1770–1790*
(Philadelphia, 1951); Philip L. White, *The Beekmans of New York in
Politics and Commerce, 1647–1877* (New York, 1956); and James B.
Hedges, *The Browns of Providence Plantation: Colonial Years* (Cambridge, Mass., 1952).

based commercial studies outlined the long-term movement of tobacco prices, the transatlantic flow of African slaves and white indentured servants, the amazing growth of exports in wheat and rice, and the complete American balance of trade for the years 1768–72.[3] Second, historians used local tax and probate records to describe the structure of property ownership in the colonies, and Jackson T. Main attempted to link the extent of wealth inequalities to participation in commercial activity.[4] Finally, demographic studies raised the specter of a Malthusian subsistence crisis in the dominant rural sector. As Kenneth A. Lockridge suggested in his brief but influential survey "Land, Population, and the Evolution of New England Society, 1630–1780," "this part of America was becoming more and more an old world society; old world in the sense of the size of farms, . . . an increasingly wide and articulated hierarchy [with] . . . the poor ever permanent and in increasing numbers."[5]

---

3. Jacob M. Price, "The Economic Growth of the Chesapeake and the European Market, 1697–1775," *Journal of Economic History* 24 (1964): 496–511; U.S. Bureau of the Census, *Historical Statistics of the United States: Colonial Times to 1970*, 2 vols. (Washington, D.C., 1975), ser. Z441–72; Philip D. Curtin, *The Atlantic Slave Trade: A Census* (Madison, Wis., 1969); David W. Galenson, *White Servitude in Colonial America: An Economic Analysis* (Cambridge, England, 1981); Paul G. E. Clemens, *The Atlantic Economy and Colonial Maryland's Eastern Shore: From Tobacco to Grain* (Ithaca, N.Y., 1980); James F. Shepherd and Gary M. Walton, *Shipping, Maritime Trade, and the Economic Development of Colonial North America* (Cambridge, England, 1972).

4. Jackson T. Main, *The Social Structure of Revolutionary America* (Princeton, N.J., 1965); Alice Hanson Jones, *Wealth of a Nation to Be: The American Colonies on the Eve of the Revolution* (New York, 1980).

5. Kenneth A. Lockridge, "Land, Population, and the Evolution of New England Society, 1630–1780," in *Colonial America: Essays*

This new scholarship holds immense significance for the Revolutionary era. To bring it to bear on the interpretation of the wartime economy requires the creation of an analytical hypothesis similar to that constructed by Cochran. Let us ask, therefore, Did the War for Independence accelerate the process of American economic growth? and, Did it encourage the transition to a more capitalistic society? To answer these questions, we must first examine the character of the prewar economy both in terms of traditional mercantilist theory and with reference to the new literature on European proto-industrialization. With this conceptual framework in place, we can then proceed to an analysis of wartime events. Finally, a short discussion of economic change and political policies after 1790 will suggest the similarities and the differences between the economic impact of the Civil and the Revolutionary wars.

I

In many respects, the British mainland colonies constituted a classic case of a mercantilist economy. In the southern plantation colonies, freemen and slaves produced tobacco, rice, and wheat for export to Europe, and they consumed manufactured goods imported from the mother country. By the 1740s the Middle Colonies likewise boasted a strong export sector. Increased production of wheat for European mar-

---

in Politics and Social Development, ed. Stanley N. Katz (Boston, 1971), 484. Also see Philip J. Greven, Jr., *Four Generations: Population, Land, and Family in Colonial Andover, Massachusetts* (Ithaca, N.Y., 1970).

kets and corn for the West Indies permitted the importation of consumer goods—textiles, ironware, and ceramics. In New England, merchants sold meat, timber, and fish to the West Indies to pay for British manufactures.

The *absolute* size of the mercantilist economy grew rapidly during the eighteenth century. The American mainland population doubled each generation, stimulating export and import markets. Between 1750 and 1810, the number of people per square mile in most seaboard counties tripled.

Greater population density also prompted the *relative* growth of the domestic economy. Unlike the staple-producing export sector, American domestic production has received little scholarly attention. Yet the proportion of the mainland's gross output that was produced by American farmers, artisans, and merchants was undoubtedly higher in 1775 than ever before. Despite their astounding growth, imports composed an ever-smaller component of the American economy.

Just as mercantilism provides a framework for the study of the export economy, so the theory of proto-industrialization offers a conceptual perspective on the domestic sector. As a set of interpretative propositions, proto-industrialization focuses on the putting-out system of handicraft production organized by merchant capitalists. The logic of the system, Sidney Pollard has recently written, consisted

> on the one hand, of capital and entrepreneurship able and willing to grasp the opportunities of distant markets . . . and supply them on a large scale; and, on the other, dispersed manufacture in the countryside enjoying low costs of production . . . by the widespread use of "inferior labour," i.e., women and children, by the depression of real wages made possible by the

agricultural part-incomes of the workers, and by an advanced division of labour.[6]

The initial studies of the outwork system in pre-industrial Europe focused on the activities of merchants, skilled entrepreneurs who managed the distribution of raw materials and finished products. Then, in the 1950s, Joan Thirsk and H. J. Habakkuk linked the emergence of the rural textile industry with the rapid population growth encouraged by the custom of partible inheritance. In his study of economic development in Flanders, Franklin F. Mendels gave these demographic propositions a theoretical cast. He carefully delineated the process whereby "areas which turned to cottage industry tended to attract immigration, had earlier and more marriages, and had higher fertility than other rural areas." "An impressive growth of this type of manufacturing" was hardly salutary, Mendels concluded, for it "was accompanied by an equally impressive poverty," by the loss of peasants' control over land and other means of production, and, ultimately, by the appearance of a substantial rural proletariat.[7]

The existence of cottage industry was one precondition for proto-industrialization. The presence of an impoverished rural labor force was usually (but not necessarily) another. The final ingredient was intrare-

---

6. Sidney Pollard, *Peaceful Conquest: The Industrialization of Europe, 1760–1970* (Oxford, 1981), 65.

7. Joan Thirsk, "Industries in the Countryside," in *Essays in the Economic and Social History of Tudor and Stuart England*, ed. F. J. Fisher (Cambridge, England, 1961); H. J. Habakkuk, "Family Structure and Economic Change in Nineteenth-Century Europe," *Journal of Economic History* 15 (1955): 1–12; Franklin F. Mendels, "Proto-Industrialization: The First Phase of the Industrialization Process," *Journal of Economic History* 32 (1972): 203.

gional specialization. As Mendels and a trio of German historians—Hans Medick, Peter Kriedte, and Jürgen Schlumbohm—have described it, proto-industrialization involved the simultaneous appearance, in adjacent areas, of rural industries and a symbiotic commercial agriculture. This specialization of function increased the level of intraregional exchange as well as extraregional trade, resulting in a significant expansion of production for market.

Other scholars have suggested even broader theoretical perspectives. Charles Tilly has pointed to the complementary nature of rural and urban manufacturing and underlined the importance of local or regional (rather than distant) markets for manufactured goods. For Frank Perlin, proto-industrialization was part of the massive expansion of capitalist relations of production in the early modern world. In his study of the subcontinent of India in the late eighteenth century, Perlin found that "local economic life was becoming more dense and vigorous even in essentially agricultural hinterlands." There was an increased use of money, he explained, with "a knowledge of quantity, calculation, attribution of value, widely dispersed among ordinary people." What were the structural preconditions, Perlin asked, "that made it possible for manufactures to exist as an aspect of a greater organization of production and marketing relationships embracing towns, production of foodstuffs, and financial institutions" at this particular historical moment?[8]

---

8. Peter Kriedte, Hans Medick, and Jürgen Schlumbohm, *Industrialization before Industrialization: Rural Industry in the Genesis of Capitalism*, trans. Beate Schempp (Cambridge, England, 1981); Charles Tilly, "Flows of Capital and Forms of Industry in Europe, 1500–1900," *Theory and Society* 12 (1983): 123–42; Hans Medick,

Perlin's question, raised with respect to one region affected by British commercial activity in the late eighteenth century, applies to North America as well. As on the Indian subcontinent, a combination of increased foreign trade and home manufacturing created a more dense, vigorous, and prosperous economic system in the American colonies.

II

Proto-industrial theory must be applied to British North America with careful attention to its distinctive social character. The colonies lacked "the poverty of the peasantry [that] was a major precondition for the expansion of cottage industry" in many parts of Europe. Living standards for the 500,000 enslaved blacks on the American mainland were as low as those of poor peasants, but slaves mainly produced agricultural crops for export to Europe and not manufactured goods. While increasing numbers of the "strolling poor" wandered through the countryside on the eve of American independence, these whites amounted to less than 5 percent of the rural population. In times of economic downturn, the poor in the towns numbered between 15 and 20 percent of the residents. Those urban centers were small, however, and few in number. And the mainland colonies completely escaped the subsistence crises that devastated parts of Europe.

"The Proto-Industrial Family Economy: The Structural Function of Household and Family during the Transition from Peasant Society to Industrial Capitalism," *Social History* 3 (1976): 291–315; Frank Perlin, "Proto-Industrialization and Pre-Colonial South Asia," *Past and Present* 98 (1983): 84, 70, 51.

In proto-industrial Saxony, for example, sixty thousand people (6 percent of the population) starved to death or succumbed to disease in the 1770s.[9]

These differences between Europe and the American mainland colonies can be stated more precisely in terms of the traditional theoretical distinctions applied to the putting-out system. Virtually none of the inhabitants of colonial America worked within the rigid confines of the *Verlagsystem*. In this highly developed form of cottage industry, capitalist merchants dominated the manufacturing process. They owned all the raw materials and held rural workers in a position of nearly complete economic dependence. Some American farmers and rural artisans, however, participated in a *Kaufsystem*. These rural families owned most of the means of production and enjoyed considerable economic autonomy. Yet they had to sell their domestic manufactures (and crops) at the prices set by local storekeepers and seaport merchants. Those commercial middlemen charged commissions for their services and often extracted excess profits through their knowledge of the market system. Many areas of the European cottage industry, such as Flanders, participated in a *Kaufsystem* and a set of market relationships similar to those in British North America.[10]

Recent scholarship has revealed both the causes

9. Catherina Lis and Hugo Soly, *Poverty and Capitalism in Pre-Industrial Europe* (Atlantic Highlands, N.J., 1979), 149, 171–93; Karl Tilman Winkler, "Social Mobility in Eighteenth-Century North America" (paper presented at the Krefeld Conference, Krefeld, Germany, June 1983); and Paul G. E. Clemens, "Commerce and Community: Reflections on the Social History of Early American Agriculture" (unpublished paper, 1984).

10. See Robert E. Mutch, "Yeoman and Merchant in Pre-Industrial America: Eighteenth-Century Massachusetts as a Case Study," *Societas: A Review of Social History* 7 (1977): 279–302.

of the emergence of the colonial *Kaufsystem* and its specific features. Especially in long-settled towns in New England, but in Pennsylvania and the Chesapeake as well, the rapidly increasing population pressed heavily on existing agricultural resources. Prime arable land grew scarce. As a consequence, tenant farming and western migration were everywhere on the increase.

The Malthusian crisis postulated by Lockridge did not materialize, however, for creative adaption averted inexorable decline. As we found in chapter 5, families in some communities adopted a "stem family" pattern of inheritance, in which one heir received land while the others received money or other assistance; families in other communities divided the farm among all the heirs, creating an abundance of marginal farms that relied on communal economic practices for survival.

In the latter case, the creation of an interdependent economic community increased productivity through a more complete utilization of resources. Diaries and account books reveal an elaborate exchange of female labor, especially for the production of textiles. They also document the diversification of male economic activity and the increase of year-round labor. Jonathan Burnham, the owner of a relatively large farm of seventy acres in Ipswich, Massachusetts, sold his surplus grain and livestock. To make ends meet, he also fished and dug clams for sale, plowed his neighbors' fields, and made leather clothes and shoes during the winter. In the western Massachusetts town of Northampton, Ebenezer Hunt presided over a store and hatmaking enterprise that had 550 open accounts in 1773. In return for store goods and felt and worsted hats, local men and women provided Hunt with dressed deerskins and beaver pelts, meat, hoops, and barrels. They also spun and wove and lined hats for this small-scale merchant entrepreneur. The returns from domestic manufacturing thus bolstered local farm income and raised living standards. In 1776 over one-third of Northampton's families had some non-farm income.[11]

Occupational diversity appeared in more densely settled areas. In Ipswich only half the male population engaged in farming as a primary occupation; 20 percent were artisans, and another 18 percent engaged in various maritime enterprises. In the neighboring agricultural town of Andover, nearly 30 percent of the third-generation descendants of the original proprietors followed a trade or craft at some point in their lives. In Connecticut, craftsmen's estates composed 25 percent of the inventories probated in the late colonial period. The booming export trade in grain brought prosperity and occupational complexity to Pennsylvania as well. Twenty percent of the taxpayers in rural Lancaster County were craftsmen in 1758. In the small towns of Lancaster, Reading, and York, artisans numbered 30 to 40 percent of the population.[12]

While older men turned to agricultural by-employments and artisanry to cope with a shifting rural economy, younger propertyless men opted for

11. Arlen I. Ginsburg, "The Political and Economic Impact of the American Revolution on Ipswich, Massachusetts" (unpublished paper, presented at Boston Seminar in Early American History, 1976); Anne Baxter Webb, "On the Eve of the Revolution: Northampton, Massachusetts, 1750–1775" (Ph.D. diss., University of Minnesota, 1976), 223–29.

12. Jackson T. Main, "The Distribution of Property in Colonial Connecticut," in *The Human Dimensions of Nation Making: Essays on Colonial and Revolutionary America*, ed. James Kirby Martin (Madison, Wis., 1976), 70, 89, and table 4; James T. Lemon, *The Best Poor Man's Country: A Geographical Study of Early Southeastern Pennsylvania* (Baltimore, Md., 1972), table 23 and pp. 7–8, 96, 128, 139, 147.

military service whenever it was available. Both in Maryland and New Jersey, the majority of recruits into the Continental army during the Revolutionary War came from families with little or no property. The same enlistment pattern had appeared among twenty-three hundred militiamen raised in Massachusetts in 1756 for service in the Seven Years' War. A detailed analysis by Fred Anderson demonstrated that most of those recruits were young—aged seventeen to twenty-six—and "temporarily poor." They lived at or near their families' homes, working either "for themselves or to build up the family patrimony." Military service, Anderson argued, was simply a new means to achieve the traditional goal of landed independence. With the fifteen pounds in Massachusetts currency earned in the 1756 campaign, a young man could buy fifteen to thirty acres of unbroken land in an old community like Andover or as many as 150 acres of unimproved upland in Northampton.[13]

These adaptive strategies had sharp limitations. Among fishermen in Essex County, Massachusetts, the population "grew faster than the capacity of the industry to absorb it." As a result, the character of the industry changed profoundly during the mideighteenth century. Merchants no longer extended credit to trustworthy fishermen to finance their ownership of boats and their fishing voyages. Taking advantage of the labor surplus, merchant capitalists outfitted their own boats and employed wage laborers

---

13. James Kirby Martin and Mark Edward Lender, *A Respectable Army: The Military Origins of the Republic, 1763–1789* (Arlington Heights, Ill., 1982), 90–91; Fred Anderson, "A People's Army: Provincial Military Service in Massachusetts during the Seven Years' War," *William and Mary Quarterly*, 3d ser., 40 (1983): 500–527.

who were young, strong, and expendable. "The industry was no longer an effective agent for social mobility," its historian Daniel Vickers concluded. "Poor immigrants stayed poor; well-born craftsmen's sons returned to their fathers' trades; and fishermen trained up to support their parents in old age, bred sons of their own to follow them. . . . Young men . . . emerged from their stints at sea on the same level at which they had entered."[14]

The story was only slightly better in the predominant agricultural society. In the quarter century before the War for Independence, the white inhabitants of British North America maintained, and perhaps even improved, their standard of living. But the cost was high. To provide for their numerous children, many parents worked harder and in more diverse occupations. Geographical mobility left emotional scars. Winter by-employments required additional labor. The fluctuating demand for craft goods meant psychological uncertainty and physical hardship.

More significantly, this economic evolution threatened a fundamental transformation in social relationships. In the more complex environment of the late colonial period a growing proportion of rural families found themselves in positions of partial financial dependence. Some were tenants. Others owned land but fell into continuing debt to village storekeepers, landlords, or millowners. And nearly all the inhabitants of established communities increasingly de-

---

14. Daniel Vickers, "From Clientage to Free Labor: The Cod Fishery of Colonial Essex County, Massachusetts, Reconsidered as a Labor System" (paper presented at the Sixth Annual Meeting of the Social Science History Association, Washington, D.C., October 1983), 11–12.

pended on their neighbors for special craft skills, land-use rights, or labor. As Robert A. Gross has demonstrated, only affluent farmers were truly self-sufficient.[15]

Nonetheless, the new bonds of economic interdependence were mostly reciprocal and symmetrical. They tied families of roughly equal financial status to one another, often in mutually supportive relationships. "He wove for grain," a weaver testified in a court case heard in Schenectady, New York, in 1779, "and did not weave much for money."[16] Or those financial ties linked merchant entrepreneurs to "petty producers" who had some economic autonomy.

American distinctiveness stemmed, therefore, not from the absence of the *Kaufsystem*, but rather from a successful effort to avoid the oppressive *Verlagsystem*. In various parts of Europe, the spread of cottage industry increased the existing high rate of population growth stemming from partible inheritance. Deprived of their farms, landless cottagers could no longer use inheritance incentives to delay the age of marriage and thereby reduce fertility. Their children married earlier and, as a result, had even greater numbers of offspring. Even severe fluctuations in market prices for domestic manufactures did not cut fertility. Rather, high prices allowed young men and women to marry and to create new economic units. Low prices also failed to reduce fertility, for declining incomes

---

15. Robert A. Gross, "Culture and Cultivation: Agriculture and Society in Thoreau's Concord," *Journal of American History* 64 (1982): 51.

16. Quoted in Richard B. Morris, "Labor and Mercantilism in the Revolutionary Era," in *The Era of the American Revolution*, ed. Richard B. Morris (1939; reprint, New York, 1965), 129.

prompted parents to work young children harder and to urge older siblings to marry. Once they had lost control of the means of production, European cottagers were caught in a process of "self-exploitation" that increased the rate of demographic growth and the extent of impoverishment.[17]

In America, by contrast, the availability of land guaranteed the primacy of agriculture and traditional family patterns. Moreover, colonial parents reduced their fertility (from an average of six to seven births per completed family in 1700 to five to six births in 1800) in order to provide their sons and daughters with land, either nearby or in a newly settled community. As Toby Ditz has demonstrated, farm families both in lowland and in upland communities in the Connecticut River valley provided some land for 70–75 percent of *all* their children on the eve of the American Revolution. Confronted by land shortages, some of these parents excluded daughters from landed inheritances or wrote wills that required favored heirs to provide financial assistance to their siblings.[18]

Thus the circumstances of American life and the cultural values of its inhabitants militated constantly against the preconditions of the *Verlagsystem*: widespread landlessness, grinding poverty, and overdependence on cottage industry. As a result, the American revolt against Great Britain stemmed more from mercantilist pressures, such as imperial administrative reform and trade imbalances, than from an oppressive proto-industrial economy.

---

17. Kriedte, Medick, and Schlumbohm, *Industrialization*, 99.
18. Toby Ditz, "Proto-Industrialization and the Household Economy in the American North: Inheritance Patterns in Five Connecticut Towns, 1750–1820" (paper presented at the Eighth International Congress of Economic History, Budapest, 1982), 15.

III

Yet British mercantilism intersected with the nascent American *Kaufsystem* in important ways, notably in the textile industry. Historically, cloth production was the major activity in European proto-industrial regions. The industry spanned the Continent and encompassed a wide range of fabrics and markets. Some French weavers specialized in high-quality silks. German, Flemish, and Irish peasants fabricated durable linens. And English cottagers wove wool into cloth of many varieties and prices. Merchants marketed these rurally produced textiles in cities, in other European regions, and throughout the world. On the eve of the American Revolution, the mainland colonies imported 10 to 13 million yards of linen and woolen cloth from Great Britain each year, at a cost of £800,000 sterling. In addition, the colonists consumed a significant quantity of German linens.[19]

At this point it is impossible to estimate the proportion of American cloth consumption met by imports. There are no reliable data (from probate inventories or other sources) indicating requirements for clothing or the amount of heavy linen used for other purposes, such as sacking and bagging. Nor have the records of storekeepers been carefully analyzed to determine the extent of cloth purchases by ordinary artisans or farm families. Literary sources, such as letters and diaries, indicate extensive use of imported cloth in urban and commercial agricultural areas. They also suggest heavy reliance on domestically manufactured homespun by the rest of the rural population.

---

19. Shepherd and Walton, *Shipping*, 110–13, 182, and appendix 2.

The statistical evidence is equally contradictory. The per capita volume of British imports increased between 1740 and 1775, but probate records also suggest a rising number of female spinners and weavers and of rising domestic production. Apparently, increased imports and higher American output went hand in hand—resulting in a better-clothed population over the course of the eighteenth century. It seems probable that in 1775 Americans manufactured more textiles per capita than ever before. Even stronger evidence indicates that per capita domestic production increased significantly between 1775 and 1825.[20]

Three excellent studies published between 1916 and 1926 provide a wealth of information about the American textile industry both before and after the War for Independence. In *Household Manufactures in the United States, 1640–1860*, Rolla Milton Tryon focused primarily on goods made in the household from farm-produced goods and intended for home use. His account offers a comprehensive survey of family production and consumption, including an extensive discussion of the manufacture of woolen cloth. Because Tryon assumed that only agricultural products—and not home manufactures—were sold or bartered, he minimized the extent to which those handicrafts were exchanged.

Percy Wells Bidwell likewise deemphasized the importance of home manufactures in the exchange systems of early America. "The real meaning of the term 'manufactures,' " Bidwell wrote in "Rural Econ-

---

20. Clemens argues that involvement in international trade and population increase brought "a growth in rural demand that allowed the establishment of more rural retailing, manufacturing, and food processing operations" ("Commerce," 11).

omy in New England," and "the only sense in which it is significant for the purposes of this essay, and indeed, for any economic history . . . includes only articles produced for a wide market, by persons who depend entirely upon the income derived from such activity for their support." "Of manufactures in this sense," he concluded, "there were practically none in New England in 1810." These studies thus systematically underestimated the production of textiles for exchange or sale. Nevertheless, along with Arthur Harrison Cole's exemplary analysis, *The American Wool Manufacture*, they offer a fairly complete description of textile production in the late colonial period.[21]

"The custom of making Coarse Cloths in private families prevails throughout the entire province," Sir Henry Moore, the governor of New York, reported to the Board of Trade in 1767, "and almost in every House a sufficient quantity is manufactured for the use of the family." "Every house swarms with children," he continued, "who are set to work as soon as they are able to Spin and Card; and as every family is furnished with a loom, the itinerant weavers who travel about the country, put the finishing hand to the work." However, Moore added, there was not "the least design of sending any of it to market." Governor William Tryon of North Carolina also stressed the widespread production of textiles and their consumption within the family. "I have not heard of a piece of

21. Rolla Milton Tryon, *Household Manufactures in the United States, 1640–1860: A Study in Industrial History* (Chicago, 1917), 1–12; Percy Wells Bidwell, "Rural Economy in New England at the Beginning of the Nineteenth Century," *Transactions of the Connecticut Academy of Arts and Sciences* 20 (1916): 275; Arthur Harrison Cole, *The American Wool Manufacture*, 2 vols. (Cambridge, Mass., 1926).

woolen or linnen cloth being ever sold that was the manufacture of this province," he told the Board of Trade.[22]

Given the mercantilist character of the southern economy, the local production of textiles even for household consumption is surprising. In times of high export prices, well-to-do planters preferred imported cloth for themselves and for their slaves. In the 1740s Lieutenant Governor William Bull of South Carolina reported the annual importation of 500,000 yards of "Welch plains" for use by the black population. When export income fell, however, local output increased. In 1710 Lieutenant Governor Alexander Spotswood of Virginia indicated the domestic manufacture of "above 40,000 yards of diverse sorts of Woolen, Cotton, and Linnen Cloth." A poor market for tobacco, Spotswood explained, placed the people "under the necessity of attempting to Cloath themselves with their own Manufactures . . . planting Cotton and Sowing Flax . . . mixing the first with wool to supply the wants of coarse Cloathing and Linnen, not only for their Negroes, but for many of the poorer sort of housekeepers."[23]

The testimony of later observers suggests that this experience generated a strong tradition of household cloth production among poor and middling white farm families in the southern colonies. There was "no grand manufactory" in Virginia (where he had lived for twenty-five years), a London merchant told Parlia-

---

22. Moore quoted in Victor S. Clark, *History of Manufactures in the United States* (New York, 1929), 1:16; Tryon quoted in Cole, *American Wool Manufacture*, 1:32.

23. Clark, *History of Manufactures*, 1:210; Spotswood quoted in Tryon, *Household Manufactures*, 49–50.

ment in 1776, "but all the people do manufacture."
"The planters' wives spin the cotton of this country,"
Lieutenant Governor Francis Fauquier reported from
Virginia the following year, and "make a coarse strong
cloth with which they make gowns for themselves and
their children. And sometimes they come to this town
and offer some for sale."[24]

The existence of a local market for domestic cloth
in the Chesapeake is even more surprising. Yet a
variety of evidence clearly indicates its presence. John
Pemberton lived on the Eastern Shore of Maryland.
His account book for 1722 records the purchase of five
yards of "country cloth" and a pair of "country-made
stockings" for a slave. Fifty years later, William Sharp,
who lived in the same region, left an estate that
included ten pounds' worth of wearing apparel and
seventeen yards of country-made cloth.[25]

These cases are not unique. Probate records
clearly reveal the growth in domestic textile-making
capacity. In Prince George's County, Maryland, 32
percent of estate inventories in the 1730s and 1740s
indicated cloth-making capacity—sheep and a combination of spinning wheels, looms, or cards for comb-
ing cotton or wool.[26] And, as table 6.1 demonstrates,
the proportion of estates in six Chesapeake counties
with these craft tools (but not necessarily sheep) increased steadily in the succeeding decades.

Spinning and weaving had become agricultural

---

24. Merchant and Fauquier quoted in Clark, *History of Manufactures*, 1:209, 211.
25. Clemens, *Atlantic Economy*, 92, 142, and table 15.
26. Allan Kulikoff, "Economic Growth and Opportunity in Eighteenth-Century Prince George's County, Maryland" (paper presented at the Cliometrics Conference, Madison, Wis., April 1976),
table 1.

Table 6.1. *Percentage of Maryland and Virginia Estates with Yarn- or Cloth-Making Tools*

			COUNTY			
DATE	Somerset	Anne Arundel	Prince George's	St. Mary's	Talbot	York
1665–77	11	3	0	3		3
1678–87	14	0	0	5		0
1688–99	53	8	9	15		8
1700–1709	53	17	9	16		17
1710–22	66	20	11	32	46	20
1723–32	74	33	29	43	58	33
1733–44	72	57	55	50	73	57
1745–54	89	61	81	71	80	61
1755–67	82	56	75	75	76	56
1768–77	80	59	94	78	78	59

Source: Adapted from Lois Green Carr, "Diversification in the Colonial Chesapeake: Somerset County, Maryland, in Comparative Perspective," in *Colonial Chesapeake Society*, ed. Lois Green Carr, Philip D. Morgan, and Jean B. Russo (Chapel Hill N.C., 1989), figure 2 and table 2.

by-employments for many women in the Chesapeake. Many households spun yarn from wool or flax and sold or exchanged it with weavers, receiving cloth in return. Some merchants and planters had significant investments in home industry. When the merchant Isaac Handy died in 1762, he owned sheep and raised flax and cotton. In addition, his inventory listed "a wheel for spinning wool and two wheels for spinning linen; hackles for preparing flax; 43 pounds of washed wool ready for carding, 30 pounds of hackled flax ready for spinning, 30 pounds of tow, and ten pounds of cotton" as well as a loom and a tackle for weaving.[27]

The families of small-scale freeholders and tenant farmers provided the labor for textile production. Most white planters in the Chesapeake operated on a very narrow economic margin. A family of four might produce an annual crop of 2,000 pounds of tobacco and pay taxes of 140 pounds. To purchase clothing would take an additional 840 pounds of tobacco, leaving about 1,000 pounds (worth about £4.5) for needed food, supplies, and farm equipment. Among tenant farmers rent averaged 500–600 pounds of tobacco, cutting disposable income even further. In these circumstances many white women spun yarn, wove or bartered it for country-made cloth, and sewed it into clothes for their families. By the 1760s the estates of poor planters (worth less than £50) usually contained spinning wheels, and their wives and daughters wove cloth on the looms owned by richer planters. "Among the poor," Thomas Jefferson noted during the War for

---

27. Lois Green Carr, "Diversification in the Colonial Chesapeake: Somerset County, Maryland, in Comparative Perspective," in *Colonial Chesapeake Society*, ed. Lois Green Carr, Philip D. Morgan, and Jean B. Russo (Chapel Hill, N.C., 1989), 375–76.

Independence, "the wife weaves generally and the rich either have a weaver among their servants or employ their poor neighbors." For his part, George Washington expected the wives of white overseers, carpenters, and other workers to make clothes for his slaves.[28]

Cloth manufacture was even more widespread in the Middle Colonies and New England. Many farm families in rural New England produced few export crops. They accumulated specie or credits to pay for imported goods only with great difficulty and had no option but to make their own yarn. Forty percent of the household inventories in York County, Maine, listed spinning wheels in the 1730s, as did 38 percent of those in more highly commercialized Essex County, Massachusetts.[29]

The Middle Colonies exported substantial quantities of wheat, corn, and flour, especially after 1740, and imported large amounts of British dry goods. They also received thousands of Scotch-Irish, German, and Swiss settlers from proto-industrial regions of Europe. Weavers from Krefeld in Germany were among the original settlers of Germantown, Pennsylvania. (Many of their relatives must have been among the six thousand cloth outworkers employed by the firm of Johann Heinrich Scheibler in the Krefeld region in 1762.) These migrants carried their craft skills to America. Working in their own handicraft

---

28. Clemens, *Atlantic Economy*, 159–60; Jefferson quoted in Tryon, *Household Manufactures*, 121; Julia Cherry Spruill, *Women's Life and Work in the Southern Colonies* (1938; reprint, New York, 1972), 75, 78, 83.
29. Laurel Thatcher Ulrich, "Martha Ballard and Her 'Girls': Women's Work in Eighteenth-Century Maine," in *Work and Labor in Early America*, ed. Stephen Innes (Chapel Hill, N.C., 1988), 94.

shops—probably with small networks of female outwork spinners—Germantown weavers produced high-
quality worsted fabrics and stockings. They sold these
goods both locally and in the Chesapeake colonies.
Other German migrants pursued similar economic
strategies. Palatinate Germans settled in Frederick,
Maryland, in the 1740s and carried on a commerce
in domestic linen, woolen, and leather goods. To
clothe their slaves, some tidewater planters purchased
Osnaburg-type fabrics woven by Germans in the western county of Augusta, Virginia. Part of that production took place outside artisans' shops. In 1772 weavers
in Somerset County, New Jersey, asked the assembly
"to prohibit Farmers and others keeping Looms in
their Houses and following the weaving Business."[30]

Linen production had a particularly strong base
in the agricultural countryside. Middle Colony farmers formed part of a transatlantic system of textile
production. To make soft, high-quality linens, Irish
manufacturers harvested their flax before it was fully
mature. To plant the next year's crop, they imported
thousands of bushels of flaxseed from America. This
mercantilist-inspired export system unwittingly encouraged colonial production of rough linens for local
use. By seeding an acre with one bushel of flaxseed, a
Middle Colony farmer harvested four to ten bushels
of seed (worth 12 shillings a bushel). Each acre also
yielded eighty to two hundred pounds of hackled fiber
for the production of coarse cloth.[31]

30. Lis and Soly, *Poverty,* 151; Jeffrey M. Diefendorf, "Social
Mobility in the Rhineland in the Eighteenth Century" (paper
presented at the Krefeld Conference, Krefeld, Germany, June
1983); Clark, *History of Manufactures,* 1:206–7, 223; weavers quoted
in Morris, "Labor," 81.
31. Lemon, *Best Poor Man's Country,* 158, n. 33; Shepherd and
Walton, *Shipping,* appendix 4, table 2.

New England farmers grew flax as well. They exported some to Ireland but used even more for domestic textile production. Scotch-Irish communities in New Hampshire fabricated high-quality linens. Farmers of English ancestry in Massachusetts and Connnecticut mixed flax with wool from their abundant flocks of sheep to make durable linsey-woolsey. In addition, the New England colonies imported 300,000 pounds of West Indian cotton annually between 1768 and 1772, presumably for use by home manufacturers.[32] Throughout the mainland settlements, textile production was an integral part of the yearly activities of most of the white population.

Suddenly, rough homespun garments became fashionable, as the colonists protested against restrictions imposed by the British mercantile system. Following the Stamp Act crisis of 1765 and the nonimportation agreements, political leaders advocated the wearing of American-made cloth. Previously, affluent colonials had shunned the coarse fabrics made and worn by rural folk. Now they laid away their smooth imported cloth and elevated the humble fabricators of homespun to the status of patriotic heroines. Newspapers celebrated the spinning and weaving exploits of worthy "Daughters of Liberty" and reported their productive achievements. One Massachusetts town claimed an annual output of 30,000 yards of cloth, East Hartford, Connecticut, reported 17,000, and the borough of Elizabeth, New Jersey, declared an output of "upwards of 100,000 yards of linnen and woolen cloth." For individual families, an annual output of 500 yards of cloth became a newsworthy event. From

---

32. Shepherd and Walton, *Shipping*, appendix 4, table 8.

Woodbridge, New Jersey, the Freeman, Smith, and Heard families proudly announced they had attained that goal.[33]

In the past some domestic cloth produced in households or in ethnic communities had entered regional markets. Boston merchants sold "white and striped homespun" in the 1740s and shipped two hundred homespun jackets to Albany a few years later. By the late 1760s documentary evidence of production for sale becomes much more abundant. Governor Benning Wentworth of New Hampshire estimated the annual sale of 25,000 yards of high-priced but durable linen in his province. Merchant Enoch Brown advertised that he took "all Sorts of Country-made Clothes" at his store on Boston Neck, "either on Commission, or in Exchange for any kind of West India Goods at a reasonable Rate." In Philadelphia, middling traders and artisans (and not transatlantic mercantile houses) formed the "United Company for Promoting American Manufactures." By employing three hundred women and children in their homes, the company avoided the capital expenditures and worker unrest that had doomed earlier urban manufactory ventures. Two years after its creation, the company declared a dividend.[34]

The United Company was nearly unique. Even after the nonimportation agreements American merchants and entrepreneurs did not develop an extensive

---

33. Tryon, *Household Manufactures*, 108–9; Cole, *American Wool Manufacture*, 1:191.

34. Clark, *History of Manufactures*, 1:207; Cole, *American Wool Manufacture*, 1:31n, 62n; Gary B. Nash, *The Urban Crucible: Social Change, Political Consciousness, and the Origins of the American Revolution* (Cambridge, Mass., 1979), 336.

putting-out system. Their hesitancy did not reflect the absence of skilled and willing workers. As early as 1762 the merchant William Pollard reported that many older people in Lancaster, Pennsylvania, had turned to linen making. By 1776 the *Pennsylvania Gazette* argued that "many poor people (old and young) would spin a little if they knew where to turn it into ready money at the end of the week or month."[35] The availability of cheaper and better textiles from proto-industrial regions of England and Germany represented a more significant barrier. Ocean transport was inexpensive, and the skilled but impoverished cottagers of Europe had no choice but to accept low prices for their fabrics.

In fact, colonial merchants generally avoided the mobilization of rural households for market production. They relied primarily on consumer demand for West Indian or British goods to secure a supply of goods. Merchant houses invested significantly in production only in the New England fishing industry, backcountry Chesapeake tobacco-growing regions, and low-country South Carolina rice plantations. Mostly they used their surplus income in other ways. As Virginia D. Harrington has demonstrated, New York merchants bought provincial bonds, extended loans to individuals, and purchased real estate—both urban rental properties and speculative frontier tracts. Some merchants invested in urban industries directly related to commerce, such as distilling, shipbuilding, and sugar refining. A few devoted capital resources to the production of iron for export, thus providing rural

---

35. Lemon, *Best Poor Man's Country*, 96; Clark, *History of Manufactures*, 1:217.

by-employment in woodcutting and hauling. And, during the Seven Years' War, merchants with military contracts systematically tapped the agricultural market for grain and meat. Even then, however, most mercantile capital flowed into the more speculative (and potentially more lucrative) enterprises of marine insurance and privateering.[36]

Thus, on the eve of the War for Independence, textile manufacture in the American mainland colonies was extensive, but its marketing was limited. Most rural folk made some or all of their own cloth, thereby restricting the demand for fabrics. The availability of imported textiles, both cheap cloth for slaves and fine fabrics for the well-to-do, similarly discouraged entrepreneurs from mobilizing rural producers in a putting-out system. Finally, the traditional merchant preference for investment in financial instruments, real estate, and speculative maritime ventures deprived the textile industry of commercial leadership. Even so, a *Kaufsystem* of textile production existed among Germans in the Middle and Southern Colonies and Scotch-Irish settlers in northern New England, and many English households exchanged or sold some textile products. The *Verlagsystem*, however, was conspicuously absent because of mercantilist policies and an abundance of fertile land.

IV

The Revolutionary War severely disrupted established commercial patterns. The royal navy and British pri-

---

36. Virginia D. Harrington, *The New York Merchant on the Eve of the Revolution* (1935; reprint, Gloucester, Mass., 1964), chapter 4.

vateers destroyed the New England fishing industry and seized hundreds of American ships bound for Europe and the West Indies. British troops occupied major American ports and raided towns and supply depots along the coast. The court system functioned erratically, making it difficult to collect debts. Revolutionary armies requisitioned goods and offered increasingly worthless notes and currency in return. Merchants of a conservative temperament, such as James Beekman of New York, retired to the countryside to await the return of financial stability. They lived off the proceeds of prewar profits and returned to trade only as inflation sapped their incomes.

More adventurous merchants exploited the speculative opportunities provided by the wartime economy. They braved capture to trade with Europe, charging high fees and selling scarce goods at exorbitant prices. Many merchants profited handsomely from privateering early in the war. Then, after 1777, they lost many of their ships to the royal navy. Agile entrepreneurs began speculating in the financial paper spewed forth by the printing presses of the state governments and the Continental Congress. By 1781 in Maryland, merchants offered soldiers immediate credit for store goods, taking currency and western land patents at one-seventh their face value. "Speculation, peculation and an insatiable thirst for riches," Washington complained, had infected "every order of Men."[37]

Speculation in depreciated currency indicated the

37. White, *Beekmans*, 480–515; Edward C. Papenfuse, *In Pursuit of Profit: The Annapolis Merchants in the Era of the American Revolution, 1763–1805* (Baltimore, Md., 1975), 94; Washington quoted in East, *Business Enterprise*, 30.

growing financial importance of the state governments. The government of Maryland spent £500,000
between 1776 and 1779, twelve times its prewar expenditures. The drain on Maryland's treasury doubled
during the following three years. Supplying military
needs became a major enterprise. Before 1779 clothing, munitions, and other military supplies consumed
60 percent of the state's budget.

Those imported manufactures came primarily
from new European sources. The location of Nantes
on the Loire River "makes it the only port for the
American trade," noted one French trader, "as we
draw the linen and woolen manufactures of the North
by water carriage and even those of Flanders and
Switzerland." Maryland army contractors promptly
dispatched orders for "oznaburgs, coarse linens and
woolens, Russian drabbs and sheeting, some shoes if
they can be had good and reasonable." Most European
manufactures cost more than English goods and were
of lower quality. Nevertheless, they commanded high
prices in wartime America. French and German fabrics sold quickly in Baltimore at three times their
invoice value, which already included charges for
freight and insurance. Such a markup was double or
triple that on prewar English imports.[38]

Neither this trade nor the fortuitous capture of
British supply ships met civilian or military demand.
To insure adequate supplies for its military forces, the
Revolutionary government of Connecticut placed an
embargo in 1776 on the export of cloth, shoes, and
tanned leather. In New Haven the committee of in-

---

38. Papenfuse, *In Pursuit of Profit*, 92–93, 118, 100, 128; Cole,
American Wool Manufacture, 1:50.

spection urged merchants to purchase domestic wool and flax and to promote the manufacture of cloth. "Clothing is what we are deficient in," the *Connecticut Journal* complained, while from Maryland Charles Carroll lamented that "arms are still wanting and cloathing still more so."[39]

Household producers increased their output in a brave but futile attempt to compensate for the annual loss of 10 to 13 million yards of imported fabrics. As early as 1776 Revolutionary forces in New York City wore country linens from Pennsylvania. The steady parade of British victories and American retreats accentuated existing shortages. In the Battle of Long Island, Captain Edward Rogers of Cornwall, Connecticut, lost "all the shirts except the one on my back & all the stocking except thos on my legs" as well as two coats and a blanket. "The making of cloath . . . must go on," he wrote plaintively to his wife. "I must have shirts and stockings & a jacket sent me as soon as possable & a blankit."[40]

Throughout the rebellious provinces the production of domestic cloth increased, both for private and military purposes. When the Marquis de Chastellux visited a farmstead in Farmington, Connecticut, he found its residents "making a sort of camblet, as well as another woolen stuff with blue and white stripes for women's dress. . . . The sons and grandsons of the family were at work; one workman can make five yards a day." Encouraged by the state government, a Mary-

---

39. Linda Susan Luchowski, "Sunshine Soldiers: New Haven and the American Revolution" (Ph.D. diss., State University of New York, Buffalo, 1976), 82–85; Papenfuse, *In Pursuit of Profit*, 97.

40. Quoted in James P. Walsh, *Connecticut Industry and the Revolution* (Hartford, Conn., 1978), 22.

land clothing contractor set up a small factory with sixteen looms. Soon he had engaged enough outwork spinners to produce one hundred yards of linen per day. Yet production remained both limited and expensive. Weavers in "great numbers in our parts have enlisted," he complained; "those that remain have advanced their prices." To cope with soaring prices (the result, in this case, both of currency inflation and the scarcity of cloth), town authorities in New England regulated the cost of homemade fabrics and the rates charged by spinners and weavers.[41]

State governments likewise attempted to obtain adequate supplies of military clothing at reasonable prices. The requisition system employed in Connecticut was the most elaborate and successful. In July 1776 the governor and council of safety imposed a clothing levy. They called upon the citizens of Hartford to provide 1,000 coats, 1,000 vests, and 1,600 shirts and assessed smaller towns on a proportionate basis. The council assumed that these items would be mostly "homemade" and authorized additional purchases of shoes, hats, and blankets. In October state officials requisitioned tents, iron pots, wooden bowls, and canteens. A year later the state government asked the towns to provide shirts, woolen "overhalls," stockings, and shoes for each of their men serving in the Connecticut Continental Line.[42]

While the authorities promised to pay a "fair

---

41. Clark, *History of Manufactures*, 1:225; Morris, *Government*, 300–303; Papenfuse, *In Pursuit of Profit*, 89–90; Cole, *American Wool Manufacture*, 1:20n.

42. Walsh, *Connecticut Industry*, 19–20; Albert E. Van Dusen, "The Trade of Revolutionary Connecticut" (Ph.D. diss., University of Pennsylvania, 1948), 187–88, 266, 299.

price," they gathered these military supplies through the political process rather than the market system. Town meetings delegated responsibility for these levies to special committees of fifteen to thirty men. The committees sent the clothing to the state's purchasing clothier; he immediately dispatched it to the state clothier, who traveled with Connecticut's Continental troops. The state clothier distributed the goods and received payment from Congress, which deducted the cost from the soldiers' pay.[43] Initially, this requisition process worked smoothly. Local committees encouraged domestic manufacturing and paid for clothing at prices determined by the wages of Continental troops. Waterbury provided shirts, frocks, shoes, and tow cloth worth seven hundred pounds. The town charged the state government only 28 shillings in constables' fees for impressing various items. As wartime demands increased and inflation spiraled, the supply of clothing steadily diminished. By October 1779 Norwich had to pay interest on clothing "loaned" to the town, and the town meeting issued a mandatory order requiring citizens to contribute goods.[44]

Direct requisition of clothing worked as well as it did for a number of reasons. Many Americans made their own fabrics and shoes or obtained them by barter with friends or neighbors. They were therefore accustomed to a nonmarket exchange system. Moreover, the inhabitants of many towns had traditionally paid local taxes in labor or in kind. Finally, the existing market for clothes was even smaller than that for cloth fabrics. Families either sewed their own garments or

---

43. Walsh, *Connecticut Industry*, 20–21.
44. Ibid., 23–25.

employed the services of a tailor. This absence of a commercial market for shirts, trousers, and other items of clothing encouraged families to comply with political requisitions.

More important yet, these levies provided patriot women with the opportunity to contribute directly to the war effort. Women and daughters traditionally handled many aspects of cloth manufacture. Men usually sheared sheep and hackled flax, but women washed and combed these fibers, spun them into thread and yarn, and sewed the finished fabrics into garments for each family member. The nonimportation agreements of the 1760s momentarily wrapped these mundane female activities in patriotic glory. The real contribution of women to American independence came during the Revolutionary War, however, when it attracted less public attention (and, subsequently, much less study by scholars). As patriot and loyalist soldiers and militiamen marched back and forth across the countryside, fighting occasional battles, their wives and children worked constantly on farms and in workshops. In general, they maintained a sufficient level of production to supply the state governments with the grain, meat, and clothing requisitioned for military purposes.

Documentary records from the 1780s and early 1790s suggest that the wartime experience broadened the scope of women's work. Many women now added weaving to their repertoire of domestic skills. In 1785 the daughters of Martha Ballard of Hallowell, Maine, were spinning flax and carrying it to three women to weave. Two years later the Ballards acquired their own loom. During the next five years their teenage daughters (and young female servants) wove a variety of fabrics, often assisted by the skilled women of the neighborhood. By the 1790s, 50 percent of the probate inventories in Hallowell listed looms, a clear indication that weaving had become a normal female household responsibility.[45]

A similar evolution took place in the Hudson River valley, despite easy access to imported goods. Alexander Coventry, a relatively well-to-do Scottish immigrant living on a riverfront property in Columbia County, New York, employed a series of spinners and weavers in the early 1790s and had a "short coat and trousers . . . made from wool off my own sheep." Twenty-three of the forty-four itemized probate inventories in nearby Ulster County between 1788 and 1792 contained one or more spinning wheels. In addition, the inventories listed twenty-one woolen wheels and sixteen looms. The production of cloth in Ulster County increased steadily in subsequent decades, reaching 6.1 yards per capita in 1820 and peaking at 8.6 yards in 1825. By that time, the county's cloth industry supported thirty fulling mills and thirty-eight carding machines. Even as early as the end of the War for Independence, clothmaking had become part of the production and exchange systems of a majority of rural families.[46]

The political requisition of foodstuffs was a less successful aspect of the war effort. Established mar-

---

45. Ulrich, "Martha Ballard," 94–95, provides some interesting data, but there is no systematic and detailed study of women's productive activities during the revolution. See, in general, Mary Beth Norton, *Liberty's Daughters: The Revolutionary Experience of American Women, 1750–1800* (Boston, 1980), and Nancy F. Cott, *The Bonds of Womanhood: "Women's Sphere" in New England, 1780–1835* (New Haven, Conn., 1977), chapter 1.

46. Alexander Coventry, *Memoirs of an Emigrant: The Journal of Alexander Coventry, M.D.*, 2 vols. (Albany, N.Y., 1978), 1:450, 536, 620, 629, 645; David M. Ellis, *Landlords and Farmers in the Hudson and Mohawk Region, 1790–1850* (Ithaca, N.Y., 1946), 110; Michael Merrill, "The Transformation of Ulster County, 1750–1850" (unpublished paper, 1985).

kets for food existed both in the West Indies and in Europe. British occupation of American ports and the depredations of privateers partially closed those export markets, but military demands provided new outlets for farmers. Originally the British ministry planned to supply its army completely from American sources, but patriot domination of the countryside made that impossible. The ministry therefore shipped flour and salted meat from Britain, as well as tents, clothing, and munitions. Even so, the British army depended on local farmers for fresh food, fodder, horses, and fuel. Each day the main army of thirty-five thousand men and four thousand horses consumed thirty-seven tons of food, thirty-eight tons of hay and oats, and (during the winter) huge supplies of wood. To attract those supplies, British officials paid in specie—not the depreciating currency offered by patriot merchants and the commissariat of the American army. Merchants and farmers with access to British encampments in New York, Newport, Philadelphia, Savannah, and elsewhere frequently traded with the British.[47]

This lucrative commerce provoked accusations of treason and, on many occasions, armed confrontations with Revolutionary militiamen. Yet the flow of British specie aided the rebel cause. Eventually this hard currency found its way into the hands of patriot merchants, who used it to purchase desperately needed arms, clothing, and other supplies in Europe. Connecticut authorities frequently bowed to this economic reality. In 1781, for example, they allowed the

---

47. R. Arthur Bowler, *Logistics and the Failure of the British Army in America, 1775–1783* (Princeton, N.J., 1975), 30, 57, 156.

town of Windsor to export one thousand bushels of corn and used the specie to purchase linen cloth.[48]

To supply its own forces, the Continental Congress created an army commissariat. This new bureaucracy was not large. The office of the clothier general employed only a few purchasing clothiers in each state. Yet locally based merchant-agents extended the reach of this administrative system into hundreds of counties and townships. Farmers in the Hudson River valley would sell only a part of their wheat in the winter of 1776–77, a local correspondent told General Philip Schuyler: "The remainder they are determined to Grind themselves and sell the Flour to the Army in the Spring when they expect the price will be much higher."[49]

Beginning in late 1777 there were consistent and, at times, severe shortages of grain throughout the Middle Atlantic and New England states. After Saratoga, General John Burgoyne's army of five thousand men and their fifteen hundred patriot guards depleted supplies of food and fuel near Boston. The return of the main British army to New York in 1778, trailed by a sizable force of Continentals, likewise created shortages. In conjunction with the arrival of a French expeditionary force in Rhode Island, these troop movements set off a mad scramble for scarce resources. Military contractors estimated the French demand for flour for the five months beginning in May 1779 at forty-five thousand barrels. This total was more than triple the amount of bread and flour shipped annually from New England to the West

---

48. Van Dusen, "Trade," 349.
49. Schuyler quoted in East, *Business Enterprise*, 101–2.

Indies between 1768 and 1772. It composed one-fourth of annual exports of bread and flour exported from the grain-rich Middle Colonies during the same years.[50] Commissariat agents, merchants with French military contracts, and traders engaged in illicit commerce with the British army competed for food, wood, and fodder across a four-state region.

That extraordinary military demand may have increased the commercial orientation of many farming communities in the northern states. Before the Revolutionary War farmers in some regions were closely tied to the market, but others participated in the commercial world in only a limited fashion. Their families consumed most of the output of their farms or bartered it within the local community. Only the surplus, a relatively small proportion of total production, entered into the wider market. During the war, state officials requisitioned food, clothing, and other supplies from every village and hamlet. Army contractors roamed the countryside, offering high prices for food, horses, and wagon transport. By the end of the war more farm households undoubtedly understood the potential opportunities (and dangers) offered by the market exchange system.

This economic change involved shifts in the realms of production, distribution, and credit. In the first place, the upward movement of prices prompted some farm families to increase their output. In Massachusetts, for example, Winifred B. Rothenberg's weighted index of on-the-farm prices demonstrates

---

50. Richard Buel, Jr., *Dear Liberty: Connecticut's Mobilization for the Revolutionary War* (Middletown, Conn., 1980), 150, 159; Shepherd and Walton, *Shipping*, appendix 4, table 5; East, *Business Enterprise*, 153–63.

that producers received from 30 percent to 50 percent more between 1776 and 1783. Farmers had to pay higher prices for supplies and equipment as well, cutting their profits from increased sales. Yet many families raised more crops for sale and expanded their winter by-industries. Farmers in Windham, Connecticut, increased their production of saltpeter for gunpowder, while the manufacture of shoes became a major enterprise in New Jersey and Massachusetts.[51]

The specialization of work and the intensification of labor continued after the war. In Concord, Massachusetts, the proportion of the population engaged in crafts and trade increased from 15 percent to 33 percent between 1771 and 1801. And the farmers of the town, Robert Gross has argued, now "labored more intensively than ever . . . chopping wood, reclaiming land for English hay, digging potatoes, making butter."[52]

Significant changes in the distribution system occurred as well. Stimulated by wartime opportunities, country traders and local entrepreneurs became more avid and aggressive in the pursuit of business. These small-scale traders now had greater freedom, for the war broke the hold of established merchants and their backcountry trading networks. In 1766 major New York City merchants had secured legislation that prohibited peddlers from plying their trade. In 1770 the colonial assembly removed that absolute ban

51. Winifred B. Rothenberg, "A Price Index for Rural Massachusetts, 1750–1855," *Journal of Economic History* 39 (1979), table 2; Alan Dawley, *Class and Community: The Industrial Revolution in Lynn* (Cambridge, Mass., 1976), 14–15, appendix A.
52. Gross, "Culture," 57.

(probably because it was unenforceable) but continued to discourage itinerant trading through licensing fees.[53] These legal restraints evaporated during the Revolutionary War, and many small-scale traders and storekeepers became prominent military contractors.

The career of Oliver Phelps of Granville, Connecticut, indicates the new opportunities created by the wartime demand. In 1777 Phelps won appointment as state superintendent of army purchases. Once a mere shopkeeper, Phelps now prospered by supplying the state through his own firm and through newly formed partnerships with other entrepreneurs. In 1780 Phelps emerged as a leading supplier of beef to the French army, working as a subcontractor for the resourceful Jeremiah Wadsworth.[54]

Wadsworth himself rose through the ranks of the wartime bureaucracy. His ascent to a position of great wealth and prominence began in 1775. As a young man of thirty-two (with an inherited estate of two thousand pounds from his minister-father), Wadsworth became commissary of supplies for Connecticut. By 1776 he had advanced to the post of deputy commissary general, responsible for the requisition of Continental army supplies throughout New England. Recognizing his superb administrative talents, the Continental Congress elevated Wadsworth to the rank of commissary general. Wadsworth held this position from April 1778 to December 1779, and it made him a wealthy man. As commissary general, he received a commission of 0.5 percent on all purchases. Equally

---

53. White, *Beekmans*, 467.
54. East, *Business Enterprise*, 56.

important, his post provided Wadsworth with the political leverage to win the lucrative supply contract for the French army in America.[55]

Scores of country traders pursued similar, if less glorious, administrative and mercantile careers during the Revolutionary War. Their entrepreneurship expanded the *Kaufsystem* of proto-industrial production during and after the war. In the Connecticut River valley, for example, merchants, peddlers, and itinerant traders appeared in growing numbers during the 1780s. They bought cheese, potatoes, and salted meat from farmers, as well as substantial quantities of household manufactures. While traveling through Berlin, New Hampshire, in 1797, Timothy Dwight learned that, before independence, locally produced tinware had been sold by peddlers with a "horse and two baskets." "After the war," he reported, "carts and wagons were used for this purpose. . . . A young man is furnished by the proprietor with a horse, and a cart covered with a box. . . . This vehicle within a few years has, indeed, been frequently exchanged for a wagon; and then . . . these young men direct themselves to the Southern States."[56]

As a result of the system of wartime finance, these traders operated in a world filled with new and diverse monetary instruments. In 1784 merchants in New Haven advertised goods for sale in return for specie or for "banknotes, Morris' notes, Mr. Hillegas'

---

55. Ibid., chapter 4, esp. pp. 80–92.
56. Christopher S. Clark, "Household Economy, Market Exchange, and the Rise of Capitalism in the Connecticut Valley, 1800–1860," *Journal of Social History* 13 (1979): 170; Bidwell, "Rural Economy," 259; Dwight quoted in Tryon, *Household Manufactures*, 265–66.

notes, Pickering's certificates, soldiers' notes, state money." Major merchants, such as the Burrells of Boston, speculated heavily in these paper certificates. In December 1784 the Burrells purchased £2,445 in Pierce's Continental notes, paying three to five shillings on the pound. Redemption at face value would yield a 400 percent profit. Panicked by Shays' Rebellion, the Burrells settled for a smaller return, selling their notes at seven shillings on the pound in 1786.[57]

The uncertainties of the Revolutionary era prompted many men and women to adopt this calculating form of economic behavior. While relatively few Americans were speculators, everyone had to contend with the flood of paper currency. Most rural folk tried to avoid cash transactions; instead they expanded their reliance on traditional nonmarket systems of exchange among families and neighbors. If farmers did sell their grain, meat, and household manufactures, they demanded specie—or a premium for currency transactions. Local traders would accept printed notes in return for store goods, but only at a substantial discount. The greatest inflationary spiral in American history forced nearly every family to look out more carefully and more persistently for its economic self-interest.

The War for Independence, the Pennsylvania *Centinel* suggested in 1785, had removed that "great reluctance to innovation, so remarkable in old communities." David Ramsay, the contemporary historian of the revolution, argued that the demands of war had encouraged—at times, even forced—Americans to act

---

57. East, *Business Enterprise*, 271–73.

"in a line far beyond that to which they had been accustomed."[58]

While the most dramatic transformations came in the political sphere, economic change was not insignificant. Household manufacturing and artisan production increased substantially throughout the Middle Atlantic and New England states during the war. And greater quantities of rural manufactures now entered the commercial exchange system. The experience of the Reverend Medad Rogers, minister of the small town of New Fairfield, Connecticut (population 742 in 1790), offers a humble but instructive example. As his salary, Rogers received the use of a hundred-acre farm and an annual stipend of one hundred dollars, payable in cash or in kind. During one eighteen-month period in the early 1790s, the minister traded for store goods with no less than 450 pounds of cheese—made by his parishioners, paid as salary, and distributed through his barter into the wider world of commerce.[59]

The sum of thousands of similar local transactions had a significant impact on the American economy. The British consul at Philadelphia, Phineas Bond, reported in 1789 that "among the country people in Mass. Bay coarse linens of their own making are in such general use as to lessen the importation of checks and even of coarse Irish linens nearly ⅔rds." "In the 4 Eastern States viz. New Hampshire, Mass. Bay, Rhode I. and Connect.," Bond continued, "the people manufacture much larger quantities of woolens for their own use than they did before the war. . . .

---

58. Quotations from ibid., 323; Duane Ball and Gary M. Walton, "Productivity Change in Pennsylvania Agriculture," *Journal of Economic History* 36 (1976): 113.

59. Bidwell, "Rural Economy," 366–67.

40,000 yards of coarse New England linen have been sold in Philada within the last year." "Here then is a *surplus* of household manufactures sold *out of the state*," Tench Coxe noted with evident satisfaction a few years later; "it is an acknowledged fact that New England linens have affected the price and importation of that article from New York to Georgia."[60]

Nonetheless, demand far outstripped domestic supplies. "America must always look to other countries for a supply of woolen manufactures," Bond concluded in his detailed state-by-state survey. At the same time he warned that "many useful domestic manufactures . . . have lately been resumed in the Eastern and middle States from motives of economy."[61] In the winter season, one traveler to Massachusetts noted, "the inhabitants of Middleborough are principally employed in making nails, of which they send large quantities to market. This business is a profitable addition to their husbandry; and fills up a part of the year, in which, otherwise, many of them would find little employment." By expanding their by-industries during the wartime crisis, northern farm families had found yet another way to cope with the traditional problem of population growth. Moreover, their efforts partially offset the decline in foreign trade during the Revolutionary War and nearly maintained traditional living standards.[62]

This process of "internal" economic development

---

60. Report enclosed in Phineas Bond to the Duke of Leeds, 10 November 1789, in American Historical Association, *Annual Report . . . 1869*, 2 vols. (Washington, D.C., 1897), 1:651; Coxe in Tryon, *Household Manufactures*, 134.

61. Bond, *Report*, 1:632, 631.

62. Quotation from Bidwell, "Rural Economy," 272n.

resembled that described by Diane Lindstrom for the Philadelphia region in the early nineteenth century. The rural, small-town, and urban settlements in this area "reaped the highest per capita incomes of any section," she explains, "by producing an abundance of agricultural, extractive, and in some cases manufactured commodities" and by increasing "the quantity of trade" among themselves. A similar, if more limited, diversification of economic activity and exchange had taken place during the Revolutionary War. When Brissot de Warville visited Worcester County, Massachusetts, in 1795, he found "almost all these houses . . . inhabited by men who are both cultivators and artisans; one is a tanner, another a shoemaker, another sells goods; but all are farmers."[63]

V

Thus Americans emerged from the Revolutionary era with an expanded domestic industrial base. They participated as well in more active systems of local exchange and commercial markets. In fact, they were now full members in a system of proto-industrial production that spanned the North Atlantic Ocean. Like their European counterparts, American households processed a greater variety of farm products for market sale: salted beef and pork, hides for shoes, wool and flax for cloth, and milk for cheese. Rural manufacturers also processed increasing quantities of

---

63. Diane Lindstrom, *Economic Development in the Philadelphia Region, 1810–1850* (New York, 1978), 8–12; quotation from Bidwell, "Rural Economy," 263.

nonagricultural goods, such as tinware, nails, and furniture.

As of 1790 or even 1815, however, the United States had only experienced one mode of proto-industrialization. Unlike parts of Britain and Europe, the American countryside still did not contain a large population of impoverished cottagers. Most domestic manufacturers remained members of economically viable farm families. The *Kaufsystem* of proto-industrialization remained the norm. As various historians of the European experience have demonstrated, this type of cottage system often maintained or even raised rural incomes. As yet, merchant capitalists did not dominate rural production through an oppressive *Verlagssystem*. The appearance of dependent outworkers and a capitalist-run system of production in New England and parts of the Middle Atlantic states occurred mainly after 1815, with the massive expansion of the shoe, palm-leaf hat, and button industries. By that time as well, the growing production of yarn and thread in factories had generated additional rural outworkers, especially weavers.[64]

A few studies, based on careful research in local records, describe the *Kaufsystem* of proto-industrialization that predominated during the first half century of American independence. They demonstrate increased agricultural by-employments and cottage industry in many seaboard areas and hint at the existence of intraregional zones of production. This defining characteristic of proto-industrialization ap-

---

64. Clark, "Household Economy," 169–80; Thomas Dublin, "Women and the Dimensions of Outwork in Nineteenth-Century New England" (paper presented at Berkshire Conference, Smith College, June 1981).

pears in the evolution of "differing economic areas" based on "soil resources, new crops, and the development of local crafts and home industries" in late colonial Maryland.[65] It is suggested as well by the emergence of new inheritance patterns in the commercial agricultural town of Wethersfield, Connecticut, in the early nineteenth century and the continuation of traditional practices in "subsistence plus" agriculture and craft towns in the nearby uplands.[66]

The best-documented case of intraregional specialization also comes from Connecticut. The research of Edward S. Cooke indicates the evolution of distinct types of socioeconomic structures and furniture-making traditions in the adjoining Connecticut towns of Newtown and Woodbury.[67] As table 6.2 suggests, Newtown residents developed a strong craft orientation within a diversified agricultural economy in the early nineteenth century. The value of the artisanal equipment in Newtown rose, while production of wheat declined sharply and the output of dairy goods and meat remained steady. In contrast, Woodbury farmers maintained, and perhaps expanded, their agricultural output.

If economic upheavals during the Revolutionary era initiated these structural changes, they nevertheless took more than a generation to come to fruition. Various factors account for the slow maturation of proto-industrial regions in the United States. First, the absence of a substantial and concentrated market for finished goods

---

65. Carr, "Diversification," 343, 342.
66. Ditz, "Proto-Industrialization" and *Property and Kinship: Inheritance in Early Connecticut, 1750–1820* (Princeton, N.J., 1986), 1–2.
67. Edward S. Cooke, Jr., "Rural Artisanal Culture: The Preindustrial Joiners of Newtown and Woodbury, Connecticut, 1760–1820" (Ph.D. diss., Boston University, 1984).

Table 6.2 Production in Newtown and Woodbury, Connecticut, 1770–1824

	MEAN VALUE OF ARTISANAL EQUIPMENT		ESTATES WITH WHEAT IN THE INVENTORY		INVENTORY VALUE OF MEAT AND DAIRY PRODUCTS	
DATE	Newtown	Woodbury	Newtown	Woodbury	Newtown	Woodbury
1770–74	£ 1.0	£ 3.3	53%	46%	£19.12	£ 4.11
1780–84	2.9	1.0	50	55	9.2	12.5
1790–94	5.7	1.1	47	35	4.19	8.4
1800–1804	2.10	3.6	17	35	9.2	14.14
1810–14	7.6	1.19	15	25	8.12	11.12
1820–24	10.6	3.13	6	28	5.0	8.17

Source: Adapted from Edward S. Cooke, Jr., "Rural Artisanal Culture: Preindustrial Joiners of Newtown and Woodbury, Connecticut, 1760–1820" (Ph.D. diss., Boston University, 1984), tables 6, 8, and 11.

discouraged merchant investment in rural industry. Fewer than 4 million people lived in the United States in 1790, and they were dispersed over a large geographic area. Significantly, the first market for American manufactures emerged in the plantation regions of the Chesapeake and South Carolina, with the demand for cheaply made shoes for the large population of enslaved blacks. Second, rigorous British competition inhibited domestic production of textiles. An advanced *Verlagsystem* of proto-industrialization and a highly skilled work force in various regions of England enabled merchants to flood the American market with low-priced, high-quality fabrics.

However substantial, these obstacles were not insurmountable. In the aftermath of independence, purposeful action by American merchants and governments could have fostered domestic manufacturing and a much more diverse and substantial putting-out system. The experience of two textile enterprises suggests both the potential for the development of a *Verlagsystem* and the reasons for its failure. Both the Hartford Manufactory and the Massachusetts Woolen Manufactory owed their genesis to the investment capital generated by the Revolutionary War. In 1788 Jeremiah Wadsworth, the driving force behind the Hartford enterprise, organized production on a putting-out basis, using a central workshop (staffed by English army deserters and former prisoners of war) for wool sorting and cloth finishing. When President Washington visited the manufactory in 1792, he reported that most of the spinning and weaving was done "by the country people, who are paid by the cut."[68]

Dr. John Manning organized a similar enterprise in Ipswich, Massachusetts, in 1794. "The Town's poor

---

68. Cole, *American Wool Manufacture*, 1:65–69.

. . . are daily increasing," Manning informed the state legislature. "Almost all the farms have been divided and subdivided so as to yield little more than a supply of provisions for the owners, and being so full of inhabitants, is well calculated for a manufacturing town." Manning's almost classic description of the preconditions for a substantial cottage industry neglected to mention that Ipswich was already a manufacturing center. In 1790 six hundred women and children employed by local entrepreneurs had fabricated twenty-eight thousand yards of lace and thirteen thousand yards of edging.[69]

Taking advantage of this ample labor supply, Manning invested the returns from his Massachusetts state securities in looms. He housed them in both private homes and a central factory and began the production of coarse woolens, blankets, and flannels. By 1800, however, Manning and Wadsworth were out of the textile business. Both fledgling enterprises were the victims of competition from British goods, as were earlier American textile ventures. On 4 July 1788 calico printers joined other artisans in a Philadelphia parade celebrating the ratification of the new U.S. Constitution. Their intricately designed flag carried the motto "May the union government protect the manufacturers of America."[70]

In fact, as John R. Nelson, Jr., has argued, the Hamiltonian Federalists largely ignored the pleas of these textile workers and of other domestic manufacturers. Indeed, Hamilton's financial policies deprived

---

69. Ginsburg, "Political and Economic Impact," 16.

70. Motto quoted in David J. Jeremy, *Transatlantic Industrial Revolution: The Diffusion of Textile Technologies between Britain and America, 1790–1830s* (Cambridge, Mass., 1981), 20.

the handicraft and putting-out industries of funds and of tariff protection. The treasury secretary's ingenious schemes for debt redemption and assumption ignited a fierce speculation in Continental and state securities. Merchants and urban investors used their capital to buy war certificates and bonds rather than to invest in rural manufacturing. Moreover, Hamilton's funding program depended on tariff revenues to pay interest on the national debt. The treasury secretary therefore opposed high duties, for they would cut revenues as well as imports.[71]

Even Hamilton's "Society for Establishing Useful Manufactures" did not assist proto-industrial entrepreneurs like Wadsworth and Manning. Rather, the society encouraged mercantile capitalists to invest in factory production using the latest English technology. Most Federalist merchants had no financial incentive to invest in manufacturing until the embargo of 1807, and every reason not to do so. For these American traders were still tied, by their past experience and present shipping investments, to the old British mercantile system. As in England itself at an earlier time, "commercial capitalism inhibited the growth of domestic manufacturing capacity because its greatest profits came from trade in imported goods."[72]

VI

Like the Civil War, the War for Independence disrupted the existing systems of production and ex-

---

71. John R. Nelson, Jr., "Alexander Hamilton and American Manufacturing: A Re-Examination," *Journal of American History* 65 (1979): 971–95.

72. John R. Gillis, *The Development of European Society* (Boston, 1977), 13 and 15.

change. The Revolutionary War likewise altered the character of the American economy. The end of British mercantilist restrictions and wartime exigencies brought the expansion of traditional home manufactures, the creation of new rural enterprises, and the appearance of domestically oriented traders and entrepreneurs. Other developments, however, delayed the emergence of a strong manufacturing sector. By opening western lands for settlement, the treaty of 1783 drained off the surplus agricultural population, inhibiting the expansion of rural industries. By providing American merchants with the status of neutral carriers, independence also diverted capital into maritime investments during the wars of the French Revolution. Unlike the Civil War, the War for Independence did not vest political and financial power in the hands of an elite committed to domestic industrial development.

This comparison provides an answer to the two questions posed at the beginning of this essay. The net effect of those contradictory events was to *accelerate* American economic development but to *delay* the emergence of a *more* capital-intensive system of manufacturing. The War for Independence expanded the *Kaufsystem*, thereby increasing the number of independent household producers and the overall level of market activity. Yet merchants continued to invest primarily in foreign trade, inhibiting the emergence of the *Verlagsystem* of manufacturing. The United States was well on its way to becoming a commercial agrarian society by 1790, but the triumph of a fully capitalist system of manufacturing was not yet assured.

7

The Transition
to
Capitalism in America

Thousands of men and women—most of them unknown to posterity—were active agents in the American transition to a full-fledged capitalist economic
system between 1770 and 1800.

In 1773 Sylvanus Hussey, the owner of a dry
goods store and twelve-acre farm in Lynn, Massachusetts, entered into a barter agreement with Nicholas

I presented earlier versions of this paper to the History Department at Johns Hopkins University, the Philadelphia Center for
Early American History, and as the Burke Inaugural Lecture at
the University of Maryland. I am grateful for the criticisms and
suggestions offered by those audiences, graduate students in History 668, and the following individuals: Philip Morgan, Lorena
Walsh, Daniel Vickers, Lois Green Carr, Paul Clemens, Stephen
Innes, Laurel Thatcher Ulrich, and Lucy Simler.

Brown, a prominent merchant of Providence, Rhode Island. Hussey exchanged one hundred pairs of shoes, accumulated from local artisans in return for store goods, for one hundred pounds of imported tea. Such transactions were not new; for decades shopkeepers had run a complex system of barter linking local producers with transatlantic merchants. But Hussey was less a sedentary storekeeper than an enterprising entrepreneur. He and dozens of other Massachusetts traders were actively mobilizing labor, advancing credit and raw materials to induce their customers to make hand-sewn shoes during slack times in the agricultural cycle. The success of these creative architects of the first major American putting-out system was phenomenal. By 1800 the male journeymen and female outworkers employed by merchants and manufacturers in the town of Lynn produced nearly half a million pairs of shoes each year.[1]

Agricultural entrepreneurs near Philadelphia were equally assiduous in directing labor, rationalizing production, and expanding markets. In 1781 Caleb Brinton, an established farmer in Chester County, Pennsylvania, proposed a contract to George Henthorn. Brinton offered to rent Henthorn a small house and garden plot for £4.15. In return, Henthorn had to assist "with all the hay and wheat harvest" at "three shillings Per day without Liquor . . . the whole to go towards the rent" and to do all Brinton's weaving "at the same price . . . James Rolins did."[2]

---

1. Alan Dawley, *Class and Community: The Industrial Revolution in Lynn* (Cambridge, Mass., 1976), 20, 15–16.

2. Paul G. E. Clemens and Lucy Simler, "Rural Labor and the Farm Household in Chester County, Pennsylvania, 1750–1820," in *Work and Labor in Early America*, ed. Stephen Innes (Chapel Hill, N.C., 1988), 106–8. The quoted material is from Brinton's 1781 contract, which is cited in 108n.

Once again, this contractual relation was not new. Henthorn and Rolins were cotters, landless men who bartered their skills as weavers and husbandmen for a house and garden. They were familiar figures in the social landscape of eighteenth-century England and, increasingly, in the American Middle Colonies. By the 1780s cotters and other landless workers accounted for half the population in many districts of southeastern Pennsylvania. Enterprising, improving farmers like Caleb Brinton now used their labor in an ever more efficient manner—producing a variety of goods, grain, butter, and textiles for sale or exchange in the market economy.

The market-driven use of dependent labor grew more pervasive in the Chesapeake Tidewater region as well. In 1784 Mary Mallory, an affluent widow in Elizabeth City County, Virginia, used thirteen adult slaves and nine slave children to farm her property of 250 acres. She also hired out, for the term of a year, five male slaves, four females, and four children, receiving approximately sixty-five pounds in labor rent for their services.[3]

Hiring out was not new in the 1780s, but its extent was. For the first time, many Chesapeake slave owners had more laborers than they needed to farm their plantations in a traditional manner. Some proprietors became agricultural improvers, using Enlightenment knowledge to raise productivity and diversify output. Others emulated major English landowners, becoming agricultural capitalists by leasing their plantations to prosperous tenant-middlemen. Still others,

---

3. Sarah S. Hughes, "Slaves for Hire: The Allocation of Black Labor in Elizabeth City County, Virginia, 1782–1810," *William and Mary Quarterly*, 3d ser., 35 (1978): 270.

like Mallory, hired out their slaves in a capitalist labor market.

These quotidian business deals by Hussey, Brinton and Henthorn, and Malloy took place in widely separated locales yet formed a common pattern. Each transaction was not merely an *event*, the exchange of goods in a market "place." Rather, it was part of an increasingly prevalent *process* that involved the conscious and active mobilization of labor "time."[4] Northern merchants and traders no longer derived profits only from control of market exchange; as capitalist entrepreneurs they organized the productive process itself. Similarly, Scottish merchant houses subsidized the rapid expansion of the Piedmont tobacco economy, advancing credit in "futures" contracts for subsequent crop harvests. In the Tidewater, enterprising planters raised profits by devising new forms of plantation management and work discipline. Even the Indian trade changed in character. Before 1750 American Indians carried pelts and skins directly to merchants in Albany or Montreal and returned with manufactures. Thereafter, European and American merchant houses dispatched their own agents into the forests. These white traders negotiated price bargains and exchanged goods directly with Indian producers, bypassing tribal intermediaries or chiefs. Like Lynn shoemakers and Piedmont planters, American Indian hunters and trappers were becoming, as Eric Wolf has argued, "specialized laborers in a putting-out system, in which the entrepreneurs advanced both production

---

4. Jean-Christophe Agnew, "The Threshold of Exchange: Speculations on the Market," *Radical History Review* 21 (1980): 115, develops this distinction between a marketplace and the market process.

goods and consumption goods against commodities to be delivered in the future."[5]

The dimensions of economic existence had changed. Thousands of farm families and artisan households were now more deeply embedded in profit-oriented exchange relationships. Thinking in causal terms, calculating financial outcomes, they were not merely "in" the market but "of" it. Many thousands more, a full tenth of the free labor force, worked for wages; they had to engage the market simply to earn their daily bread. Finally, thousands of enslaved southern blacks experienced new capitalist intrusions into their lives through hiring out, a task system of production, and sale to new owners. The intensity and diversity of market relationships in the domestic economy was everywhere on the rise.[6] Partly in consequence, American foreign trade changed in character and declined in relative importance. As early as 1770 American merchants earned more from the "invisible" export of shipping services than from the sale of any single commodity export. Moreover, foreign trade amounted to 15–20 percent of total output

---

5. Eric Wolf, *Europe and the People without History* (Berkeley, Calif., 1982), 194. For the transforming effect of merchant capital, see note 46 below.

6. Stanley Lebergott, "The Pattern of Employment since 1800," in *American Economic History*, ed. Seymour E. Harris (New York, 1961), 292 and passim. For a broader perspective on these issues, see Immanuel Wallerstein, *The Modern World-System*, vol. 1, *Capitalist Agriculture and the Origins of the European World-Economy in the Sixteenth Century* (New York, 1974), and vol. 2, *Mercantilism and the Consolidation of the European World-Economy, 1600–1750* (New York, 1980). Steven J. Stern, "Feudalism, Capitalism, and the World-System in the Perspective of Latin America and the Caribbean," *American Historical Review* 93 (1988): 829–72 proposes an alternative interpretive framework that is similar, in some respects, to the approach I develop here.

in 1770, but only 10–15 percent in 1800 and less than 10 percent by 1820.[7] The creation of a "national" American economy was part of the process of capitalist transformation.

This transition to a more intensive system of domestic capitalism was the product of four interrelated developments. First, a buoyant transatlantic demand for agricultural products encouraged thousands of ordinary Americans to sell more goods in the market. Second, rapid population growth—from natural increase and immigration—created a surplus of workers, facilitating the emergence of wage labor. Third, many American merchants, landowners, and artisans became aggressive entrepreneurs, reorganizing production to exploit the new market opportunities and labor supply. Finally, as a result of American independence, the political state became increasingly responsive to the needs and interests of these "monied men." At the same time, newly politically conscious farmers, artisans, and planters advanced an alternative set of economic policies. The struggle for home rule had pushed forward the transition to capitalism, setting in motion, to paraphrase Carl Becker, a fifty-year battle between monied men and rural smallholders over which group—and which system of political economy—would rule at home.[8]

---

7. James F. Shepherd, "British America and the Atlantic Economy," in *The Economy of Early America: The Revolutionary Period, 1763–1790*, ed. Ronald Hoffman et al. (Charlottesville, Va., 1988), 10; Robert E. Lipsey, "Foreign Trade," in *American Economic Growth: An Economist's History of the United States*, ed. Lance E. Davis et al. (New York, 1972), 554.

8. My contrast between these two systems of political economy draws upon Michael Merrill, "The Anti-Capitalist Origins of the United States," *Review: The Journal of the Fernand Brandel Center* 13 (1990): 465–97.

I

The legacy of the past was particularly apparent in mid-eighteenth-century New England. The original migrants to New England came from a society in the midst of a capitalist agricultural revolution. As early as 1700, owner-occupiers cultivated less than 30 percent of the arable land in England and propertyless cotters or wage laborers formed a majority of the rural population. Aristocratic and gentry landlords benefited most from the enclosures that dispossessed tens of thousands of peasants from their common-field use rights, but less affluent property owners profited as well. Nearly three-fourths of the yeomen families in seventeenth-century England and one-half of the husbandmen hired the labor of one or more servants-in-husbandry. While not averse to large holdings and servant labor, most early settlers in New England favored widespread landownership. The land distribution policies of general courts and town meetings provided farms for most families, inhibiting the development of the English system of agricultural capitalism based on wage labor. Servants numbered only 5 percent of the population during most of the seventeenth century and worked in fewer than 20 percent of rural households. Daily hired labor was equally scarce and expensive. Day laborers received twenty to thirty pence per day, nearly twice the English rate of twelve to fifteen pence.[9]

Settlers in Essex County, Massachusetts, adapted to the abundance of land and the shortage of labor in

---

9. Daniel Vickers, "Working the Fields in a Developing Economy: Essex County, Massachusetts, 1630–1675," in Innes, *Work*, 52–59.

three ways. First, middling farmers relied on their own labor, and that of their sons and daughters, as they set farm tasks and production goals. Second, wealthier farmers called upon poorer property owners to assist them with the spring planting and the hay and grain harvests. They paid for their neighbors' labor with money, produce, or access to pasture land. Third, land-rich settlers used attractive "developmental" leases to attract tenants to their holdings. Most leases were short, ten years or less, and permitted tenants to sell their capital improvements—houses, barns, fences—to the next occupant. Low annual rents also assisted tenant families, who numbered no more than 10 percent of the population, to accumulate moveable property and capital and eventually to acquire property.[10]

This system of family-run farms, labor exchange, and life cycle tenancy shaped the character of rural New England well into the nineteenth century. Even rapid population growth did not undermine the "household mode of production" (as Michael Merrill has termed it). In Andover, Massachusetts, for example, there were 435 people in 1680, but 1,425 in 1730, and over 2,900 in 1780. Despite a growing surplus of workers, most middling farmers continued to rely primarily on family (rather than hired) labor. Deacon John Abbot of Andover, who died in 1754, indentured two of his eight children; the other six worked full-time on the family property from age sixteen to the time of their marriages. Four sons provided Abbot with sixty-eight years of labor, while two daughters contributed twenty-seven years of labor to his wife.[11]

---

10. Ibid., 59–60, 63–65, 67.
11. Michael Merrill, "Cash Is Good to Eat: Self-Sufficiency and

The ethic of economic cooperation likewise remained vital, in part because of the historic pattern of property ownership. One-half of the nineteen thousand farms listed on the Massachusetts valuation list for 1772 did not have plows or oxen; 40 percent lacked enough cultivated acres to be self-sufficient in grain; and two-thirds did not have enough pasture for their livestock. Interdependence was an economic necessity and created a productive system (and cultural values) based primarily on local barter, not commercial markets. "Many farmers undoubtedly entered into exchange, not for profit or to raise their standard of living," Bettye Pruitt has argued, "but simply to be able to feed their families." As in the seventeenth century, poorer farmers (or their sons) worked regularly for their more affluent neighbors, the five thousand farmers on the valuation list who owned more than twenty acres of tillage and hay land.[12]

As in the past, land-poor families sought low-cost "developmental" leases. Beginning in the 1730s they migrated in large numbers to newly founded communities in central and western Massachusetts, eastern Connecticut, and eventually southern Maine. To accumulate the cash to purchase frontier farmsteads from land speculators, young men sought military bounties in the Seven Years' and Revolutionary wars,

---

Exchange in the Rural Economy of the United States," *Radical History Review* 9 (1977): 42–72; Richard S. Dunn, "Servants and Slaves: The Recruitment and Employment of Labor," in *Colonial British America: Essays in the New History of the Early Modern Era*, ed. Jack P. Greene and J. R. Pole (Baltimore, Md., 1984), 185–86.
12. Bettye Hobbs Pruitt, "Self-Sufficiency and the Agricultural Economy of Eighteenth-Century Massachusetts," *William and Mary Quarterly*, 3d ser., 41 (1984): 338, 339–40, 349; Richard L. Bushman, "Family Security in the Transition from Farm to City, 1750–1850," *Journal of Family History* 6 (1981): 242.

lived at home while working as day laborers, or went to sea as sailors or fishermen.[13]

The pressure of population growth thus pushed some men and women into capitalist markets for land and labor. By the late colonial period, one-half of the ordinary hands in the Nantucket whaling fleet were the sons of mainland farmers. Enterprising merchants induced those young men to become whalers by advancing cash and goods to them or their families; in return, traders received a written labor contract obligating the recruit to turn over his "lay" (his proportionate share of the profits). Those contracts then circulated as bills of exchange, and as Daniel Vickers has argued, the whaler's "labor now belonged to his creditor."[14]

Many New England families sought to avoid such "dependence." Their goal was neither self-sufficiency nor profit maximization, but autonomy. They wanted to preserve the traditional system of local political power and economic interdependence that inhibited control over their lives by outside agents, be they merchants, creditors, or government officials. Consequently, Pruitt has concluded, farmers participated in the market but would not accept "specialization and large-scale investment." Storekeepers and merchants had to accumulate goods for export "through innumerable small-scale purchases and exchanges." "The farmers have the game in their hands," an exasperated

---

13. Fred Anderson, "A People's Army: Provincial Military Service in Massachusetts during the Seven Years' War," *William and Mary Quarterly*, 3d ser., 40 (1983): 499–527.

14. Daniel Vickers, "Nantucket Whalemen in the Deep Sea Fishery: The Changing Anatomy of an Early American Labor Force," *Journal of American History* 72 (1985): 292–93.

Alexander Hamilton complained in 1781 while trying to amass food for the Continental army. Living in virtually self-sufficient communities, rural producers "are not obliged to sell because they have almost every necessary within themselves." Patriotic residents of New England equated this economic and political autonomy with republicanism itself. As the Northampton town meeting put it during a debate on the Massachusetts Constitution of 1780, no man should have "any degree or spark of . . . a right of dominion, government, and jurisdiction over [an]other."[15]

Autonomy required increasing ingenuity, as land in coastal New England grew scarce and expensive. The economic strategies of the land-poor family of Caleb Jackson, Sr., provide a case in point. The creative expedient of using the family's ample supply of labor on neighboring farms, as described in chapter 2, was only partially successful. To ensure a comfortable subsistence for his family, Mr. Jackson "made a bargain with Captain Perley to make shoes for him" in 1802. Every winter thereafter, he dispatched his two sons to an outbuilding to make one hundred pairs of shoes for a variety of local traders. Unlike husbandry, shoemaking was an unpleasant obligation, a task "we have got to [do]," Caleb, Jr., complained in his journal. While such outwork "was better than regular day labor," Daniel Vickers has argued, the Jackson family had compromised its cherished "independence" and had begun "to cross the frontier of

15. Pruitt, "Self-Sufficiency," 363; Hamilton quoted in Merrill, "Anti-Capitalist Origins," 487; town meeting quoted in Rowland Berthoff, "Independence and Attachment, Virtue and Interest: From Republican Citizen to Free Enterprise, 1787–1837," in *Uprooted Americans: Essays to Honor Oscar Handlin*, ed. Richard Bushman et al. (Boston, 1979), 114.

what rural New Englanders considered a satisfactory way of life." Other young men considered even more drastic alternatives. Far off in western Massachusetts, an advertisement in the Hampshire County *Gazette* promised "good wages in CASH" to "able bodied . . . industrious, sober men . . . to labor at the town of *Patterson*, in the state of *New Jersey* . . . in the greatest manufacture going on in America."[16]

As young men worked more for employers outside the household, women and young girls labored harder within it. The life of Martha Ballard, a midwife who migrated with her family from densely settled eastern Massachusetts to Hallowell, Maine, in 1777, was typical. Ballard's husband operated saw and grist mills with his sons and worked as a land surveyor. In 1790 he earned thirty-eight pounds for three months' survey work for the Kennebec Proprietors, one of the many groups of speculators who claimed much of the best land in southern Maine. In the same year Martha Ballard's cash income was twenty pounds, the return for her labor as a midwife (at six shillings a delivery) and as the manager of a household textile manufactory. At first, the work force consisted of her two daughters, ages seventeen and twenty-one. The Ballard girls spun flax and wool for neighboring women weavers. Mrs. Ballard acquired a loom in 1787 and her daughters quickly learned to weave a variety of textiles. The family kept most of the cloth for its own use

---

16. Daniel Vickers, "Competency and Competition: Economic Culture in Early America," *William and Mary Quarterly*, 3d ser., 47 (1990): 6, 9–10, 12; *Gazette* quoted in Gregory H. Nobles, "Hardship in the Hilltowns: Agricultural Development and Economic Conditions in Pelham, Massachusetts, 1740–1790," (paper presented to the Organization of American Historians, Chicago, April 1980), 30.

but exchanged some textiles for goods, labor services, and cash. When her daughters married in the early 1790s, Ballard replaced them with servant girls who received room, board, and six pounds per year.[17]

Ballard's textile manufactory was not unique. Weaving had become a normal female household responsibility, one with a significant impact on the local economy. Ballard and other women traded with blacksmiths for iron parts and repairs for their looms, with timbermen for potash to process flax, and with shopkeepers for goods from Boston. Their activities, and those of thousands of other women and girls, expanded the productive base of the American economy, in part by increasing the domestic supply of cheap cloth. Yet the Ballard women also used large quantities of imported cloth, making dresses from English chintz and quilting imported calico. The expansion of the market economy simultaneously increased domestic production and foreign imports.

This system of cloth production was not organized directly by merchants in an oppressive *Verlagsystem*. Nor was the increasingly prevalent by-employment of nail making. Instead, American farmer-artisans enjoyed considerable economic freedom. Even hired workers maintained some autonomy. In July 1799 Sally Fletcher abruptly left her servant's position in Martha Ballard's modest household textile manufactory. Her parting threat to Ballard and her

---

17. Laurel Thatcher Ulrich, "Martha Ballard and Her 'Girls': Women's Work in Eighteenth-Century Maine," in Innes, *Work*, 90–92. Allan Kulikoff argues that "women so disliked this added work that they willingly permitted their daughters to work in textile factories as soon as they were established" ("The Transition to Capitalism in Rural America," *William and Mary Quarterly*, 3d ser., 46 [1989]: 139).

husband, to "sue us in a weak from this time if we did not pay her what was her due," echoed the traditional cultural value of independence.[18]

As in European regions with a similar *Kaufsystem* of proto-industrialization, the family income of many rural workers rose. They lived better as a result of new work opportunities outside the household or more systematic exploitation of labor within it. Yet their economic lives were increasingly intertwined in a market system that altered their behavior and values. Some farmers fell into debt to commercial middlemen, who often extracted excess profits through their knowledge of the market system. Other farmers beat traders at their own game by careful calculation and astute bargaining. Ultimately, both groups became more conscious of "profits" and of "costs." Traditionally, merchants had used high markups to defray inventory costs and to offset delinquent accounts. Beginning in the 1780s they reduced profit margins but charged interest on overdue bills. Farmers likewise began to levy interest on personal loans to friends and neighbors. Only 5 percent of a sample of rural estates probated in Middlesex County, Massachusetts, before 1780 contained charges for interest. The proportion jumped to 20 percent between 1780 and 1800 and to 33 percent in the first decade of the nineteenth century. Simultaneously, affluent farmers and investors formed an array of profit-seeking voluntary associations (banks or canal, bridge, and turnpike companies), some of which issued securities that paid more than the "lawful rate" of interest.[19]

---

18. Ulrich, "Martha Ballard," 98.
19. Winifred B. Rothenberg, "The Emergence of a Capital Market in Rural Massachusetts, 1730–1838," in Hoffman et al., *Economy*, 137–40. Richard D. Brown, "The Emergence of Urban Society in

The transition to a robust capitalist economy had begun in New England by 1800 but was far from complete. Merchants and entrepreneurs had expanded their activities and devised new capitalist institutional structures. But as yet they lacked more than a modicum of control over the production of rural farmer-artisans. In economic affairs as in political life, the yeoman legacy remained strong, personifying the Democratic-Republican vision of the ideal American future. "The class of citizens who provide at once their own food and their own raiment," James Madison argued, "may be viewed as the most truely independent and happy . . . [and] the best basis of public liberty."[20]

II

Both merchants and landlords controlled the productive system with far greater success in the mid-Atlantic region. From the outset, large property owners in New York, Pennsylvania, and New Jersey relied less on family members and yeomen neighbors than did their counterparts in New England and more on "bound" labor. They regularly used slaves, indentured servants, convicts, and tenants to work their businesses and farms. The arrival of tens of thousands of Scotch-Irish and German migrants in the mid-eighteenth century created new opportunities for established

Rural Massachusetts," *Journal of American History* 61 (1974): table I, shows that Massachusetts residents founded only seven "profit-seeking" voluntary associations before 1790, but then created thirty in the 1790s and seventy-eight in the following decade.
20. Quoted in Merrill, "Anti-Capitalist Origins," 492.

property owners and for ambitious entrepreneurs. Peter January was a case in point. In 1767 January appeared on the Philadelphia tax list as a propertyless master cordwainer. Over the next eight years he used his craft skills and managerial energies to organize a shoe manufactory. By 1775 January was the master of seven servants (mostly Scotch-Irish) and two apprentices. By renting a building, directing servant labor, and selling shoes, he made the jump from artisan to entrepreneur. January called himself a "merchant" on the 1780 tax list.[21]

The continuing influx of migrants prompted the transition to a capitalist system of work discipline in Philadelphia. The ample supply of workers pushed down wage rates, thereby encouraging employers to replace bound men and women with free wage laborers. Servants and slaves accounted for 38 percent of the Philadelphia work force in 1751, but only 13 percent in 1775; simultaneously, the proportion of "laborers" on the tax lists rose from 5 to 14 percent. By 1800 the proportion of bound workers had fallen to less than 2 percent, and more than a quarter of the work force labored for wages. As employees came to be paid by the day or week (or on a piecework basis), their lives became less secure. No fewer than forty-nine journeymen woodworkers passed through the five positions in Samuel Ashton's cabinet shop between 1795 and 1803; they averaged only 145 days of work. The paternalistic labor system of the early eighteenth century, when even free workers boarded with their employers on year-long contracts, had given way to a

---

21. Billy G. Smith, " 'The Vicissitudes of Fortune': The Career Patterns of Laboring Men in Philadelphia, 1756–1798," in Innes, *Work*, 230; Dunn, "Servants," 180–83.

more flexible and transient pattern of work relations. The new system of wage labor aided entrepreneurs, who could now respond more quickly and efficiently to changing market conditions.[22]

The surplus of labor, in combination with the booming transatlantic market for grain, had an equally dramatic effect on productive relations in the countryside. The population of Europe rose steadily after 1750, bringing a sharp increase in cereal prices and land values throughout the Atlantic world. Wheat prices on the Amsterdam and Philadelphia markets jumped 30 percent between 1740 and 1760 and then rose even more dramatically after 1790.[23] Philadelphia merchants responded to the opportunity for windfall profits in the cereal trade with "a vigorous spirit of enterprise." One firm dispatched ships to Quebec to buy surplus wheat; many others hired factors in Maryland and Virginia to purchase huge quantities of wheat and corn. Still other merchants specialized in the procurement of agricultural goods from the countryside. Indeed, by 1785 there were no fewer than fifteen "flour merchants" in Philadelphia. These firms stimulated production for market by contracting with hundreds of large-scale farmers; Levi Hollingsworth, the most successful, drew from a network of four hundred producers that spanned the mid-Atlantic region. Enterprising merchants also created a reliable

---

22. Sharon V. Salinger, "Artisans, Journeymen, and the Transformation of Labor in Late Eighteenth-Century Philadelphia," *William and Mary Quarterly*, 3d ser., 40 (1983): 71; Stern, "Feudalism," 838.

23. B. H. Slicher Van Bath, *The Agrarian History of Western Europe, A.D. 500–1850* (London, 1963), 226–33; Marc Egnal, "The Economic Development of the Thirteen Continental Colonies, 1720–1775," *William and Mary Quarterly*, 3d ser., 32 (1975): 208–10.

and efficient land and water transportation system to handle bulky grains and encouraged the construction of mills to grind it into flour. As early as the 1770s the Brandywine River in Delaware was dotted with mills, "8 of them in a quarter of a mile," noted one traveler, "so convenient that they can take the grain out of the Vessels into the Mills."[24]

The aggressive pursuit of profits by Philadelphia merchants played a major role in the transition to a capitalist agricultural system. They encouraged greater production and created the infrastructure to carry it to market. British merchant houses likewise promoted trade by extending liberal terms of credit. Beginning in the 1750s, they allowed colonial merchants a year (rather than six months) to remit payment for the flood of goods—dry goods, ceramics, ironware—pouring out of the workshops and factories of England's increasingly industrialized economy. American merchants now had greater financial incentives to penetrate the rural market, where 90 percent of sales were on credit and payments waited until the harvest. Many rural producers responded with enthusiasm to the new market opportunities. They increased their output of wheat, flaxseed, and meat and used the returns to purchase imported manufactures. The per capita consumption of British goods in the Middle Colonies doubled between the 1720s and the 1770s (from £0.8 to £1.5 sterling). Equally significant,

---

24. Thomas M. Doerflinger, *A Vigorous Spirit of Enterprise: Merchants and Economic Development in Revolutionary Philadelphia* (Chapel Hill, N.C., 1986), 113–14, 122–24; idem, "Farmers and Dry Goods in the Philadelphia Market Area, 1750–1800," in Hoffman et al., *Economy*, 189–90; idem, "Commercial Specialization in the Philadelphia Merchant Community, 1750–1790," *Business History Review* 57 (1983): 20–49.

per capita exports from the region increased during the disruptions of the Revolutionary era, rising from £1.01 sterling in 1768–72 to £1.11 in 1791–92.[25]

The life histories of George Henthorn and Caleb Brinton reveal the spectrum of opportunities in this expansive rural environment. In 1781 Henthorn was recently married. Over the previous four years he had moved from one farm job to another in search of advancement. He declined to sign the contract drawn up by Brinton for housing and labor service. Instead, Henthorn negotiated a better deal for himself with a landholder in a nearby township, beginning a slow climb up the agricultural ladder. In 1799, after two decades as a cotter and tenant, he purchased a six-acre property for £165. At his death in 1815, Henthorn left personal possessions valued at $426.25; sundry clothes and household furnishings; a few farm implements; a mare, two cows, and four pigs; and two spinning wheels and three looms. Through hard work and careful calculation, Henthorn had achieved his goal of a "competence." He ended as his life as a relatively autonomous property owner. His small farmstead provided shelter, pasture, and land for a truck garden and a small orchard, while the sale of his labor as a weaver provided a modest but respectable standard of living.[26]

Caleb Brinton did not suffer greatly when Henthorn refused to enter his service. The supply of labor for hire was ample in Chester County, and Brinton had the resources and the enterprise to employ it

---

25. John J. McCusker and Russell R. Menard, *The Economy of British America, 1607–1789* (Chapel Hill, N.C., 1985), table 13.1; Shepherd, "British America," table 2.
26. Clemens and Simler, "Rural Labor," 109–10; Bushman, "Family Security," 240.

advantageously. Brinton was the fourth-generation descendant of two of the first Quaker immigrants to Pennsylvania. In 1783 he owned at least two farms (of 190 and 260 acres) and sizable herds of cattle and sheep. At his death in 1826, at the age of ninety-eight, Brinton's probate inventory listed his personal financial assets at a spectacular $303,000 in cash, bank balances, mortgages, and bonds at interest. If Brinton began his working life as a land-rich, market-oriented farmer, he ended it as a capitalist landlord.

The account books and journals of George Brinton, Caleb's son, reveal the capitalist agricultural practices that accounted, in part, for this impressive accumulation of wealth. In 1788 George and his bride, Elizabeth Yeatman, received a 282-acre farm from Caleb Brinton. By 1793 the young couple had three children. They hired one full-time and one part-time female worker to assist with house and dairy work. George Brinton himself employed two propertyless male field hands, renting them cottages at four pounds per year and paying them for farm labor. To keep his hired field hands busy, he planned an intensive year-round agricultural regime. His workers planted nitrogen-rich clover in the early spring and, to improve productivity further, carted dung and lime to newly plowed fields. Then Brinton sheared his sheep, selling the wool or sending it out to be woven into cloth, and sowed flax, spring wheat, and corn in succession. In June the workers harvested hay, since Brinton's large dairy herd needed winter fodder. Meanwhile, Brinton engaged in a variety of market transactions, selling some of his sheep and the first batch of the seven hundred pounds of cheese that he would produce in 1794. His workers then planted buckwheat, pulled flax, and harvested the spring wheat. Brinton saved twenty-six bushels of wheat for seed, reserved twenty bushels for family use, and sent one hundred bushels to the mill to be ground and sold as flour. In October he directed the planting of winter wheat, the harvest of potatoes and apples, and the making of cider. As the days grew cooler and shorter, he mobilized his workers to break and dress flax and to spin tow yarn.[27]

The extent of Brinton's commitment to the market marked him out as a capitalist rather than as a yeoman farmer. He invested heavily in the labor, livestock, and capital equipment needed to produce cheese, cider, and yarn, as well as wheat and meat. And he used these resources in a calculating and risk-taking manner. Unlike Caleb Jackson, Brinton sought to maximize profits, regardless of his consequent "dependence" on others—recalcitrant workers, hard-bargaining merchants, or fickle consumers. He relied on his managerial skills and his well-placed confidence in continuing agricultural prosperity to see him through.[28]

Many of Brinton's propertied neighbors likewise moved toward a capitalist productive system based on wage labor and market sales. In 1799 fifty-one property-owning farmer and artisan families resided in East Caln Township in Chester County. They employed the labor of twenty-four married inmates or cotters and forty-eight propertyless freemen. The

---

27. Clemens and Simler, "Rural Labor," 127-31.
28. Kulikoff, "Transition," 141-42, likewise contrasts "yeomen" and "capitalist" farmers. The top thirteen farmers (of the sixty-seven whose wills were probated in three Delaware Valley counties in 1774) were probably capitalist farmers; the average value of their crops and livestock was £251. Another fourteen farmers owned animals and farm commodities worth over £100; some may have been capitalists. The remaining forty farmers (60 percent) were probably yeomen. See Doerflinger, "Farmers," 188.

money wages—and goods—paid to those landless laborers enabled some of them to become small property holders, like George Henthorn. Yet their labor also provided substantial profits for their employers, and their need for clothing, land, mortgages, and other services augumented the wealth of other merchants and landowners.

Like Caleb Brinton, the property owners of southeastern Pennsylvania were becoming not only a privileged economic class but also the capitalist managers of hired labor and substantial financial assets. By the 1780s bonds, mortgages, and other paper instruments accounted for nearly 50 percent of the value of all probated estates in Chester County and nearly 30 percent in nearby Bucks County. As Winifred Rothenberg has argued with regard to the increasing importance of financial assets in Massachusetts after 1780, "The enhanced liquidity of rural portfolios *is* the transformation of the rural economy . . . [and] must loom large in whatever is meant by the coming of capitalism to the . . . village economy."[29] In the mid-Atlantic region, that transition was the product of aggressive merchants exploiting a buoyant transatlan-

---

29. Rothenberg, "Emergence," 161. Also see Duane E. Ball, "Dynamics of Population and Wealth in Eighteenth-Century Chester County, Pennsylvania," *Journal of Interdisciplinary History* 6 (1976): 634–35, table 5; Carole Shammas, Marylynn Salmon, and Michel Dahlin, *Inheritance in America: From Colonial Times to the Present* (New Brunswick, N.J., 1987), table 1.4 and p. 68, document the new practice of paying a widow's dower as annual interest on one-third of the value of the husband's landed estate. Doerflinger notes similar gains in the liquidity of business assets in Philadelphia between 1750 and 1790: the appearance of banks and "commercial paper" allowed merchants "to transact more business with the same amount of property" (*Vigorous Spirit*, 305–7).

tic market for grain and entrepreneurial landowners mobilizing European migrants for market production.

III

Planters in the southern colonies had long used co-erced labor to produce staple crops for the capitalist world economy. During the seventeenth century Chesapeake planters ruthlessly exploited tens of thousands of English indentured servants. Subsequently, they (and the low-country planters of South Carolina) used physical violence to extract labor from hundreds of thousands of African slaves, expropriating the crops, goods, and children that they produced. Social oppression yielded economic prosperity. Per capita exports from the tobacco colonies of Virginia and Maryland averaged about three pounds sterling per free resident around 1770, while exports of rice brought nine pounds to each white in South Carolina. These systems of coerced-labor, staple-crop production underlay the political power of the Virginia gentry and the fabulous wealth of low-country planters. Of the ten wealthiest men who died in the mainland colonies in 1774, nine had made their fortunes in South Carolina.[30]

The traditional rice economy of South Carolina persisted until the 1820s, but the productive system of the Chesapeake region changed in fundamental ways beginning around 1750. To take advantage of the boom in cereal prices, large-scale planters in Maryland

---

30. Shepherd, "British America," 7; Russell R. Menard, "Slavery, Economic Growth, and Revolutionary Ideology in the South Carolina Lowcountry," in Hoffman et al., *Economy*, 265.

and the Northern Neck of Virginia grew wheat and corn for export to Europe and the West Indies. Like Caleb and George Brinton and "improving" landlords in England, they became "vigilant managers." Many planters introduced new technology and a more intensive year-round work routine. They boosted production by using plows (rather than less-efficient hoes). To feed the greater number of draft animals required by plow agriculture, they expanded the acreage devoted to hay, oats, and other fodder crops. Planters rotated crops and introduced clover and other "English grasses" to increase yields. These "gentlemen farmers" likewise made more efficient use of their labor force, training male slaves as plowmen and women as spinners and weavers. By adopting a different crop mix, new technology, and a sexual division of labor, many planters increased productivity and profits.[31]

Other Chesapeake planters emulated the estate management practices of English aristocratic landlords. They leased their lands to middling tenants, who then managed the property and its work force. In the early 1790s Robert Carter personally supervised only two of his eighteen plantations. He leased the rest to tenants, fully stocked with slaves, livestock, and equipment. The tenant-managers of Carter's six plantations in eastern Frederick County paid their absentee landlord £490 in rent annually. Finding the direct exploitation of his five hundred slaves to be distasteful, Carter became an urban capitalist. He

---

31. Doerflinger, *Vigorous Spirit*, 356–65; Lois Green Carr and Lorena S. Walsh, "Economic Diversification and Labor Organization in the Chesapeake, 1650–1820," in Innes, *Work*, 175–83.

moved to Baltimore, buying and renting out urban properties and investing in banks and stock.[32]

Other wealthy planters pursued somewhat similar strategies, renting out some of their slaves and land to middling planters and tenant farmers. In Elizabeth City County, Virginia, the top 10 percent of white property owners owned 40 percent of the county's slaves and hired them out with increasing frequency. Rates varied according to sex and age, with male adults fetching about ten pounds per year, adult females about four pounds, and young boys and girls from ten shillings to 1 pound. Hiring out was profitable for owners, for the average rental was one-fifth of the assessed value of the slave. Ambitious smallholders benefited as well from the ample supply of labor and land; by 1810 tenants cultivated at least the 30 percent of the land in the county that was owned by absentee landlords and perhaps considerably more.[33]

Blacks gained little from the new management practices. In fact, their lives may have become harder and less secure. Hiring out freed some slaves from close patriarchal control by their masters and gave them somewhat more autonomy in their work lives. But it did not usually result in emancipation through self-purchase. Hiring out also separated parents from one another and probably resulted in an earlier and more systematic exploitation of the labor of their

32. Robert D. Mitchell, *Commercialism and Frontier: Agriculture and the Settlement of the Shenandoah Valley* (Charlottesville, Va., 1977), 127; Hughes, "Slaves," 265. J. R. Wordie, "Rent Movements and the English Tenant Farmer, 1700–1838," *Research in Economic History* 6 (1981): 193–243, traces the effect of the cereal boom on English agricultural capitalism.
33. Hughes, "Slaves," 269, 275, 277–79; see, in general, Robert Starobin, *Industrial Slavery in the Old South* (New York, 1970).

children. Likewise, vigilant management by profit-minded owners or tenants meant harder year-round labor for many slaves. Most important of all, the labor surplus prompted the sale or forced migration of thousands of slaves. Between 1755 and 1780 over seventeen thousand Tidewater slaves were moved to newly opened Piedmont plantations. Most of these forced migrants were young and unmarried; a majority were female, purchased either for their tobacco- and corn-planting skills or as capital goods whose offspring would increase the size of the plantation work force. Thus, the Tayloe family sold fifty slaves from its Mount Airy, Virginia, plantation in 1792, and John Tayloe III sold as many more, mostly young girls, between 1809 and 1828. In subsequent decades Tayloe's sons forcibly moved another 364 slaves from Mount Airy to a brutal life on cotton plantations in Alabama.[34]

The increased emphasis on efficiency and profitability in the late eighteenth-century Chesapeake may also account for the expansion of the "task system." By the eve of the American Revolution, many slaves in South Carolina already worked under this system of work discipline. Philip Morgan has suggested that tasking represented a partial victory for slaves in the struggle with their masters over the conditions of work. As a contemporary observer noted,

> Their work is performed by a daily task, allotted by their master or overseer, which they have generally done by one or two o'clock in the afternoon, and have

---

34. Philip D. Morgan and Michael L. Nicholls, "Slaves in Piedmont Virginia, 1720–1790," *William and Mary Quarterly*, 3d ser., 46 (1989): esp. 222–38; Dunn, "Servants," 179.

the rest of the day for themselves, which they spend in working in their own private fields, consisting of 5 or 6 acres of ground, allowed them by their masters, for planting of rice, corn, potatoes, tobacco, &c. for their own use and profit, of which the industrious among them make a great deal.[35]

By creating work incentives for slaves, the task system may have increased planters' profits. The annual rate of return on a two-hundred-acre South Carolina rice plantation with forty slaves was about 25 percent. Alternatively, the high profit margin may simply have reflected the expanding demand and high prices for rice on the transatlantic market. In any event, slave owners in other regions gradually introduced the task system, using it to increase the output of their labor force. Around 1800 some sugar plantation managers in the British Caribbean formed their workers into "jobbing or task gangs." They hired them out to planters, who paid a fixed amount per acre of ground cleared, holed, or cut. This piecework system made those laborers the hardest worked of any West Indian slaves.[36] Chesapeake planters likewise adopted the task system. By the 1770s many masters regularly assigned nightly tasks to their slaves. After dusk, a visitor to a Virginia plantation reported in 1789, each slave "has a task of [tobacco] stripping allotted which takes them up some hours, or else they have such a quantity of Indian corn to husk, and if they neglect it,

35. Quoted in Philip D. Morgan, "Work and Culture: The Task System and the World of Lowcountry Blacks, 1700–1880," *William and Mary Quarterly*, 3d ser., 39 (1982): 579.

36. Morgan, "Work and Culture," 576; Philip D. Morgan, "Task and Gang Systems: The Organization of Labor on New World Plantations," in Innes, *Work*, 201.

are tied up in the morning, and receive a number of lashes."[37]

Trapped by their own racism and their privileged position in society, Southern planters refused to abolish slavery despite its moral shortcomings and relative economic inefficiencies. Instead some became rentier-capitalists, leasing their plantations to tenant-middlemen and living from their rents. Others remained personally involved with their estates. They became "vigilant managers" who used the market and incentives of hiring out, tasking, and crop diversification to enhance their profits. Longtime participants in the capitalist world markets, buying slaves and selling staple crops, they now applied capitalist methods to the productive process itself.

This use of "capitalist" incentives within a coerced labor system underscored the changing character of the slave regime. Like employers in late colonial Philadelphia, planters were exploring indirect means of coercion to extract work from laborers. Upland cotton planters established individual tasks for plowing, hoeing, and picking the crop. West Indian planters eventually introduced individual tasking into the cane-holing operation, a job traditionally performed by labor "gangs" under the close supervision of a "driver." Indeed, planter Jonathan Steele of Barbados offered financial inducements to slaves to perform a variety of tasks in a given day. As a British journal, *The Quarterly Review*, noted in 1823, these Caribbean labor experiments were a "means of paving the way for the introduction of voluntary labor on the part of

---

37. Carr and Walsh, "Economic Diversification," 159; Morgan, "Task and Gang Systems," 201–2.

the negroes." In the antebellum southern United States, commentators placed less emphasis on the "ameliorative" aspects of the task system than on its superior economic efficiency. "The advantages of this system," the editor of *Southern Agriculture* suggested, are "the avoidance of watchful superintendence and incessant driving." Whatever the reason, the task system became ever more widespread. "By the 1830's," Philip Morgan has concluded, "a majority of slaves in the Anglo-American world were working by the task."[38]

Despite these changes, slavery remained a coerced, cash-crop system of labor. Masters continued to own property rights in their workers and their offspring and, ultimately, they used physical force (rather than wage incentives or dismissal) to extract labor. The task system worked to the advantage of slaves only in a few regions. The overwhelming numerical dominance of blacks in the South Carolina low country, combined with absentee ownership and a lucrative crop, gave slaves enviable and unusual opportunities. By the late eighteenth century they were able not only to regulate their work lives but also to acquire property rights—in garden plots, in cash or goods exchanged for vegetables and chickens, and in mules and horses—and to pass them to their offspring. They lived both as coerced laborers and as protopeasants, producing food for market sale.[39] In other areas the task system served the masters' interests, maintaining output while reducing the supervision costs of "gang" labor. Even so, the transition to tasking gave

---

38. Morgan, "Task and Gang Systems," 208, 202.
39. Morgan, "Work and Culture," 590–96.

slaves the chance to bargain over work loads and, like dependent peasants elsewhere, to win privileges or to establish "customs" limiting exploitation.

By the early nineteenth century tens of thousands of rural white workers in the northern states were also doing task work. Like the Jackson boys, they worked for storekeepers or merchant entrepreneurs on a piece-work basis, fabricating shoes, or brooms, or straw hats, or cloth. As the rising corporation lawyer and politician Daniel Webster noted perceptively in 1814, these men and women lacked autonomy. Although formally free, a worker employed in a factory or an elaborately subdivided putting-out system was "nec-essarily at the mercy of the capitalist for the support of himself and his family . . . [for he was] utterly incapable of making and carrying to market in his own account the smallest entire article."[40]

Slave hiring out or tasking, handicraft piecework, and agricultural or factory wage labor were hardly identical forms of work discipline. Yet they may be viewed as regional versions of an emergent capitalist system of social relations that was less paternalistic and less overtly coercive than "traditional" labor prac-tices. The specific character of each regional labor system reflected local customs and the balance of power among social groups. As Robert Brenner has argued with respect to the transition from feudalism to capitalism in early modern Europe, the influence of new causal forces—demographic, commercial, or po-litical—in a given region depended upon "certain *his-torically specific* patterns of the development of the contending agrarian classes and their relative strength

---

40. Quoted in Berthoff, "Independence," 114.

. . . their relationship to the non-agricultural classes
. . . and to the state."[41]

IV

The American Revolution accelerated the transition to
a regionally diverse capitalist society in various ways.
The war disrupted the import trade, prompting the
expansion of traditional home manufactures and the
appearance of new rural enterprises. Wartime opportunities likewise sharpened the acquisitive instincts of
thousands of farmers, both capitalist and yeoman.
"The raised price of grain," the assistant foragemaster
of the Continental army complained in 1779, had
created an "unwillingness of the Farmers to part with
it while there is a prospect of a still greater advance in
the Price." Merchants invested both in speculative
ventures, such as privateering and government bonds,
and new productive enterprises—banks, textile factories, wagons, ships, equipment, gristmills, and sawmills. The new American republic came out of the
war with more household producers, more domestic
traders, and a more highly developed market economy.[42]

Nonetheless, the results of the war also inhibited
the expansion of domestic capitalism. By opening
western lands for settlement, the Paris Treaty of 1783

---

41. Robert Brenner, "Agrarian Class Structure and Economic
Development in Preindustrial Europe," *Past and Present* 70 (1976),
52.
42. Quotation from E. Wayne Carp, *To Starve the Army at Pleasure:
Continental Army Administration and American Political Culture,
1775–1783* (Chapel Hill, N.C., 1984), 65.

drained off part of the surplus agricultural population, retarding the expansion of rural industry. By providing American merchants with the status of neutral carriers, independence also diverted capital into maritime investments during the wars of the French Revolution. Finally, as Michael Merrill has argued, the war increased the political influence of a "self-conscious class of small property holders" who demanded government policies "designed to enrich 'producers' rather than 'moneyed men.' "[43]

Conflict between yeomen farmers and capitalist entrepreneurs were not new in the 1790s, but the context was. Independence revealed the potential power of the state legislatures to advance American economic development and, in the process, to favor one social group over others. A comparison of the dynamics of economic change in North Carolina in the 1760s and Rhode Island in the 1790s suggests the dimensions of this transition to a locally controlled system of political economy.

The North Carolina backcountry initially stood at the periphery of the transatlantic capitalist economy. Most settlers in Anson, Granville, and Orange counties were subsistence-plus farmers. They grew enough food to feed their families and bartered the surplus for imported salt, sugar, cloth, and farm implements. Beginning in the 1750s, enterprising planters invested heavily in slaves to take advantage of the rising market prices for wheat and tobacco. The number of slaves in Anson County multiplied by a factor of 14.5 between 1754 and 1767. To buy slaves, land, and equipment, they went into debt to newly resident

---

43. Merrill, "Anti-Capitalist Origins," 466.

Scottish traders. When tobacco prices collapsed between 1759 and 1763, less able planters, or the less lucky, found themselves in court. Merchants brought an average of ninety suits per year in Orange County between 1763 and 1765, as opposed to only seven per year during the previous decade.[44]

Legal confrontation prompted political upheaval. Led by Herman Husband, a migrant from Maryland with investments in milling, land speculation, and iron production, local planters formed a regulation movement. Regulators attacked "Scotch merchants" with verbal abuse and physical force, threatening "to kill all the Clerks and Lawyers" who were their political allies. Between 1768 and 1771 regulators closed courts, harassed lawyers and judges, and destroyed the stores of merchants. Finally, in 1771 Royal Governor William Tryon mobilized the eastern militia and suppressed the regulators with armed force.[45]

The North Carolina regulation movement illustrated the difficulty of capitalist agricultural transformation in a labor-scarce region by dramatizing the links among cultural values, political conflict, and economic change. Market production required the purchase of imported slaves with British credit.[46]

---

44. James P. Whittenberg, "Planters, Merchants, and Lawyers: Social Change and the Origins of the North Carolina Regulation," *William and Mary Quarterly*, 3d ser., 34 (1977): 225, 226–28. Jacob M. Price, "Reflections on the Economy of Revolutionary America," in Hoffman et al., *Economy*, 306, notes that high transportation costs increased the effect of falling prices on North Carolina producers.

45. Whittenberg, "Planters," 237.

46. Ordinarily, merchant capital is "conservative," invested in trade among existing producers. But, as Stern argues, "under colonial conditions, which allied merchant capital with imperial political power in the fluid environment of a frontier 'outpost,'

Some entrepreneurial planters in Orange County joined the regulators because they resented the economic and political ascendency of the new creditor class of merchants and lawyers, who filled one of the county's two assembly seats from 1762 to 1776. Yeomen farmers were equally hostile. Depicting themselves as "poor families" and "industrious peasants," they used the regulation movement to protest against the new structure of credit. Like smallholders in New England, they expected flexible debt relationships; local creditors usually carried unpaid debts for two or three years and rarely charged interest. Yeomen therefore allied with their entrepreneurial neighbors to oppose the demands of "foreign" merchants.[47] Finally, the regulation movement pointed to the ultimate importance of government power in upholding bargains made in the marketplace. Governor Tryon's intervention decisively upheld the authority of the court system and the legally sanctioned system of capitalist credit.

Tryon acted to protect the interests of Scottish merchants and the British mercantile system. For similar reasons Parliament passed the Currency Act of 1764, which protected British merchants from currency depreciation schemes in Virginia and other colonies. Parliament likewise considered a ban on British migration to America in the 1770s, a measure that would have undermined the labor supply of Caleb Brinton and other mid-Atlantic farmers. And a long series of Parliamentary statutes sought to prevent the

---

merchant capital could exercise an aggressive, organizing, and transformative impact on technologies and social relations of production" ("Feudalism," 869).

47. Whittenberg, "Planters," 234–35.

fabrication and sale of American manufactures. The entrepreneurial activities of Sylvanus Hussey and Martha Ballard could not expect encouragement from the home government. Within the British mercantile system, Americans were doomed to positions of inferiority and exploitation. "Every shilling gained by America" through the tobacco trade, Daniel Dulany noted bitterly in 1764, "hath entered in Britain and fallen into the pockets of the British merchants, traders, manufacturers and land holders, and it may therefore be justly called the British commerce." The rapid maturation of the American economy after 1775 proceeded in part from the demise of British mercantilism.[48]

The speed and character of economic development now depended on the balance of social and political power between yeomen farmers and capitalist entrepreneurs in the new American states. In 1734 the Rhode Island General Assembly had passed a Mill Act, which allowed mill owners to flood upstream agricultural land in return for court-assessed "rent" payments. That measure prevented farmers from using the traditional common-law remedies of trespass or public nuisance to protect their property. As Gary Kulik has argued, the act "was a form of eminent domain, sanctioning the enforced loan of privately-held land." Most farmers accepted this loss of their

---

48. Dulany quoted in Joseph A. Ernst, "The Political Economy of the Chesapeake Colonies, 1760–1775: A Study in Comparative History," in Hoffman et al., *Economy*, 213; Robert E. Mutch, "Colonial America and the Debate about the Transition to Capitalism," *Theory and Society* 2 (1980): 847–63; Oscar Handlin and Mary Handlin, *Commonwealth: A Study of the Role of Government in the American Economy* (Cambridge, Mass., 1945), chapters 1–2; Morton J. Horwitz, *The Transformation of American Law, 1780–1860* (Cambridge, Mass., 1977), chapter 1.

property rights because the dams usually powered much-needed sawmills or gristmills. Moreover, Rhode Island's Fish Acts explicitly directed mill owners to provide fish runs around the dams, so that upstream farmers and their neighbors would continue to have a free supply of protein-rich food.[49]

Beginning in 1765, entrepreneurial iron masters waged a fifty-year struggle for complete control of Rhode Island's rivers and streams. To make the most efficient year-round use of their blast furnaces and iron forges, they successfully sought exemptions from the Fish Acts. Farmers fought back. In 1773 their representatives secured passage of "an act making it lawful to break down and blow up Rocks at Pawtucket Falls to let fish pass up." The statute affirmed the common-law right of the populace to remove "public nuisances"—in this case a milldam built of "Rocks"— by public action.[50]

The balance of power within Rhode Island shifted in the aftermath of the American Revolution. To encourage domestic manufactures, the General Assembly sacrificed the interests of farmers and grist-mill operators to those of cotton mill owners. In 1793, for example, the assembly specifically exempted the cotton mill constructed by Samuel Slater on the Paw-tucket River from the Fish Act. In neighboring Mas-sachusetts, a development-minded General Court chartered the Massachusetts Bank in 1784, lending the prestigious name of the commonwealth to a private,

49. Gary Kulik, "Dams, Fish, and Farmers: Defense of Public Rights in Eighteenth-Century Rhode Island," in *The Countryside in the Age of Capitalist Transformation*, ed. Steven Hahn and Jonathan Prude (Chapel Hill, N.C., 1985), 30–33.

50. Ibid., 39.

capitalist institution. The court granted an exclusive franchise to the Charles River Bridge Company in 1785; allowed mill owners to rent (rather than have to purchase) flooded agricultural lands in 1796; and granted millions of acres of land in the district of Maine to well-connected capitalist speculators.[51] In nearly every state, enterprising capitalist merchants, manufacturers, and speculators won government support for their projects.

The success of those "projectors" was never assured and always difficult, for yeomen farmers and planters were now a formidable political force. Responding to smallholder demands, the New York legislature issued £250,000 in paper currency in 1786, earmarking it to buy soldiers' warrants and pay interest on war bonds previously issued by the state loan office. This measure ignored the demands of "stockjobbers" who wanted the state to pay off Loan Office certificates at face value. In Pennsylvania, farmers condemned the "amazing desire to accumulate wealth" of Robert Morris and other merchant backers of the Bank of North America. Arguing that "the commercial interest is already too powerful, and an overbalance to the landed interest," rural assemblymen repealed the bank's charter in 1785, only to see it restored two years later.[52]

---

51. Handlin and Handlin, *Commonwealth*, 100, 102, 71–72, 82–86; Alan Taylor, " 'A Kind of Warr': The Contest for Land on the Northeastern Frontier," *William and Mary Quarterly*, 3d ser., 46 (1989): 3–26.

52. Cathy Matson, "Public Vices, Private Benefit: William Duer and His Circle, 1776–1792," in *New York and the Rise of American Capitalism: Economic Development and the Social and Political History of an American State, 1780–1870*, ed. William Pencak and Conrad Edick Wright (New York, 1989), 98–99; Doerflinger, *Vigorous Spirit*, 270–71, 300–301.

For the next generation, state and national legislators continued to divide over two rival systems of political economy. One set of policies, favored by Alexander Hamilton and the Federalist party, would use the power of the state to assist "monied men," merchants and financiers, and to pursue a "capitalist" path of commercial development. Some state legislatures actively embraced this approach, enacting hard-money laws and liberally granting economic privileges to aspiring entrepreneurs. Such measures often brought public as well as private benefits. "Our monied capital has so much increased from the Introduction of Banks, & the Circulation of the Funds," Philadelphia merchant William Bingham noted in 1791, "that the Necessity of Soliciting Credits [from England] will no longer exist, & the Means will be provided for putting in Motion every Species of Industry."[53]

Other state governments pursued the public good by spreading political favors more broadly. Their policies, advocated by Thomas Jefferson, James Madison, and the Democratic-Republican party, favored "producers," yeoman farmers and artisans, and embodied an "agrarian" model of commercial society. To assist land-hungry tenant farmers and credit-hungry yeomen families, legislatures created state land banks, gave legal rights to "squatters," and divided frontier districts into small, affordable tracts. That legislation was the product, in many cases, of petitions from scores, even hundreds, of ordinary Americans. The

---

53. My argument follows that of Merrill, "Anti-Capitalist Origins," 469, on the distinction between "capitalist" and "agrarian" paths of commercial development. Bingham quoted in Doerflinger, *Vigorous Spirit*, 333.

"true Policy of a Republic," argued ninety Virginians who wanted land "in moderate Quantities, by Way of Head Rights," consisted in laws that assisted "the Poor and Needy to raise their Families to be reputable and useful Members of Society."[54]

Whatever their differences, these two systems of political economy assumed the existence of a vibrant market system. The newfound centrality of the "market" in American ideology and society foreshadowed the eventual triumph of the monied interest. For the market, along with private property, wage labor, and sophisticated financial instruments, constituted the institutional core of early modern capitalism. In the short space of the fifty years between 1750 and 1800, these ingredients of a capitalist order had risen in prominence as the traditional limitations on economic development in America—the shortage of labor, of extensive markets, of entrepreneurs, and of political purpose—had been overcome. For better or for worse, perhaps a little of both, the United States would confront the nineteenth century as an increasingly capitalist commercial society.

---

54. Quoted in Ruth Bogin, "Petitioning and the New Moral Economy of Post-Revolutionary America," *William and Mary Quarterly*, 3d ser., 45 (1988): 405.

Suggested Reading

The best general study of the early American economy is John J. McCusker and Russell R. Menard, *The Economy of British America, 1607–1789* (Chapel Hill, N.C., 1985), while Jack P. Greene, *Pursuits of Happiness: The Social Development of the Early Modern British Colonies and the Formation of American Culture* (Chapel Hill, N.C., 1988), offers a fine synthesis of colonial social history.

These topics are treated in greater scholarly detail in four important collections of essays: Robert Blair St. George, ed., *Material Life in America, 1600–1860* (Boston, 1988); Jack P. Greene and J. R. Pole, eds., *Colonial British America: Essays in the New History of the Early Modern Era* (Baltimore, 1984); Ronald Hoffman, John J. McCusker, Russell R. Menard, and Peter Albert, eds., *The Economy of Early America: The Revolutionary Period, 1763–1790* (Charlottesville, Va., 1988); and Stephen Innes, ed., *Work and Labor in Early America* (Chapel Hill, N.C., 1988).

Other studies that provide a broad overview of American economic and social development include: Bernard Bailyn, *The Peopling of British North America:*

An Introduction (New York, 1986); Stuart Bruchey, *The Roots of American Economic Growth, 1607–1861* (New York, 1965); Ralph Davis, *The Rise of the Atlantic Economies* (Ithaca, N.Y., 1973); James A. Henretta and Gregory H. Nobles, *Evolution and Revolution: American Society, 1600–1820* (Lexington, Mass., 1987); Alice Hanson Jones, *The Wealth of a Nation to Be: The American Colonies on the Eve of the Revolution* (New York, 1980); Allan Kulikoff, *Tobacco and Slaves: The Development of Southern Culture in the Chesapeake, 1680–1800* (Chapel Hill, N.C., 1986); Curtis P. Nettels, *The Emergence of a National Economy, 1775–1815* (New York, 1962); Edwin J. Perkins, *The Economy of Colonial America* (2d ed., New York, 1988); and Richard B. Sheridan, *Sugar and Slavery: An Economic History of the British West Indies, 1623–1775* (Baltimore, 1973).

Reference should also be made to works that offer a comparison with other early modern societies or that place events in America in a broader Atlantic and European context. See, for example, Nicholas Canny, *Kingdom and Colony: Ireland in the Atlantic World, 1560–1800* (Baltimore, 1988); D. C. Coleman, *The Economy of England, 1450–1750* (New York, 1977); T. M. Devine and David Dickson, eds., *Ireland and Scotland, 1600–1850: Parallels and Contrasts in Economic and Social Development* (Edinburgh, 1983); Peter Laslett, *The World We Have Lost: England before the Industrial Age* (New York, 1973); Neil McKendrick, John Brewer, and J. H. Plumb, eds., *The Birth of a Consumer Society: The Commercialization of Eighteenth-Century England* (Bloomington, Ind., 1982); Peter Marshall and Glyn Williams, eds., *The British Empire before the American Revolution* (London, 1980); J. H. Parry, *Trade and Dominion: The European Overseas Empires in the Eighteenth Century* (London, 1971); and Immanuel Wallerstein, *The Modern World System* (2 vols., New York, 1974–80).

Index

Abbot, Deacon John, 263
Abbot, George, 34
Abbot, Samuel, 145
Account books, xxiii, xxiv,
    xxix, 67, 97, 194, 213
Adams, Henry, 26
Adams, Herbert Baxter, xvii
Adams, James Truslow, 149
Adams, John, 69
African-Americans, 211
Africans, 171, 278
Age
    at death, 17
    and inheritance, 101
    at marriage, 18, 19, 21, 191–
        92, 217
    of military recruits, 215
    and officeholding, 178
    in rural society, 76–77
    of selectmen, 78
    and social structure, 78
    and wealth, 77–78, 178–79
Agricultural crisis, 160–61
Agricultural ladder, 80, 105,
    274
Albany, N.Y., 95, 259
All Hallow's Parish, Md., 175,
    189, 190

Allen, David Grayson, 185,
    188
Allen, Deacon Henry, 132
Amenia, N.Y., 32
American Revolution, xxvii,
    24, 41, 57, 60, 84, 121,
    146, 218, 219
    causes of, 161
    and economy, 199–200
American Slavery, American
    Freedom, 185
American Wool Manufacture, 221
Anderson, Fred, 215
Anderson, Terry, 166
Andover, Mass., 16, 17, 18,
    20, 21, 22, 23, 25, 27, 32,
    34, 78, 82, 111, 159,
    214, 215, 263
Andrews, Charles McLean,
    xxxv
Andros, Sir Edmund, 12
Anglicization, 187
Annapolis, Md., xxxi
Anticapitalist values, xxv, 43,
    62
Antifederalism, 152
Antinomian Controversy, 50
Appleby, Joyce, 61n

Apprenticeship, 33, 124–25
Ariès, Philippe, 14
Aristocracy, English, 187
Arminianism, 64
Army
    British, 239, 240
    Continental, 240, 266, 286
    French, 240, 244
Artisans
    in Boston, 122, 125–26
    and exchange system, 194
    ideology of, 183
    increase in, 23, 214
    and *Kaufsystem*, 212, 250
    rural, 84, 91, 214
    urban, 183, 184, 271
    weavers, 227
Ashton, Samuel, 271
Assembly
    and debtor laws, 51, 53
    and local politics, 31
    in Massachusetts, 31, 151
Augusta County, Va., 227
Autonomy, 265, 266, 280, 285

Bacon's Rebellion, 152
Bailyn, Bernard, xix, 8n, 152,
    153, 162, 187, 188
Ballard, Martha, 237, 267, 290
Baltimore, Md., xxxi, 233, 280
Bank of North America, 292
Barnstable, Mass., 110
Barrett, John, 145
Barrett, William, 146
Bartering, xxiii, 91, 92, 141,
    236, 241, 257, 264
Beard, Charles A., xviii, 148
Becker, Carl, 261
Beekman, James, 232
Beer, 170
Behavior, of farm population,
    xxxii, xxxvi, 100
Bendix, Reinhard, 48, 156, 157
Benevolence, 64
Benezet, Anthony, 64
Bentley, Rev. William, 78
Berlin, N.H., 244

Berthoff, Rowland, xx, 187,
    188
Berwick, Me., xxiii
Bezanson, Anne, 205
Bidwell, Percy Wells, xxxii,
    89, 90, 93, 220
Bills of exchange, 265
Bingham, William, 293
Birth intervals, 18, 22
Birthrate
    black, 171
    in New England, 19, 22, 171
Blacks
    in Boston, 134n
    hiring-out, 258–59
Blacksmiths, 125, 268
Board of Trade, 221, 222
Bond, Phineas, 246
Book of Martyrs, 57
Boorstin, Daniel, 186
Boston, Mass., xx, 31, 38, 39,
    53, 63, 122, 123, 150,
    161, 182, 183, 240, 268
Boston Associates, 70
Bradford, William, 21, 52
Brandywine River, 273
Brattle, Thomas, 55
Brenner, Robert, 285
Brinton, Caleb, 257, 274, 277,
    279, 288, 289
Brinton, George, 275, 279
Brissot de Warville, Jacques-
    Pierre, 41, 248
Brown, Katherine, B., 151
Brown, Nicholas, 256–57
Brown, Robert E., 150, 153,
    158
Brown thesis, 156, 160
Bulfinch, John, 146
Bull, Lt. Governor William,
    222
Burgoyne, General John, 240
Burnham, Jonathan, 213
Burrell, Sidney A., 47
Bushman, Richard L., 15, 28,
    83, 161
Button industry, 249

By-employments, 214, 216, 225, 231, 247–48, 249, 268. *See also* Putting-out system
Byrd, William, II, 89

Cabot family, 70
"Calling," 35, 37, 39, 40, 43, 50
  and benevolence, 64
  and evangelicals, 65–66
  among farmers, 59
  and Lutheranism, 44
  among merchants, 54
Calvinism
  and "calling," 39, 50
  in England, 44
  in New England, 62
  in Scotland, 43
Capital formation, 175, 179–80
  in Boston, 127, 141–43
  rural, 100, 104, 105–7
  and speculation, 244–45, 254
  and war, 242–44
Capitalism
  agricultural, 180, 258, 262, 275–77, 279–280
  causes of, 45, 47, 61–62
  definition of, 42, 46–47, 259–60
  in India, 210
  institution of, 269–70, 294
  and legal system, 66–69
  in Massachusetts, 45, 53
  in Pennsylvania, 45
  and plantations, 279–80
  and politics, 288–94
  and population, 261–65
  and putting-out system, 208, 249
  and religion, 41, 43, 48, 65–66
  rentier, 283
  in Rhode Island, 289–94
  rural, 96, 266–67, 269, 273–78
  urban, 280–81

Carding machines, 117, 238
Carr, Lois Green, xxx, xxxi, 186
Carroll, Charles, 234
Carter, Robert, 279
Catholicism, 44
Centuries of Childhood, 14
Chalkley, Thomas, 35, 36, 37, 40, 42, 46
Chandler, Rev. Samuel, 111
Charles River Bridge Company, 292
Chastellux, Marquis de, 234
Chauncy, Charles, 64
Chebacco, Mass., 193
Cheese, xxvii, 244, 246, 275
Chesapeake colonies, xxx, 167, 175
  economy of, 165, 179–80, 278–81
Chester County, Pa., 75, 76, 167, 170, 257, 274, 276, 277
Children
  in Boston, 134
  and inheritance, 186
  labor of, 218, 221, 266
  mortality of, 27
  naming of, 113–14
  property rights of, 113
  as servants, 14
  during war, 237
Christian at His Calling, 56
Church membership, 10, 53
Cities
  and class, 182–83
  and wealth distribution, 178
Civil War, 203, 254, 255
Class. *See* Social class
Classical republicanism, xx
Clemens, Paul, 173
Cloth
  for army, 234, 235–36, 240
  cost of, 235
  homespun, 219, 221, 235
  imports of, 219, 222, 252–53, 268

Cloth production, xxvii, xxx,
    116–17, 194, 196, 200
  in England, 226, 228, 252–
    53
  in Europe, 219, 230, 233
  in factories, 252–53
  increase of, 219–231, 238,
    267–68
  in Maine, 267
  in Middle Colonies, 226–27
  in New England, 226, 228,
    252–53
  in New York, 221, 238
  in North Carolina, 221–22
  among poor, 222
  and tenancy, 225–26
  in Virginia, 222
  during war, 226, 228–29,
    234–35, 238
  and women, 194, 220, 223–
    29, 237–38, 267–68
Clover, 275, 279
Cochran, Thomas C., 203,
    204, 207
Cole, Arthur Harrison, 221
Colman, Rev. Benjamin, 64
Columbia County, N.Y., 238
Commissariat, 240, 243
Common field system, 85n
Commonwealth, 32, 51
Community, 4, 9, 10, 28, 29,
    73, 75
  in Boston, 121, 136
  conflict in, 31–32
  consensus in, 29–32, 59
  and English customs, 185
  inequality in, 181, 195
  interdependence of, 193, 264
  and kinship, 22, 33–34
  and legal rules, 67–69
  in New England, xxx, xxxvi,
    4, 7, 10, 13, 23, 24
  self-sufficiency in, xxiii, 175,
    217, 265–66
  social morphology of, 23, 25
  Winthrop's vision, 50, 53,
    56, 60

"Competence," 274
Concord, Mass., 77, 111, 112,
    118, 242
Congress, Continental, 232,
    236, 240, 243
Connecticut, 28, 69, 93, 94,
    214, 239, 246
  artisans in, 250
  furniture industry, 250
  legal system, 66–69
  and war, 234, 235–36, 239,
    242, 243
Connecticut River valley, 218,
    244
Consciousness. See Mentalité
Consensus history, xviii, xx
Constitution
  Massachusetts, 266
  United States, 152
Constitutional Convention, 148
Consumer revolution, xxvi,
    xxvii, xxviii, xxx, xxxii
Continental Line, 235
Continental notes, 245
Contractors, military, 240–44
Cooke, Edward S., 250
Corn, 87, 94
Cottage industry, 196, 217,
    253. See also Putting-out
    system
Cotton, John, 37, 56
"Covenant of grace," 63
"Covenant of works," 50, 63
Coventry, Alexander, 238
Coxe, Tench, 247
Craftsmen. See Artisans
Credit, British, xxxii, 172,
    273, 288
Creditors, xxiv, 51, 56, 67
"Critical period," 165
Crop yields, 87
Currency, 232, 239
Currency Act, 289

Daughters, and inheritance,
    112
Daughters of Liberty, 228

Davenport, James, 65
David, Paul, 164, 204
Debt, xxiv, 51, 56, 60, 67, 216, 232, 287, 289
Debts
    and American Revolution, 161
    in Kent, Conn., 93n
    in rural economy, 92, 93n, 105
Declension, 7, 32
Dedham, Mass., 9, 10, 11, 12, 16, 21, 25, 26, 78
Delaware, 181, 273
Democracy, 26, 150
Democracy in Kent, 83, 160
Democratic-Republicans, 270, 293
Demographic change, 27. *See also* Population
Demos, John, 12, 14, 15, 19, 109, 159
Dependent people, 171, 265, 276
    in Boston, 124–25, 134
Diaries, 194, 213, 219
Diet, 170, 171
Diphtheria, 17
Discipline, of Quakers, 35, 41
Distilling, 126, 230
Distribution of wealth, 58, 77–81, 155, 176–84, 195, 196
    in Boston, 122, 125, 126, 127–32, 139–43, 176
    among merchants, 143–44, 183
    and shipping ownership, 142, 143n
Ditz, Toby, xxiv, 218
Dominion of New England, 12, 55
Dower rights, 77, 113, 186
Dulany, Daniel, 290
Dunn, Richard, 190
Durkheim, Emile, 8n
Dutch, 38, 74, 189
Dwight, Timothy, 244
Dyer, John, 136

Earle, Carville, 173
East, Robert A., 205
East Caln Township, Pa., 276
East Guilford, Conn., 78
East Hartford, Conn., 228
East Riding, Yorkshire, 40
Eastern Shore, Md., 223
    and war, 207
Economic development, 4, 154, 255
    extensive, 166, 170, 173, 184
    intensive, 257–59, 266–69
    internal, 247–48
    rate of, 164–70
    and social class, 136, 155
Economic growth, 85, 121, 164–70, 199–200, 204, 207
Economic Interpretation, 148
Economy, xxvii, 100, 232
    Chesapeake, 278–81
    domestic, xxxiii, 208, 268
    limited, 90–92, 98–99
    and moral principles, 39–40, 49, 52–57
Education, 33, 162
Education and American Society, 162
Edwards, Jonathan, 65
Egnal, Marc, 167
Elite groups, 146, 152–53, 179
    in Boston, 126, 132, 140
Elizabeth City County, Va., 258, 280
Elizabeth I (1533–1603), 57
Embargo of 1807, 254
Enclosures, 262
England, xxvii, 10
    persecution in, 40
    social class in, 152, 157
Enlightenment, 41, 258
Entail, 110, 114
Entrepreneurs, 102, 259, 271, 272
    agrarian, xxii, 257
    and manufacturing, 116, 257
Epidemics, 16, 27
Erikson, Erik, 14, 15

Erving, John, 123
Essex County, Mass., 191,
    215, 226, 262
Ethnic identity, 73–74
Europeanization, 163, 188
Exchange system, xxiii, xxiv,
    59, 60, 67, 91–93, 193–94,
    216–17, 236, 245, 263–67
Exports, 93, 227–28, 241, 260–
    62, 278
  and economic growth, 164,
    169, 200, 297–8

Factory system, 117, 196
"Families and Farms," xxii,
    xxiv, xxxii
Family, xxx, 13, 15, 16, 17,
    109, 118–19, 162, 191,
    216
  in Boston, 134–146
  and economy, 96–98, 100,
    103–7, 109–10, 194
  farm, xxviii, 96–98, 113–15
  as institution, xxv, 4, 101,
    103
  lineal, xxx, 108–10, 113–15
  and manufacturing, 212,
    220, 234
  values of, xxii, xxiv, xxv,
    xxxii, 5, 12–13, 33, 119
Family factory, 116–17
Farmers, 39, 80–81, 225, 248
  enterprising, xxii, xxxi, 72,
    83–88, 95–96, 274–
    77, 279–81
  homespun cloth, 219, 221,
    222–29
  subsistence, 91–93, 287
  yeoman, 263, 288, 289
Farming, 96–97, 241, 263
  in Concord, Mass., 161
  and economic development,
    164, 210
  entrepreneurial, 72, 82–83,
    86–88, 93–96, 275–77
  in Kent, Conn., 83–88
  in New England, 262–67

subsistence, xxiii–xxiv, 28,
    67, 84–87, 96–98
  tenant, 75, 80–81, 189–93
Faulkner, Harold U., 204
Fauquier, Gov. Francis, 223
Federalists, 253, 293–94
Fee simple, 52
Fertility, 20, 209, 217, 218
Feudal revival, xx, 187, 188
Feudalism, 285
First Church, Boston, 36, 39
Fischer, David Hackett, xvii
Fischoff, Ephraim, 47
Fish Acts, 291
Fishing industry, 215–16, 232
Fithian, Philip, 110
Flanders, 212, 233
Flax, 225, 227, 267
Fletcher, Sally, 268
Franklin, Benjamin, 41, 45,
    134
Franklin and Hall Printers, 42
Frederick County, Md., 190,
    227, 279
Free grace, 50
Freehold tradition, 59, 61, 76,
    79, 98, 103–5
  in colonies, 189–90, 191, 195
  in England, 189, 262
  in New England, 215, 262,
    269
  and republicanism, 161–62,
    266
  and yeoman, 270
From Puritan to Yankee, 83
Frontier, 19, 32, 55, 76, 81,
    111, 175, 264
  thesis, xvii–xviii, 149
Fuller, Joseph, 101–3, 104
Fuller family, 32, 105
Fulling mills, 84, 117, 238
Fur trade, 259
Furniture industry, 250

Gallman, Robert E., 164, 204
Gang labor, 284

General Court, 21, 40, 51, 53, 111, 145, 291
General Will, 29
Generations, 10, 14, 16, 18, 20
  and land, 102–6, 179
  and social change, 58, 134
Genesee Valley, N.Y., 82, 88
Geneva, Switzerland, 51
Gentlemen farmers, 279
Germ theory, xvii–xviii
Germans, 112, 189, 191, 226, 227, 270
Germantown, Pa., 226
Gini coefficient, 182
Goodrich, Rev. Samuel, 90
Government
  and economy, 69, 85, 233, 242, 261, 288–94
  and manufacturing, 252, 291
  in Maryland, 233, 234–35
  in wartime, 233–35
Grain, 240
  export of, 169, 172
Grant, Charles, S., 24, 84, 85, 88, 160
Great Awakening, 62, 63, 65, 83
Greene, Jack P., 187, 188
Greven, Philip J., Jr., 16, 19, 20, 33, 76, 82, 101, 159
Gross, Robert A., 76, 161, 217, 242
Gross national product, xxxiii, 155, 164–70, 204
Guilford, Conn., 166, 178, 192

Habakkuk, H. J., 209
Halfway covenant, 12
Hallowell, Me., 237, 267
Hamilton, Alexander, 74, 253, 266, 293
Hampshire County, Mass., 166
Hampshire County *Gazette*, 267
Handlin, Mary, 205
Handlin, Oscar, 205

Hartford County, Conn., 67, 68, 166
Hartford Manufactory, 252
Hartz, Louis, xviii, xix, xx, 186
Hat industry, 213
Henthorn, George, 257, 258, 274, 277
Hernadi, Paul, xxxvi
Higginson, Rev. John, 55, 69–70
Higginson, Sarah, 55
Hingham, Mass., 114, 118
Hiring-out, 258, 280, 283
Historical change, xxvi, 4, 8, 15, 45, 210
  analysis of, 152–63, 184–88, 195
  Malthusian view of, 169–70, 171, 173
  and population, 25, 61
History
  and chronology, xviii–xix, 4, 16, 27
  consensus view of, xx, 29, 150
  demographic, 16–25, 159–61
  epistemology of, xxviii, xxxi–xxxii, 10, 47–48, 88–89
  interpretation of, xvii, xxxvi, 13, 149–150, 153, 200–201
  liberal view of, xviii, xx, xxxvii, 5, 61n, 72
  methodology of, xxviii, 5, 8, 15, 31, 47–48, 152, 153, 200
  narrative, 3–4, 201
  progressive, 149–50, 152, 158n
  quantitative, xxxv, 71, 85–86, 122, 150, 152, 203, 220
Hofstadter, Richard, 88
Homespun clothes, xxviii, 219, 228, 246–47

Homestead Acts, 107n
"Honest Farmer," 103–4, 105
Hoover, Herbert, xix
Household manufacturing, 116–17, 220
Household mode of production, xxiv, xxi, 99, 263
Housing ownership, 55, 132
    in Boston, 126, 127, 137
    and social class, 128–29, 140
Howe, Daniel Walker, 63, 65
Hudson River valley, 189, 238, 240
Hughes, Stuart H., 45
Hull, John, 38, 40, 46, 54, 70
Husband, Herman, 288
Hussey, Sylvanus, 256, 290
Hutchinson, Anne, 50
Hutchinson, Elisha, 132

Ideal-types, 47, 48, 99
Imports, xxvii, 208, 233, 273–74
In English Ways, 185
Indentured servants, 96, 109, 124–25, 134, 173, 180, 190–91, 270, 278
Individualism, xxxvii, 5, 8, 29, 74, 75, 84, 85
    of farmers, 72–73
    and frontier, 115
    lack of, 32, 59
    limits on, 109, 119
    and naming patterns, 114–15
    and women, 113, 118
Industrial Revolution, xxvi, 200, 204, 273
Industrialization, 27, 115–17, 177–78, 203
Inequality, 177, 178, 195, 196
    in Boston, 137, 140
    and commerce, 179–81
Inflation, 232, 235, 236, 242, 245
Inheritance, 23, 59, 77, 79, 159, 250
    in Andover, 82

in Chesapeake, 186
in Connecticut, 218
partible, xxv, 22, 26, 112, 193, 217, 218, 253
patterns of, 23, 101, 110–13, 192
and women's rights, 186
Interest charges, 60, 269
Ipswich, Mass., 60, 193, 214, 252
Iron industry
    in Kent, Conn., 84–85
    in Rhode Island, 290–91
Isaac, Rhys, 101n

Jackson, Caleb, 276
Jackson, Caleb, Sr., 60, 266
Jackson, Colonel Joseph, 145
Jackson, Nicholas, 60
Jackson family, 70, 285
James II (1685–88), 55
Jedrey, Christopher, 57
Jefferson, Thomas, 95, 225, 293
Jensen, Merrill, 152
Johns Hopkins University, xv
Johnson, Edward, 54
Jones, Alice Hanson, 164
"Just price," 52, 98, 235

Kaufsystem, 212–13, 217, 219, 231, 244, 249, 255, 269
Keayne, Robert, 39, 40, 42, 46, 48, 57
Kennebec Proprietors, 267
Kent, Conn., 24, 28, 32, 83–88, 93n, 101–2, 111
Kent County, Md., 175
Krefeld, Germany, 226
Kriedte, Peter, 210
Kulik, Gary, 290
Kulturekampf, 44

Labor. *See also* Exchange system
    family, 263–67
    in fishing industry, 215, 265

intensification of, 213, 242, 282, 283
market for, 258–59, 271–72
slave, 171–73, 278–81
surplus, 261, 263, 272
wage, 253, 260, 261, 275–77
Lancaster County, Pa., 75, 214
Lancaster, Pa., 74, 75, 214, 230
Land, 20, 101, 106, 178–79, 190–93, 215, 218, 262
distribution of, 28, 52
ownership of, 52, 55, 59, 191
price of, 28, 172, 175, 215
speculation in, 28, 32, 84, 106, 111, 287
subdivision of, 24, 192
Land, Aubrey, 173
Laslett, Peter, xix, 10, 156
Legal system, 29
capitalist, 66–69, 113, 288–94
in Connecticut, 66–69
Lemon, James T., 72, 73, 75, 76, 80, 82, 96, 109
Leuthy, Herbert, 47n
Leverett, Gov. John, 55
Liberal outlook, 72, 76, 82
Liberal Tradition in America, xviii
Life cycle, 25, 27, 78, 119, 178
Life expectancy, 16, 17
Lindert, Peter, 177, 178
Lindstrom, Diane, 204, 248
Lineal families, 61, 108–10
Linen production, 219, 240
in Ireland, 227, 246
in Middle Colonies, 227, 228
in New England, 246–47
Lipset, Seymour Martin, 156
Little Commonwealth, 13
Livestock, 94, 193
Locke, John, xix
Lockridge, Kenneth A., xix, 9, 10, 11, 12, 20, 25, 159, 160, 187, 188, 206, 213

Logan, James, 63
London, 49
Long Island, battle of, 234
Longue durée, 4
Looms, xxx, 223, 235, 237, 238
Lord Baltimore, 190
Lowell, Mass., 70
Loyalism, 237
Luther, Martin, 44
Lynn, Mass., 116, 256, 259

McNall, Neil, 82
Madison, James, 270, 293
Main, Gloria, 177
Main, Jackson Turner, 93, 152, 153, 176, 177n, 181, 195, 206
Majority rule, 29, 30, 59–60
Mallory, Mary, 258, 259
Malthusian interpretation, 169–70, 173, 206, 213
Mann, Bruce H., 67
Manning, Dr. John, 252, 253, 254
Manufactures, xxvi, xxxiii, 196, 200, 267
domestic, xxvii, 133, 208, 247, 267
household, 116–17
increase in, 246–48
and war, 244, 246
Marital fertility, 22, 23, 102–6
Market economy, xxii, xxiv, xxviii, xxix, 32, 154, 194
and capital formation, 106–7
expansion of, 258–61, 268–70
and labor, 133–34, 258–60
lack of, xxix, xxxi, 86–90
and slavery, 258–59
and war, 240, 241
Marriage, 18, 118, 209
age at, 159, 217
arranged, 59, 108
Marx, Karl, 44

Maryland, xxxi, 94, 177, 190, 215, 233, 250
Massachusetts, 45, 55, 56, 105, 177, 241, 246
Massachusetts Bank, 291
Massachusetts Bay Colony, 12, 21, 39, 48, 50, 51
Massachusetts Woolen Manufactory, 252
Mather, Cotton, 56
Mayhew, Jonathan, 64
Medick, Hans, 210
Mendels, Franklin F., 209, 210
Mentalité
    of farmers, xxii, xxvi, 87–90, 100
    liberal, 72–73, 82
    of lineal family, 108–10, 113–15, 118–20
    profit-seeking, xxii, 83–86, 88
Mercantilism, 201, 207, 208, 218, 219, 222, 254, 255, 289–94
Merchants, xxii, 49, 51, 53, 74, 107, 133, 183, 187, 212, 232, 239–41, 242, 244, 269, 273, 287, 288–89
    in Boston, 36, 38–39, 54, 55, 126–27, 133, 143, 229
    and capitalism, 66–67, 69–70, 230–31
    entrepreneurial, 232, 242, 257, 259, 261
    and farming, 107, 180, 230, 259, 272
    and fishing industry, 215, 230, 265
    and manufacturing, 116–17, 214, 225, 230–31, 254, 257
    and putting-out system, xxvii, 62, 69, 116–17, 208, 230
Quakers, 36–41, 64, 74, 116
    religious views of, 38–39,

46, 50, 54–55, 63, 69, 74
Scottish, xxxii, 259, 289
as spectators, 230, 232, 257, 259, 261
and war, 205, 234, 242
wealth of, 55, 58, 126–27, 183, 230–31
Merrill, Michael, 263, 287
Methodism, 63
Middle class, 10, 26, 150, 160
    in Boston, 142
Middle Colonies, 58, 63, 73, 96, 112, 173, 191, 226–27, 258, 273
    exports from, 94, 207–8, 241
Middle-Class Democracy, 150, 151
Middlemen, 105–7, 212, 269
Middlesex County, Mass., 170, 269
Midwife, 267
Migration, 226, 281
Mill Act, 290
Mill girls, 118
Miller, Perry, 7
Ministers, 56, 63
Minutemen and Their World, 161
Mobility, 80, 123–24, 154, 156–57, 216, 281
    geographic, 11, 21, 24, 26, 31, 32, 33, 80, 81, 125, 154, 157, 216, 264
    in Kent, Conn., 24, 86
"Model of Christian Charity," 49, 51, 62
Money, 28, 210, 232–33
Moore, Sir Henry, 221
Moran, Gerald, 109
Moravians, 75
Morgan, Edmund, 109, 173, 185, 188
Morgan, Philip, 281, 284
Morison, Samuel Eliot, 149
Morris, Richard B., 205
Morris, Robert, 292
Mortality, 17–20, 103, 212

Mortgages, xxxiii, 105, 277
Mount Airy, Va., 281
Mount Vernon, Va., xxxi
Murrin, John, xx, 187, 188

Nail industry, 247
Namier, Sir Lewis, 153
Naming patterns, 114
Nash, Gary, xxix, 61, 183
Native Americans, 259
Nelson, John R., Jr., 253
New England, xxix, 7, 16, 29,
    111, 181, 185
  economy of, 41, 115–17,
    165–66, 173, 189, 208,
    226, 228, 246
  religion in, 37, 65, 109
  society in, 26, 32, 34, 196
New Fairfield, Conn., 246
New Hampshire, 111, 192,
    229, 246
New Haven, Conn., 65, 67,
    233
New Jersey, 63, 77, 181, 215
New Light Congregation, 65
New social history, xvi, 3,
    4, 201
New York, xxxi, 58, 82, 94,
    95, 116, 182, 183, 189–90,
    239, 240, 270
New York City, 95, 234
Newtown, N.Y., 80, 112, 250
Niebuhr, Richard H., 44n
Nonimportation, xxviii, 228,
    229, 237
Norris, Isaac, 42n
North, Douglass, 164, 204
North Carolina, 89, 221, 287–
    89
Northampton, Mass., 57, 213,
    214, 215, 266

Open-field system, 10, 22, 40
Orange County, N.C., 287,
    288, 289
Osnaburg fabrics, 227
Otis, James, 145

Outwork. See Putting-out
    system
Overseers of the poor, 145

Palm-leaf hats, 196, 249
Paris Treaty (1783), 286
Partible inheritance, xxv, 22,
    26, 112, 193, 217, 218,
    253
Paternalism, 271, 285
Patriarchal authority, 20, 21,
    23, 25, 33, 186
Patten, Matthew, 92
Peasants, 7, 211
Peddlers, 242
Penn, William, 38
Pennsylvania, 38, 58, 63, 64,
    75, 95, 181, 191, 234, 270
Pennsylvania Gazette, 230
Pennsylvania Packet, 103
Perkins family, 70
Perley, Captain, 266
Perlin, Frank, 210
Phelps, Oliver, 243
Philadelphia, xxxi, 35, 41, 63,
    74, 95, 182, 183, 229,
    239, 246, 248, 272
Philanthropy, 54
Piecework system, 282, 285
Pietism, 63
Plough Boy, 88
Plows, 279
Plymouth colony, 12, 14, 16,
    17, 18, 22, 52, 53
Pocock, J. G. A., xxxv
Political economy, xxi, 293–94
Political power, 78, 187
  and economic change, 204
  of entrepreneurs, 289–94
  and social class, 145–46, 153
  and wealth, 78, 144–45
  of yeomen, 287–94
Political system, 29, 151, 160,
    261
  elitist, 21, 149–50
"Politics and Social Structure,"
    152

Poor, 183, 185, 211, 252
Population, 25, 31, 32, 58, 61,
    93, 159–61, 169, 192, 213,
    252, 272
  of Andover, 16, 20, 263
  of Boston, 122, 132, 133,
    135n
  growth, 17, 18, 19, 77, 192,
    208, 261
  landless, 26, 75–76, 77–78,
    80–81, 123
  propertyless, 124, 135, 143,
    160, 189–90, 191, 258,
    262, 264, 275–77
  and resources, 12, 23, 77,
    105, 110, 159–161, 208,
    213
Potatoes, 170–71, 244, 276
Predestination, 42, 63
Pregnancy, premarital, 118
Prices, 11, 92, 98, 233
  regulation of, 52, 235
  tobacco, 172, 287–88
  wartime, 233, 241
  of wheat, 94, 272, 278
Prince George's County, Md.,
    171, 172, 223
Privateers, 231, 232, 239
Probate inventories, xxx, 237,
    238, 275
Probate records, 158, 166, 177,
    223
Proletariat, 193, 209
  in Boston, 123, 135–36,
    146–47
  in Kent, Conn., 26
  rural, 75–76, 77–78, 80–81,
    209
Promissory notes, xxiii, xxiv,
    67, 68
Propertyless population, 124,
    135, 143, 160, 189–90,
    191, 258, 262, 264, 275–
    77
  in Boston, 143, 234
  and geographic mobility,
    124

in Maryland, 175
  and military, 214–15
Proprietors, 10, 28, 31, 85, 187
Prosopography, 153
Protestant ethic, 5, 37, 41, 43,
    59, 70
Proto-industrialization, 195–
    96, 200, 207, 209–11,
    248–49. *See also* Putting-
    out system
Pruitt, Bettye, 181, 193, 264,
    265
Puritans, xix, 9, 15, 37, 38, 43,
    44, 49
Putting-out system, xxvii, 62,
    69, 116, 208, 231, 252,
    257, 285
  in cloth, 230
  in Europe, 209, 211
  and fur trade, 259
  and poverty, 209, 211
  and shoe industry, 266–67

Quakers, 35, 38, 41, 64, 74,
    272, 275
Quarterly Review, 283

Ramsay, David, 245
Randolph, Edward, 54
Redemptioners, 191
Redfield, Robert, 99n
Regions, 185
  and proto-industrialization,
    210, 249–50
  and tenancy, 189–93
  and wealth, 164–70, 172–73
Regulator movement, 288–89
Religion, 10, 51, 63–64, 73–74
  economic values of, xxv, 37–
    38, 40, 45, 62, 65–66
  evangelical, 63, 65–66
Remonstrance of 1646, 53
Republicanism, xxxv, 266
Requisition system, 235–41
Revolutionary War, 241, 247,
    248, 264
Rhode Island, 240, 246, 290

Rice, xxix, 200, 282
Rockefeller, John D., xix, 84
Rogers, Rev. Ezekiel, 39, 40, 57, 60
Rostow, W. W., 154
Roth, Guenther, 48
Rothenberg, Winifred, xxxiii, xxxiv, 241, 277
Rowley, Mass., 39, 57, 60
Royal Navy, 231, 232
Rural economy, xxvii, 11
    changes in, 213–19
    culture of, 90, 92, 97–98
    in Kent, Conn., 83–88
    in New England, 57–62, 77–78, 89
    in New Jersey, 77
Rutman, Darrett, 192

"Safety valve," 192
Salem, Mass., 53, 55, 60, 69–70, 78
Salt meats, 170, 244
Saugus Ironworks, 52
Saxony, Germany, 212
Scheibler, Johann Heinrich, 226
Schlumbohm, Jürgen, 210
Schumacher, Max, 95
Schuyler, General Philip, 240
Scollay, John, 145
Scotch-Irish, 184, 191, 226, 228, 231, 270, 271
Scotland, xxvii, 43
Scottow, Joshua, 36, 37, 39, 40, 46, 54, 70
Selectmen, 11, 12, 21, 25, 78
    in Boston, 127, 132
    wealth of, 127, 132, 145
Self-sufficiency, xxiii, 175, 217, 265–66
Seven Years' War, 215, 231, 264
Seventh Day Baptists, 74
Sewall, Samuel, 55
Sex ratio, 18, 186
Shammus, Carole, xxix

Shays' Rebellion, 245
Sheep, 228, 275
Shipbuilding, 126
Shipping, 122
    and social class, 126, 141–43
Shoe production, 62, 116, 135, 196, 242, 271
    in Boston, 133
    in Philadelphia, 271
    and putting-out system, 266–67
Shucking bees, 194
Sickle, inefficiency of, 95
"Significance of the Frontier," xvii
Slater, Samuel, 291
Slavery, 94, 191
    growth of, 171, 173, 175, 184
    and hiring-out, 258–59
    in Philadelphia, 271
    and white wealth, 171–73
Slaves, 96, 109, 134n, 172, 211, 222, 252, 270
    autonomy of, 280–81, 284–85
    exploitation of, 279–84
    in North Carolina, 287–88
    property rights of, 284–85
Smallholders, 261, 280, 282
Smith, Daniel Scott, 76, 169, 176
Social class, 106, 136, 149, 170–71, 177, 182–83
    in Boston, 144
    and political power, 145, 152–53
    in Virginia, 152
Social mobility, 143, 216
Social Mobility in Industrial Society, 157
Social morphology, xxxvi, 4, 8, 23, 25, 27
Social science, 8, 154–56, 200
Social structure, xxxvi, 5, 121, 163, 184, 185, 196

Social structure (*cont.*)
analysis of, 148–53, 184–89, 193–94
and American Revolution, 160–62
of Boston, 124–27, 133–37, 143
rural, 26, 52, 78–79, 85–86, 115, 119
Social Structure of Revolutionary America, 153, 154, 158, 181
Sombart, Werner, 47
Somerset County, N.J., 96, 227
Sons
and inheritance, 111–12
naming of, 114
South Carolina, 173, 222, 252, 278, 281
Southern Agriculture, 284
Specialization, process of, 91, 117, 142, 210, 242, 265–66
Speculation, 107, 254, 267, 286
in currency, 232–33, 244–45
wartime, 232–33
Spinning wheels, xxx, 117, 223, 225, 226, 238
Spotswood, Lt. Gov. Alexander, 222
Stages of Economic Growth, 154
Stamp Act, 228
Standard of living, 164–70, 216
and exports, 164, 167–68
in Middle Colonies, 58, 166–167
in New England, 58, 102, 140, 166–67
in South, 58
Staple crops, xxx, 180, 278, 283
Staple thesis, 200
Steele, Jonathan, 283
Stem family, 192, 213

Stoddard, Samuel, 57
Stone, Lawrence, 10, 157, 201
"Strolling poor," 211
Sturges family, 70
Subsistence crises, 91n, 211–12
Suffrage, 29
Sugar industry, 282, 283
Surplus production, xxiii, xxxii, 86, 87, 89, 96–97, 104

Talbot County, Md., 173, 175
Tanneries, 84
Tariffs, 254
Task system, 61, 281–84
and capitalism, 283–84
in Chesapeake, 282
in northern states, 285
in South Carolina, 281–82
spread of, 283–84
in West Indies, 282, 283
Tawney, R. H., 43
Tax lists, 102, 122, 158
Tayloe, John, III, 281
Taylor, George Rogers, 155, 156, 163, 176, 195, 204
Technology, 95, 279
Tenancy, xxx, 74, 80, 103, 107n, 270, 279
and capitalism, 279–80, 283
and cloth production, 225–26
in England, 189, 191–92
in Maryland, 190
in New England, 189, 263
in New York, 189–90
and slavery, 279–80
Textiles. *See* Cloth production
Thernstrom, Stephen, 157
Thirsk, Joan, 209
Thompson, E. P., 100n
Tidewater region, 259, 281
Tilly, Charles, 210
Tobacco, xxix, 165, 179–80, 190, 200
Town meetings, 25, 28, 30, 31, 59, 136, 236, 262

Index

INDEX

Trade
and capital formation, 141–
43
foreign, xxviii, xxix, xxxiii,
126
and inequality, 179–81
with West Indies, 126, 133
Transition to capitalism, xxi,
261, 265, 269, 272–73,
285, 286–87, 290–94
Trempealeau County, Wis.,
xxiii, 81
Tribalism, Puritan, 109
Tryon, Gov. William, 221,
288, 289
Tryon, Rolla Milton, 220
Turner, Frederick Jackson,
xvii–xviii, xix, 7, 76, 80,
115, 148, 149

Ulster County, N.Y., 238
Ultimogeniture, 110
United Company, 229

Varley, Charles, xxxi
Ver Steeg, Clarence, 156
Verlagsystem, 212, 217, 218,
231, 249, 252, 255, 268
Vickers, Daniel, 216, 265, 266
"Vigilant managers," 283
Virginia, 1705–1786, 151
"Visible saints," 52
Voluntary associations, 269

Wadsworth, Jeremiah, 243,
252, 253, 254
Wage labor, 96, 104, 109, 123,
125, 134–35, 183–84
Waldo, Captain Benjamin, 145
Walsh, Lorena, xxx, xxxi, 186
War for Independence, 195,
204, 215, 216, 220, 231,
238, 242, 245, 255
and cloth production, 226,
228–29
and economy, 165, 199–200
Warden, G. B., 176

Washington, George, 226, 232,
252
Waters, John, 178
Wealth, 169, 170–73, 178–79,
187
production of, 164–70, 196
and slavery, 171–73, 278
Weavers, 27, 223, 235, 237–38,
249, 258, 268
Weber, Max, 5, 37, 41, 42, 46,
48, 61
Weber thesis, 40
Webster, Daniel, 285
Wellenreuther, Hermann, 161
Wenham, Mass., 178, 191
Wentworth, Gov. Benning,
229
Wesley, John, 63, 66
West Indies, 166, 208, 232,
239, 279, 282, 283
Whaling industry, 265
Wharton, Richard, 54, 55
Wheat, xxix, 87, 94–97, 99,
175, 207, 272
Whitefield, George, 63
Widows, 77, 113
Willard, Samuel, 38
Williamson, Jeffrey, 177, 178
Wilson, Woodrow, xv, xvi
Windham County, Conn., 32,
93n, 242
Winthrop, John, 39, 40, 62
economic views, 51–52, 53,
56, 60
Wisconsin, University of, xvii,
152
Wolf, Eric, 98n, 259
Women, 22, 117, 118, 186,
194, 237, 280
and cloth production, 194,
220, 223–29, 237–38,
267–68
and inheritance, 112, 113
labor of, 194, 200, 213, 253,
263, 280–81
patriotic, 228, 237
and putting-out system, 195,
200, 225, 253

311

Wonder-Working Providence, 54
Woodworkers, 271
Wool, 219, 267
Woolman, John, 64
Worcester County, Mass., 111, 248
Work discipline, 271, 281, 285
World We Have Lost, xixn, 156

Yeoman values, 60–61, 81, 265–67, 269, 270, 274, 293–94
Yorkshire, England, xxxi, 40

Ziff, Larzer, 50
Zuckerman, Michael, 13, 14, 28, 29, 30, 31, 79